"The world's most neglected great wine, sherry is ancient, delicious, and still far too obscure. So it's fortunate to have its story told by Talia Baiocchi, a great young wine-writing talent with her finger on the pulse. Her clear, witty style is perfect for untangling sherry's intricacies—and for demonstrating why a whole new generation of wine lovers (and bartenders!) are so taken with it. The tastefully opinionated producer profiles make this an essential guide for anyone seeking to navigate the ever expanding sherry lists of so many new shops and restaurants."

— JORDAN MACKAY,
James Beard Award–winning coauthor of *Secrets of the Sommeliers*

• • • ———————— • ———————— • • •

"Witty, fun, relatable . . . These three words are not typically associated with sherry, but perfectly describe Talia Baiocchi and her passion for the wines of the Sherry Triangle. The cocktails and recipes are a welcome (and critical) addition to this stylish, well-written book."

— DAVID LYNCH,
owner/wine director of St. Vincent Tavern and Wine Merchant and author of *Vino Italiano*

SHERRY

A MODERN GUIDE TO THE

WINE WORLD'S BEST-KEPT SECRET

SHERRY

WITH COCKTAILS AND RECIPES

Talia Baiocchi

PHOTOGRAPHY BY ED ANDERSON

TEN SPEED PRESS
Berkeley

CONTENTS

INTRODUCTION

AS MY TRAIN pulled into the station in sherry's historic capital, Jerez de la Frontera, rain spattered against my window and onto the platform below. I was half-awake, with a mosaic of half-eaten *jamón bocadillo* stuck to the front of my sweater, classically overpacked yet without an umbrella in January, a month so rainy it makes you forget that arid Morocco is anywhere near Jerez.

I shuffled into the lavishly tiled station bleary-eyed and inelegant. In such a state only a few things were immediately clear to me. I was in Spain. Spanish was being spoken. To my right, in the train station café: the hum of the espresso machine, the faint mumble of a football game, and the clink of cups meeting saucers—a definably Spanish kind of clink and hum. Furthermore, I was in southern Spain. Nobody was in a hurry. In fact, people almost looked embarrassed to be making their trains. (And, let me tell you this now, because it's as true as anything I've learned while writing this book: never, ever come to this part of Spain and show up to a meeting on time. You will startle and confuse your host.)

I tumbled out onto the street and into a cab, cracked the window, and watched the buildings whirl by, whitewash peeling off their façades to reveal the scars of centuries. Seville orange trees lined the sidewalks, sagging with fruit so fragrant it smelled as if the streets were paved with marmalade. I was a goner, of course, but it's not hard to fall in love with the aesthetic beauty of this place and the obvious cultural bounty—the sherry, the food, the music, the everything— that has enchanted centuries' worth of thinkers, poets, explorers, artists, and (apparently) California girls. But Federico García Lorca—the great early twentieth-century Spanish poet often dubbed the Son of Andalusia—would say to look past the obvious charms, that the real Andalusia cannot be seen.

It's true that the cultural affluence smells and tastes so good that it's easy to forget the centuries of conflict buried underneath Jerez, Sanlúcar de Barrameda, and El Puerto de Santa María—both literally and figuratively. These three towns, which form the roughly 25,000-acre swath known as the *marco de Jerez*, or Sherry Triangle, have seen a tremendous amount of historical tumult and variety of cultural influence. In many ways, sherry—in its idiosyncrasies, triumphs, and failures—is an embodiment of the region's experience.

It is a wine that has endured through thousands of years of political upheaval, sacking, conquest, and economic disappointment. But sherry's highs have certainly outweighed its lows: it was practically the official drink of fifteenth- and sixteenth-century explorers; a favorite of everyone from Shakespeare to Poe to Dickens; the base of the Sherry Cobbler, one of the greatest American cocktails ever invented; and, believe it or not, one of the muses of California's nascent wine-producing industry before it set its sights on Bordeaux as a model. So it's not hyperbole when I say that sherry's story is one of the most remarkable in the history of wine.

Despite its storied pedigree, however, sherry has been maligned in America for decades—so misunderstood that one wonders whether it was the victim of an elaborate smear campaign involving all of the grandmas, everywhere. But against odds that seemed insurmountable just ten years ago, sherry—real sherry, not the warm, blended stuff still found lurking in octogenarian pantries—is undergoing a renaissance. It has become a star ingredient on the modern craft cocktail scene, beloved of bartenders who use it in pre-Prohibition-era cocktails as well as in their own contemporary drinks. It is popping up on wine lists in restaurants and bars from New York to New Orleans to San Francisco, where sommeliers have finally given sherry the real estate it deserves. And at long last, importers and wine shops are selling an unprecedented array of sherries from producers large and small, which means that the best sherry wines are available to American consumers for the first time in generations.

Sherry has, in short, been reborn. And with this rebirth, it's time that sherry's story is retold.

⊙ ••• ———— ≋•≋ ———— ••• ⊙

In simple terms, sherry is a wine produced in Jerez de la Frontera, Sanlúcar de Barrameda, and El Puerto de Santa María. It is a fortified wine, which means that a small amount of neutral grape spirit (brandy) is added to the wine to increase its alcohol content. Fortification—or, more specifically, the lingering negative connotations surrounding it (thanks, Thunderbird)—is one of the reasons sherry is so misunderstood in America. Another reason: its wide range of styles, which include both the driest and the sweetest wines in the world, and numerous points in between.

There are four dry styles of sherry, each with differing modes of production: fino (in which style I include manzanilla, which though distinct in character is

simply a fino aged in the town of Sanlúcar de Barrameda), amontillado, palo cortado, and oloroso. These styles fit, in this order, along a spectrum from lightest to fullest.

In addition to the range of dry wines, the region produces two naturally sweet wines: pedro ximénez (known affectionately as "PX") and moscatel.

And those cheap, sweet bottles with the sticky labels left marinating in pantries across America? Those fit into the category of blended sherries, which are generally made by mixing one of the dry styles with either PX, moscatel, or unfermented grape must and labeled with designations like "pale cream," "cream," "amoroso," and "medium."

In America, people often equate sherry with these ubiquitous, sweetened wines. Thus, the entire category is generally considered sweet, even though the majority of it is not. That fact, coupled with a general distrust of fortified wines, has long kept sherry from the dinner table. But sherry is above all a wine, and one that should be consumed like any other wine: with food. In fact, the intense savoriness of the dry wines and their compatibility with a wide range of cuisines, from English pub fare to sushi, are what's helped drive modern interest in it.

But while sherry should be considered a wine like any other, it's also true that its production methods, especially, make it unique within the world of wine—and not in an academic or abstract way. The differences are dramatic, and visceral.

"No wine differs so much from all others, and the differences are not merely of taste or colour, of scent or sparkle, but of kind . . . it is not a variant, but a primary," writes Rupert Croft-Cooke in his 1956 book, *Sherry*. "There is Sherry, and there are all other wines."

◦ ••• ——————— ⧓ • ⧓ ——————— ••• ◦

Despite what all the vowels in my name might imply, I was not reared on the great wines of Italy and my mother, who is half Spanish, did not teach me either the art of flamenco or how to love fino sherry.

Instead, it all begins with a stoned surfer, a liquor store on Pacific Coast Highway, a carful of high school girls, and a botched request for Bailey's. That night I had my first taste of Harvey's Bristol Cream Sherry, which I stirred into a concoction that I still maintain is the worst blended drink I've ever consumed. I was sixteen.

Five years later (and no thanks to the Bristol Cream), I broke the news to my parents that I'd fallen in love with wine. Instead of going to law school as predicted (or at least as hoped), I'd taken a job as a vineyard slave in Piedmont, Italy, and I wouldn't be back until I'd spent all of the money my relatives sent for graduation. (P.S. I love you.)

I had my second sip of sherry the year after I returned from Italy, when I wandered into Bar Jamón, a pocket square of a restaurant on Irving Place in New York's Gramercy neighborhood, just down the block from the wine store where I worked. I went for the ham, but I left loving sherry. That night the bartender poured me the first *real* sherry I'd ever tasted: a chilled *copita* of oloroso. It was both incredibly foreign and totally familiar—like old Barolo laced with iodine that was amplified, reduced, and somehow elegant despite its heft. It sparked that dull, joyous pulse in the gut that travels north, gains momentum in the chest, and releases all its pent-up energy behind the eyes in the same way that good '90s rock choruses, eggs with truffles on them, love, Barolo, and log rides do. It's a variety of bliss, I guess; the kind that is best expressed through tears or dancing—or, if you've had enough sherry, both.

That was in 2007, and sherry was at the tail end of a decades-long decline that had left it nearly irrelevant—a wine best reserved for bridge games and bad jokes. In fact, the best bit of PR the wines enjoyed over the last thirty years was a nine-year stint on the sitcom *Frasier* as the object of the Crane brothers' alcoholic affection, which doubled as a backhanded jab at their stodgy Britishness. In a testament to how old-fashioned it had become, the Cranes served their sherry warm out of a decanter next to Frasier's grand piano, and sipped it pinky up.

But just a few years after *Frasier*'s run ended, rumblings of an unlikely renaissance began in the cocktail world. The modern-day craft cocktail revival inspired bartenders and consumers alike to rediscover America's pre-Prohibition-era drinking past. Bars around the country were studiously unearthing nineteenth-century recipes, many of which called for sherry as a primary ingredient. The rebirth of classic cocktails like the Sherry Cobbler gave sherry a way back into the barman's repertoire. By 2009, sherry had become a budding trend in the cocktail world, with bars from coast to coast featuring sherry prominently on their menus.

The wine world wasn't far behind. The improved distribution of smaller, high-quality sherry bottlings—including Lustau's Almacenista line, the boutique sherries of El Maestro Sierra, Hidalgo–La Gitana's Manzanilla Pasada Pastrana, and Emilio Hidalgo's La Panesa, as well as the La Bota wines from Equipo Navazos—helped hook the more progressive sommelier set. Within a few years New York and San Francisco had become incubators for an overdue American fascination with one of the first wines ever imported to the New World. Sherry, quite suddenly, was hip.

Some of this comeback is linked to a decades-long shift in flavor hierarchy in the American palate—a slow but steady decrease in the dominance of fruit flavors to an embrace of bitter and intensely savory flavors. Simply browse the greens section at Whole Foods: endive, treviso, arugula, and dandelion greens now hold court in aisles that once pledged allegiance to Bibb lettuce and spinach. Even McDonald's serves radicchio now. As it applies to beverages, this change can help us understand everything from the rise of the bitter, Campari-based Negroni cocktail to the unlikely popularity of intensely savory skin-fermented orange wines.

Enter sherry. Its various dry styles—fino and manzanilla, amontillado, palo cortado, and oloroso—are arguments for rebellion against fruit: wine's anthems about the savory. They are also wines that deserve to be on the table. And that is the great lesson we are learning in America: while sherry's production process makes it unique within the world of wine, it represents more of a convergence with table wine than a departure. And the more I taste, the more I find glimpses of other wines—the salinity of Chablis, the warmth and meatiness of northern Rhône Syrah, the earthiness and florality of Nebbiolo—in the wines of the Sherry Triangle.

It's thanks to some of the country's best sommeliers and bartenders that sherry is finally being understood as both a table wine and an element that can make a cocktail more complex. These are people like Ashley Santoro, the former wine director of Manhattan's Casa Mono and Bar Jamón, who would be a millionaire if she had a buck for every time she's heard "I thought that was for grandmas" during her years at the restaurant. She converted many of those people by slipping glasses of fino or manzanilla next to countless plates of *ibérico* ham, gratis. There's Sean Diggins, formerly of Gitane, who was pouring more than twenty sherries by the glass before most restaurants in San Francisco even thought to consider it. And Sandro Piliego, an Italian from Lazio who fell in love with sherry in the late 1990s, when collecting it was about as cool as collecting navel fuzz. When I asked him why an Italian guy would move to America to open a Spanish restaurant in Brooklyn, he said, plainly, "For the love of sherry."

There are dozens of people who helped dig sherry out of the dark ages and have pushed to prove that the wines of Jerez de la Frontera, Sanlúcar de Barrameda, and El Puerto de Santa María, as well as those of Montilla-Moriles, are some of the world's most intriguing and uniquely *terroir*-driven food wines. They are different, yes, but they require nothing but curiosity (and perhaps a little *jamón*).

In fact, thirteen years after that not-so-fateful night on PCH and more than three years after that first rainy January in Jerez, I've realized that unbridled curiosity—not knowledge, or fancy glassware, or the right vernacular—is the only thing you need to love wine. It's the one thing that led me here, and perhaps it's what's led you here, too.

1
HOW SHERRY IS MADE

very so often when the topic of sherry comes up, there's at least one person who says, "Oh, sherry. Right. So what *exactly* is it?" After plenty of contemplation (a book's worth), I've realized that the best possible answer really is, "How long do you have? A few hours?" A lifetime would really be better.

In my opinion, there is no other wine in the world whose spectrum is more versatile and wildly contrasting, and no other that defies an easy explanation quite so well. How do you succinctly sum up a wine whose range includes both the sweetest and the driest wines in the world? There's more than two hundred years of flowery prose on the subject to prove just how difficult it is.

Here goes, though.

By modern definition, sherry is a fortified wine aged in above-ground cellars called bodegas in three main towns within the Andalusian province of Cádiz—Jerez de la Frontera, Sanlúcar de Barrameda, and El Puerto de Santa María—which form the corners of the *marco de Jerez*, or the "Sherry Triangle." Though these towns are just miles from one another, each has its own distinct culture, history, and set of microclimates. What these differences breed—aside from lots of intra-Triangle towel snapping—are wines whose characteristics can vary quite significantly from one town to the next. These nuances play out within the spectrum of sherry styles, from bone-dry fino and manzanilla to dry but boldly oxidative oloroso to the two main sweet wines produced in the region, pedro ximénez and moscatel.

There are three elements of sherry's production that set it apart. The first is the solera system, a method of gradually blending new wines with older wines so that ultimately each bottle is a mixture of many wines of varying ages, rather than a single vintage.

The second unique element is flor, the layer of yeast that naturally grows on the surface of the wine and contributes to the character of every style of dry sherry except for oloroso. Flor drastically changes the wine aged under it— contributing, most famously, to the extreme dryness and textural delicacy of fino and manzanilla, which spend their life aging exclusively under the *velo*—veil—of flor. This is known as biological aging.

And third is the unique relationship between the *terroir* of the vineyard— the interplay of soil, climate, grape variety—and the *terroir* of the physical structure where the wine is aged. No other wine tradition anywhere in the world pays such detailed attention to the space in which a wine matures. The location of the bodega—near the sea or inland, partially sheltered from the winds off the Atlantic or in direct exposure to them—is one of the major factors that contributes to the character of the finished wine. Equally important is the location of each of the barrels within the bodega, and the unique population of microbial yeasts within each.

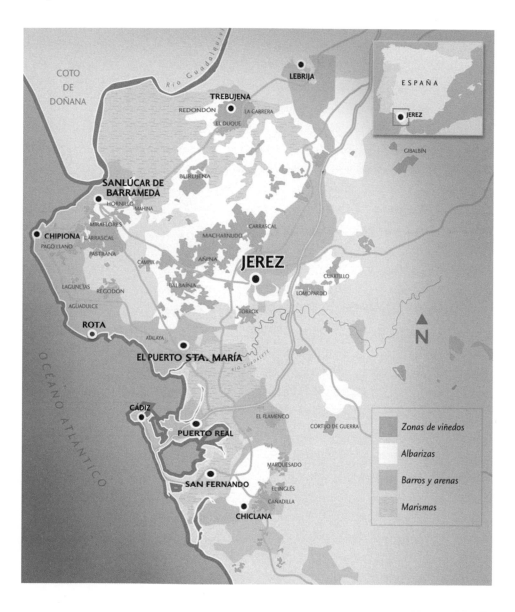

Terroir Two Ways: The Vineyard and the Bodega

In the foreword to James E. Wilson's *Terroir*, Hugh Johnson, the wine world's unofficial mystic, defines the word as the "whole ecology of the vineyard: every aspect of its surroundings from bedrock to late frosts to autumn mists, not excluding the way the vineyard is tended, not even the soul of the *vigneron*." Johnson is describing an encompassing "sense of place." Every aspect of each vineyard, including the way it is tended and even who it is tended by, determines the character of a wine produced in that place.

Vineyard *terroir* is as important to sherry as it is to the other great wines of the world. But there is another part of the equation: the bodega. The unique relationship between the *terroir* of the vineyard and the *terroir* of the bodega is both essential and difficult to quantify, comprising everything from the particular architecture of the cellar, exposure to the winds off the Atlantic Ocean, and growth (or lack thereof) of flor on the surface of the wines.

Antonio Flores, *capataz* (cellarmaster, see page 32) at González Byass, likes to say that the life of a fino (and this is true of sherry in general) begins when the life of another wine ends. This idea of reincarnation gets to the core of what sherry is: a wine that is drastically transformed by its aging process.

But the imprint of this windswept corner of southwestern Spain is not eliminated by this transformation. Like any of the world's truly great wines, great sherry comes from great soil—limestone-rich chalky soil called *albariza*, to be exact—and it is produced from a grape capable of translating the virtues of the land. Some define Palomino Fino as "vapid" or "insipid," but such claims ignore not only the history of sherry production, but also how the perfect marriage of grape and place can transcend the virtues of each on its own. Palomino, in short, belongs here.

Terroir of the Vineyard

Along the road between Jerez and Sanlúcar, the gentle slopes and narrow valleys that make up the famous *pagos*, or winegrowing districts, of Macharnudo, Balbaína, Carrascal, and Añina run into each other, undulating like the earth's version of so many hips and waists. In the spring and summer when the soils are dry and the vines are wearing their best green, the light that pinballs between the hills is nearly nuclear. The vineyards, which look as if they were paved with plaster of Paris, seem to swallow the sun, spitting it back out with a force that feels as if it could shatter you to pieces. It's bright in a blinding, biblical way.

It is this light, the sea, and this milky-white *albariza* soil that form the foundation of what makes the wines of this region great. And while there are two other main soil types in the Sherry Triangle—the clay-rich *barros* and the sandy *arenas*—the best vineyards have always been planted in *albariza*. This type of soil, which has an active limestone content of between 30 and 60 percent—with some forms of *albariza*, notably *tajón*, containing upward of 80 percent—begs comparison to the hallowed vineyards of Champagne, where the chalky soils are credited with creating some of the best white wines in the world. Champagne and sherry are kin in many ways, but in *The World Atlas of Wine*, Hugh Johnson and Jancis Robinson sum up their bond best: "They are the far-northern and far-southern interpretation of the same equation, or the same poem: the white grape from the white ground."

Albariza is extremely poor soil with very little organic matter and a particular talent for water retention, which comes in handy during the virtually rainless summer months. Palomino Fino thrives in it. It's drought resistant and ripens with relatively low acidity, but also low sugars; grapes destined to become sherry are ripe as early as mid-August with a potential alcohol of just 11 to 12.5 percent—quite a bit lower than your average table wine.

During fall and winter, when rainfall averages around twenty-four inches over the course of seven months, the vineyard workers build rectangular pits in the soil between the rows of vines to help collect water for the hot, dry months to follow via a process known as *asperia* or *alumbra*. Despite these efforts, and the spongelike water retention of *albariza*, the root systems of the vines still have to go deep to survive the summer. At just seven to eight years old many have root systems over twenty-five feet long. As the old maxim goes: the poorer the soil, the harder the vine works, the better the wine.

While the southern tip of Spain is largely defined as a Mediterranean climate, the push and pull of the cooling, humid wind off the Atlantic, called the *poniente*, and the dry, hot wind that blows from the east and northeast through the Strait of Gibraltar, called the *levante*, form a drastically shifting microclimate unique to the Sherry Triangle. In the summer months when the levante whips up from Africa, the whole city of Jerez hangs its clothes out to dry and evacuates to the beach. In this climate, which is decidedly southern, overworked wine adjectives like "finesse" and "crisp" aren't exactly the first words that come to mind when envisioning what the wines might be like. Yet fino and manzanilla defy their latitude to the degree that, as Rupert Croft-Cooke writes in his 1956 book, *Sherry*, it's as though "their pale gold had been mined not grown here."

THE GRAPE AND SOIL TYPES OF THE SHERRY TRIANGLE

LIKE MANY OTHER WINEGROWING regions in Europe, prior to the outbreak of phylloxera—the vineyard louse that decimated most of Europe's vineyards in the late nineteenth century—the Sherry Triangle was home to far more grape diversity than it is today. In fact, many of the *pagos* and individual vineyards within them were interplanted with a variety of grape species, both red and white, in addition to several different clones of Palomino, the region's principle grape.

While there are still small, experimental plantings of native Andalusian grapes like Tintilla de Rota—which is used in the production of red table wines, several of them very interesting—within the Sherry Triangle, today the vineyard land here is almost completely dedicated to the only three grapes now permitted in the production of sherry: Palomino Fino, Pedro Ximénez, and Moscatel.

The Grapes

PALOMINO FINO: *The* sherry grape, Palomino Fino is the only grape permitted in the production of dry sherry. In the Canary Islands, where it is also the principle white grape, it is known as Listán Blanco.

PEDRO XIMÉNEZ: Known more affectionately as "PX," Pedro Ximénez is responsible for the sherry region's inky-black sweet wine of the same name. Today most of the PX aged in the Sherry Triangle actually comes from Montilla-Moriles, where PX is used in the production of both dry and sweet wines.

MOSCATEL: The least-planted grape in the Sherry Triangle, Moscatel is responsible for the amber-colored, highly aromatic sweet wine of the same name.

The Soil

Hisorically, the land in the Sherry Triangle that produces sherry was divided into three main soil types.

ALBARIZA: The chalky, limestone-rich soil that is credited with producing the finest wines in the region. Today the great majority of the region's vineyards are planted in *albariza*.

BARROS: A darker, clay-rich soil that is more fertile and less suited to the production of quality wine from Palomino Fino. Only during boom times have vineyards been planted in these soils.

ARENAS: A sandy soil that is typically found near the sea in Sanlúcar de Barrameda. While it's not particularly well suited to the production of quality Palomino Fino, it's the preferred soil type for Moscatel.

THE WINEGROWING DISTRICTS

The Jerez-Xérès-Sherry DO (Denominación de Origen) covers, as of 2013, around 17,500 acres of vines broken up into an estimated sixty principle *pagos* (the Consejo Regulador is currently in the process of mapping those still in production), which can range from under 2 acres to over 1,500. Within these *pagos*, the finest plots of *albariza* soil—which are densely clustered to the northwest of Jerez and in smaller patches around El Puerto de Santa María, Chipiona, Sanlúcar de Barrameda, and Trebujena—are further categorized as Jerez Superior. Sadly, over the past decade the total vineyard acreage in the Sherry Triangle has shrunk dramatically. Perhaps the only silver lining, though, is that now almost all of the region's plantings—upward of 92 percent—are located within the Jerez Superior zone. In other words, although there are fewer vineyards, the ones that survived are of high quality.

But what exactly makes one *pago* of higher quality than another? This is a question that has been asked in the Sherry Triangle for centuries—perhaps even millennia. In the first century CE, Columella was already writing about chalky, sandy, and clay-rich soils, among many other things, in his book *De Re Rustica*. Admittedly, Columella wrote his books while living in Latium (Rome); however, he was born and raised in Gādēs (modern Cádiz), and there is plausible evidence to suggest that many of his observations were based on Roman winemaking practices in what is now known as the Sherry Triangle.

Fast-forward to the latter half of the nineteenth century: sherry was at the peak of its global popularity, and characterizing the best vineyards in the Sherry Triangle was all the rage. Both Diego Ignacio Parada y Barreto and Henry Vizetelly, writing in 1868 and 1875, respectively, were singling out the finest vineyards among the hundreds of *pagos* in the region. The result? Single-vineyard wines—like Valdespino's Inocente, and the now defunct Agustín Blazquez's Carta Blanca, among many others that have since disappeared—became increasingly fashionable.

The *pago* of Macharnudo, for example, was once held in the same esteem as the greatest vineyards in the world. The Englishman Richard Ford, writing in his 1846 *Gatherings from Spain*, called it "the finest of all"; another writer called it "the Lafitte of Jerez" in 1856. Dozens of similar proclamations, along with the increasingly detailed organization of vineyards, led the historian and sherry expert Álvaro Girón Sierra to believe that during this time the Sherry Triangle was looking to either Bordeaux or Burgundy as a model.

But 150 years have changed the region drastically, and today very few producers actually own vineyards; discussions about sherry rarely include mentions of vineyard designation, vine age, or farming. This is a truly modern predicament; the notion that the vineyard is somehow not important to the production of sherry would have been considered, in the words of Girón Sierra, "complete nonsense" in the late nineteenth century and even on through the first half of the twentieth.

So why did our focus on the vineyard shift so much in a little over a half-century?

As happened with many agricultural products, the scientific revolution of the 1950s and 1960s, with its emphasis on efficiency, resulted in a fundamental change in the way bodegas thought about and produced sherry. On one hand, technological developments resulted in a greater understanding of fermentation and flor; on the other, they gave birth to the possibility of producing more wine at a lower cost. This led to a boom in the production and sale of cheap, lower quality fino and blended sherry that slowly chipped away at the image of the region as a producer of *terroir*-driven, high-quality wine.

However, in recent years there has been a slow but steady backlash against the farming and production practices of the midcentury. A small group of influential growers and producers are acting on their conviction that the preservation of heritage vineyards, the genetic diversity of plants, and the quality of farming are intimately tied to the future of sherry. But economically speaking, the market has yet to provide the incentive for the industry as a whole to spend time and money to preserve old vineyards or bottle single-vineyard wines. The prices for sherry are still just too low. But demand is rising among an educated group of consumers and wine lovers—and as this interest in sherry continues to grow, the fact that the best wines still come from the best vineyards will again become both obvious and important.

Of the storied *pagos* that form a patchwork of *albariza* soil to the northeast of Jerez, Balbaína, Añina, Carrascal, and Macharnudo remain the most revered, though there are plenty of others—like Miraflores near Sanlúcar—that are equally important. Each is known for the purity of its *albariza* soil, but the character of the wines sourced from each varies drastically, not only among the *pagos* but also within them. For example, of the *pagos* to the northeast of Jerez, Balbaína—which is the furthest west of the crew—produces the lightest and most elegant wines by virtue of its direct exposure to the poniente winds, while Carrascal—located furthest inland, behind both Añina and Macharnudo—is known for being an earlier ripening zone that produces more robust wines, typically well suited to the production of oloroso. Macharnudo, whose altitude reaches the highest in this area, is known for the purity of its soil and the quality of the wines produced from it, which—even into old age—show a sort of chalky minerality and fine texture specific to the *pago*.

Because sherry's aging process is so transformative, ascertaining how the vineyard plays into the character of the wines isn't always easy. I'd been drinking sherry for years before I really understood how *terroir*, as I'd understood it in other wines, applied. How much of the character of the wines is a product of oxidative or biological aging? A lot of it, certainly, but taste fresh, unfortified *mosto* from the Miraflores *pago* in Sanlúcar de Barrameda against fresh wine from Macharnudo, and it's hard to argue that sherry isn't dependent on *terroir* in the traditional sense. These differences were once more obvious when the wines were separated by vineyard and fermented in barrel. But with the rise of large-vat stainless steel fermentation, blending sites together has become routine and these differences far less obvious as a result.

Efforts are already underway within the region's regulatory council not only to map and categorize the *pagos* in the region but also to encourage producers to source and bottle single-*pago* or single-vineyard wines. In many ways, the future of the region lies in relearning the lessons of the past, and it is efforts like these that are necessary to the Sherry Triangle's quest to reestablish itself as a region defined by *terroir*-driven wines.

Terroir of the Bodega

Applying the word *terroir* to the location and architecture of a physical structure might seem radical. The word, among wine's most sacred, is almost exclusively used in reference to the ability of a wine to speak of the place in which it was grown.

But let us consider the sherry style manzanilla, which is exclusively produced in the town of Sanlúcar de Barrameda. It's made exactly like fino (the grapes can even come from the same place), but because the town of Sanlúcar is situated closer to the sea, there is greater exposure to the cooling poniente winds off of the Atlantic, higher humidity, and more moderate temperatures. These conditions make for a more vigorous, thicker layer of flor, which in turn produces wines that are leaner than those aged just fifteen miles inland, in Jerez.

By contrast, the finos of El Puerto de Santa María are slightly more robust than those produced in Sanlúcar, though still lighter than the wines of Jerez, which is also credited to the town's proximity to the sea. While the climatic differences among these towns are incredibly important to the finished wine, even more striking are the differences that emerge within them, among different bodegas, and even within a single bodega.

BODEGA ARCHITECTURE

Walking around the three sherry towns today you get the sense that you're touring the ruins of another, grander time—or several. During the winter months, paint peels off the buildings in sheets and the cool, nutty air trapped inside abandoned bodegas spills out onto the streets, haunting dimly lit alleys with its aroma.

From the outside, the bodegas simply look like broken-down warehouses in some Spanish version of Bushwick, with few features that differentiate them. But there can be a tremendous amount of variation in the architecture of these buildings, which has a profound impact on the way the wines age. The majority of the bodegas in use today date from the nineteenth century, while a few more ramshackle examples from the seventeenth and eighteenth centuries—many converted from former mills and convents—are also in use.

As the nineteenth century progressed, sherry houses constructed larger and more practical bodegas—not only to house a greater number of barrels, but also to moderate temperatures and control humidity to promote the growth of flor. Ceilings got higher, buildings got wider, and a number of details were added to control things like light filtration and airflow. This style of bodega reached its apex in the late nineteenth century with the construction of "cathedral-style" bodegas like Barbadillo's La Arboledilla cellar, which is still fantastically preserved in Sanlúcar today. It contains one hundred columns supporting a ceiling that reaches forty-one feet above the floor at its highest point, with windows situated at the very top of the bodega's walls allowing light to ooze in with a sort of preternatural drama that certainly earns the style its moniker. During sherry's heyday in the late nineteenth century, these bodegas were some of the most prestigious cellars in the world. They stand now as monuments to a time when the Sherry Triangle was the playground of Spanish royalty and the British gentry and when top sherry was often more expensive than first-growth Bordeaux. But for all of their grandeur, these bodegas were as much about function as they were about prestige.

In order to facilitate the growth of flor, a bodega must have considerable airflow, a relative humidity of between 70 and 75 percent, and, ideally, an internal temperature somewhere between 64°F and 68°F. The thickness of the walls and the height of the ceilings work to control internal temperature, and the floors of the bodegas are covered in *albero*, a sandy, chalky dirt (also used in bullrings throughout Spain) that releases moisture well. To keep humidity and temperature constant for flor growth and to mitigate evaporation of the wine, the *albero* floors are constantly sprinkled with water.

Generally speaking, prototypical aging bodegas are oriented along their main axis northwest to southeast and are located in parts of town that allow

for maximum exposure to the cooling poniente winds off of the Atlantic. Thus the prime real estate locations are the same in the Sherry Triangle as they are in Southern California: oceanfront or on a bluff with a view of the sea. El Maestro Sierra, for example, is located at one of the highest points within the town of Jerez with direct line of sight to the sea. This position lends itself to more vigorous flor growth and is a key factor in the distinct style of the bodega's fino, which is creamier and more flor-forward than most.

The walls of most bodegas are about two feet thick, providing insulation, while other design features—like shading the south façade (which receives more sunlight and is most exposed to the devilish levante winds) with trees and vines, or the use of gable roofs—work to bring temperature down slightly. The ceilings are high to provide maximum airflow, and vents, which are generally located on the eastern and western walls, help expel the hot air that collects under the roof. The windows are small and covered with esparto grass blinds, which filter air (keeping out bugs) and light (providing terrific mood lighting).

Within the ecosystem of the bodega, particularities emerge. Temperatures vary depending on the vertical placement of barrels (higher is hotter), and different parts of the bodega are more or less suited to biological aging. Flor is a fickle thing and though the solera system does help mitigate the vast differences that emerge between barrels, part of managing it requires understanding and capitalizing on minute microclimates within the bodega.

The Young Wine: Classifying Mosto

In the Sherry Triangle, the Palomino Fino grape is king. As the sole grape used in the production of the dry sherry styles—fino, manzanilla, amontillado, palo cortado, and oloroso—it accounts for just over 90 percent of the total vineyard plantings in the region. The other two main grapes planted in the Sherry Triangle—Pedro Ximénez, or PX, and Moscatel—are responsible for the region's two sweet wines, while blended sherries, which are generally a mix of one of the dry sherry styles produced from Palomino and one of the two sweet wines, represent the only wines that can be produced from more than one grape variety.

Palomino Fino grapes for the production of sherry are generally harvested at around 11 to 12.5 percent potential alcohol in late August through early September, though hotter vintages can bring the harvest date up to as early as mid-August. Until as recently as the early 1960s, the harvested grapes were brought from the vineyard to pressing houses in the countryside and trod by foot in a square wooden trough called a *lagar*. Four treaders called *pisadores*, wearing cowhide shoes with nails on the soles (called *zapatos de pisar*), would then trod the grapes from about midnight until noon the following day in order to avoid the heat. It was grim work; Julian Jeffs, writing in the early 1960s, describes *pisadores* wading solemnly from side to side of the *lagar*, barely speaking, splattered with grape juice, legs raw from the rub of the stalks. The free-run juice, called *primera yema*, obtained through this slightly depressing if admirable process, was then added to the juice from the first press, which was obtained from the same vessel via a giant screw, at least two men called *tiradores*, and four good forearms.

Once pressed, the must (*mosto*) was acidified with gypsum, or calcium sulfate—which has been used as an acidifying (and antibacterial) agent in winemaking since Roman times. Nowadays, gypsum has largely been replaced by tartaric acid, but acidification remains a routine step in the production of wine from Palomino Fino grapes, which have a pH that makes them particularly susceptible to bacterial contamination. The juice was transferred to barrels, which were fitted with a large funnel to help ensure that the must didn't overflow as fermentation unavoidably began in muggy transit to the bodega by way of carts pulled by donkeys or oxen. Historically, fermentation would take

THE CONSEJO REGULADOR

THE PRODUCTION AND CLASSIFICATION OF sherry has since 1934 been governed by a regulatory council, called the Consejo Regulador, which oversees and enforces the regulations on wines produced within the DOs of Jerez-Xérès-Sherry and Manzanilla—Sanlúcar de Barrameda (as well as the production of vinegar under the DO of Vinagre de Jerez).

When it comes to pressing, the council has established rules to help control the quality of *mosto* used in sherry produc-

tion. The *primera yema*, or the free-run juice and the juice of the first press, makes up 65 percent of the usable *mosto* and is generally reserved for the production of biological wines, while the *segunda yema*, a light second pressing (two kilograms of pressure per square centimeter), can be used for oloroso or oxidative wine that will ultimately be blended with sweet wine. Any pressings beyond this are called *prensa* and cannot be used in the production of sherry.

place within these individual barrels, a tradition that continued well into the twentieth century. However, by the time Manuel González Gordon's *Sherry* was published in 1972, the trend of fermenting in larger vessels was becoming more widespread. Gradually, mechanical presses replaced *tiradores* and *pisadores* and, with the exception of a few wines—most notably, Valdespino's Fino Inocente and Amontillado Tío Diego—fermentation is now generally carried out in large stainless steel vats.

After fermentation the primary duty of the *capataz* is to gauge the quality of the *mosto* and decide its fate: whether it will start its life biologically (fino/ manzanilla), oxidatively (oloroso), or be blended with sweet wine. This classification occurs during what is called the *sobretablas* stage—a nursery of sorts where the wine generally rests in barrels for up to one year before entering the solera system.

During the *sobretablas* stage, the barrels are marked with chalk symbols meant to indicate the character of the wine within; the symbols roughly correspond to the wine's destined style and level of fortification. *Una raya* (/) is used to indicate a wine of particular finesse and delicacy; *raya y punto* (/.) is for a wine considered slightly less fine, but still potentially suited to biological aging; *dos rayas* (//) is for a more rough-and-tumble wine with greater tannic structure; and *tres rayas* (///) is for a wine of a quality unsuitable for sherry production. The last classification, *Ve*, is reserved for the wines that contain a high level of acetic acid—a bad thing for wine and a crucial thing for vinegar—and will immediately be transferred to the bodega's vinegar solera. As the wines rest in the *sobretablas* stage they are further classified in to palmas (finos), olorosos, and rayas (wines that will be used for blended sherry).

After classification, the wines are fortified with the *mitad y mitad* (half and half) or *miteado*, an equal mixture of grape spirit (brandy) and older, unfortified wine. Wines destined to enter an oloroso solera system will be fortified to at least 17 percent, which kills any flor that has formed on the wine and prevents it from forming again; wines slated to enter a fino or manzanilla solera system will be fortified to at least 15 percent alcohol—the level that is considered optimal for the growth of flor.

Once the wines begin their grand tour of the solera system, humidity, exposure to the winds off the Atlantic, and a number of other climatic considerations—which, in most of the world's wine regions, would apply only to the vineyard—continue to have a major impact on the wine's development. These conditions vary, as mentioned, from town to town, but also from bodega to bodega, contributing to what is ultimately each bodega's unique *terroir*.

THE VENENCIA, VENENCIADOR, AND THE LONG POUR

WHEN WINES UNDER FLOR ARE TASTED from the *bota*, they tend to require aeration to express their true range of aromas. This is one of the main reasons why the *venencia*—a long flexible rod with a tiny cup at one end—is used to sample the wine. Not only does it penetrate the barrel with minimal disruption to the flor, but the long (and very difficult to execute) pour also helps rapidly introduce oxygen to the wine.

It's a spectacle complete with fabulous wrist flicks, flying sherry, and visitors with mouths agape. It goes like this: the *venenciador* (wielder of the *venencia*, generally the *capataz*) thrusts the instrument into the center of the barrel, bypassing the layer of flor to pull out clear wine. The *venenciador* then whips the *venencia* high above his or her head into a horizontal position, allowing the wine to cascade out in a long stream into a *copita* glass, whose mouth is barely bigger than the diameter of a golf ball. Once the stream weakens, the *venenciador* thrusts the *venencia* backward (with flair) and in one fell swoop it lands back at his or her hip.

The use of the *venencia*—or a tool similar to it—to sample wine is said to date back to antiquity, but the name came later. It's derived from the noun *avenencia*, which means "agreement" or "deal" and refers to the *venencia*'s historic role in the sampling and sale of sherry.

The artistry involved in the process has inspired admiration—and even imitation—for ages. In fact, today the (arguably) most skilled *venenciadors* are from Japan, where there are a number of schools and over 100 certified *venenciadors* officially recognized by sherry's regulatory council. It's even made its way into restaurants and bars there—where sherry is often served via *venencia* straight from the barrel. The cocktail world isn't immune either. The Japanese bartender Daiki Kanetaka—a protégée of famed bartender Hidetsugu Ueno and a certified *venenciador*—uses a *venencia* to mix his version of Japan's official sherry cocktail, the Bamboo.

Traditionally, the *venencias* of Jerez and El Puerto were made with silver and whalebone; however, today fiberglass and stainless steel are more common. In Sanlúcar, the *caña*, as it is called there, is still fashioned from a single piece of a bamboo-like reed, as it has been for more than a century.

The Solera System

We don't know exactly when the solera system—the process by which young wines are gradually blended with older wines—was first introduced to the Sherry Triangle, but evidence suggests that very simple soleras first came into use in Sanlúcar de Barrameda sometime in the late eighteenth century. By the beginning of the nineteenth century, the solera system as we know it today began to grow up alongside the *añada* system, or the practice of bottling according to vintage—the way most of the world's wines are produced. Remarkably, many of these very early soleras are still in production today—which means that some VORS (very old rare sherries) may contain small amounts of wine that began its life in the 1800s or earlier.

The adoption of the solera system was largely a matter of practicality: it helped guarantee a relatively stable, predictable wine yield in spite of fluctuations in the size and quality of a harvest. It also meant that no one vintage was at risk of languishing unsold during one of the many dips in demand that plagued bodegas in the mid-eighteenth century. Today the purpose of the solera has evolved as producers gained a better understanding of flor (and wine production in a general), but its basic structure remains largely unchanged.

In simple terms, the physical solera system is a group of barrels organized by the age of the sherry inside into levels called *criaderas*. While the oldest level is traditionally placed closest to the floor, with younger levels above, one single solera system can have many *criaderas*, some with thousands of barrels in each level. As such, the network of *criaderas*, rather than always being literally stacked from oldest to youngest, is often broken up into parts that live in different areas within a bodega—or even, in the case of a very large solera system, in two separate bodegas.

The process of moving sherry through the solera system is often referred to as "fractional blending," and it occurs gradually, over the course of years (sometimes many, many years) through a repeated cycle of *saca* (extraction) and *rocío* (refilling).

When wine is removed from the solera system for bottling (that is, when a *saca* is performed), it is typically extracted in equal parts from the barrels that form the oldest level in the system—also called, confusingly enough, the solera—and is then replaced (via *rocío*) by wine from the next oldest level, called the first *criadera*. The first *criadera* will then be refilled with younger wine from the second *criadera*, and so on until the *sobretablas* stage is reached, wherein the youngest wines are classified and fortified and left to rest in barrels before entering the solera system. This process of continual rounds of *saca* and *rocío* is called, in bodega-speak, *correr la escalas*, or "to run the scales."

The function of this seemingly convoluted system of blending is twofold. Its principal purpose is to maintain consistency, allowing the *capataz* to control the style of the wine across vintages, much in the same way that a Champagne house might treat its nonvintage wines. The secondary purpose of the solera system is to keep the wine and flor levels stable across the years: some evaporation occurs with the purely oxidative styles of sherry, like oloroso, and the *rocío* replenishes barrels that have lost too much. In the case of biologically aged styles, like fino, the *rocío* literally feeds the flor.

Traditionally, moving wine through the solera system was a painstaking and inefficient task carried out with little more than the tools required to construct a beer bong. First, the wine would be extracted from a barrel using a *sifón* (siphon) and a man with a very strong mouth—a process known in the Sherry Triangle as "calling the wine." Once siphoned, the wine was then directed into metal *jarras* (jars) and transferred to the destination barrel via a canoe-shaped metal funnel called, appropriately, a *canoa* (canoe), and a tube with perforations at one end called a *rocíador* (sprinkler). These tools are meant to introduce the new wine slowly and evenly to the center of the barrel without disturbing either the layer of flor on top of the wine or the the layer of fine lees at the bottom, called the *cabezuela*, or "head of the flower."

The bodega workers who specialize in the movement of wine are called *trasegadores*, and despite the tediousness of the job, Henry Vizetelly insisted, in his 1875 *Facts About Sherry*, that these men clad in "caps, coloured shirts, light trousers, and the all-essential crimson or scarlet" looked as if "unlimited sherry agreed remarkably well with them." Today not only is drinking on the job less prevalent—though many of the bodegas maintain a spigoted barrel specifically for the workers—but also the tools have become more modern. Some bodegas, like El Maestro Sierra, still run the scales the traditional way, but many now use modern pumps and stainless steel holding tanks that have made the process of *saca* and *rocío* more streamlined.

Still, how often a bodega runs the scales in a solera system is (like most things in Spain) not on any sort of standardized schedule. Instead, it's determined solera by solera. In general, fino soleras in Jerez are typically refreshed somewhere between two and five times per year, while manzanilla soleras in Sanlúcar are generally refreshed more often, which is due, in part, to the vigor of the flor—like any feisty garden plant, the more flor grows, the more "watering" it needs to stay alive.

The Magic of Flor

Flor, the idiosyncratic "flower" that naturally blooms on the wines in this part of Spain, is, scientifically speaking, made up of several strains of *Saccharomyces* yeast that rapidly procreate to form a veil—*velo* in Spanish, *voile* in French—on the surface of the wine that looks, to the observant eye of this book's photographer, like "a 1970s popcorn ceiling."

The impact of flor aging is perhaps best understood by tasting a fino (aged under flor) and oloroso (aged sans flor), both of the same age, side by side. The fino, even after as much as ten years in barrel, is a light golden yellow and smells of sea spray, citrus, and bread dough, while an oloroso of the same age is dark brown and full-bodied and smells of caramel, nuts, and bergamot. How?

Put most simply, the flor feeds off oxygen inside the barrel, essentially vacuum-sealing the wine beneath it, preventing oxidation. (There's a common misconception that all sherry is oxidized—it's not: biological aging is an anaerobic process, defined by the *absence* of oxygen.) In the case of biologically aged sherry, in order to promote the growth of flor, the standard 600-liter sherry barrel is only filled up to roughly 500 liters and very loosely bunged so that small amounts of oxygen can flow into the empty portion of the barrel. Flor feeds on this oxygen as it creeps in, as well as on alcohol and glycerol in the wine beneath it. (Glycerol, by the way, is the compound that gives wine its viscosity, which explains why biologically aged wine—especially fino and manzanilla—can be so remarkably lean.) The flor can consume up to one percent of alcohol each year, which is yet another reason why the barrels need to constantly be refreshed with new wine via the solera system. If the alcohol level gets too low (below 14 percent) it will result in a *bota desmayada,* or "fainting cask," that is far more susceptible to bacterial contamination.

THE CAPATAZ

THE SHERRY CELLARMASTER, OR *CAPATAZ,* as Julian Jeffs writes in *Sherry,* "like the butler in England, belongs to a legendary race." In the United States we rarely think of winemakers as part of a race, let alone even part of a lineage. We are too young still. But in a region as draped in history and mysticism as the Sherry Triangle, it's no wonder that the historical *capataz* has become a sort of folk hero—part soothsayer, part hustler.

There are many stories about the most famous and fortunate among them: the legendary Juan Fuentes (*capataz* of the now-defunct Pedro Domecq) died in the mid-1800s, having apparently earned upwards of 15 million pounds in today's currency. At the industry's high point, the *capataz* was not only the keeper of the cellar's secrets, but also a middleman collecting lofty commissions from growers—the "grand lion of Xeres," as

Richard Ford wrote in *Gatherings from Spain* (1846).

But the enduring legend of the *capataz* has less to do with the apparent fortunes they could earn in the region's heyday than it does with their palates. They were the wine whisperers during a time where there were no labs or detailed manuals on managing flor—just a winemaking process that was, and still is, far less predictable than most.

Ford describes the *capataz* as the "sole possessor of the secrets of the cellar . . . celebrated for the length of their pedigrees, and the tasting properties of their tongues." And even today, in a climate where technological advancements have caused some to dismiss the importance of taste and instinct, the best *capataz* still possess the same sort of mythical intuition.

Depending on the time of year, the thickness of the veil varies from milky white and cottony (in spring and autumn) to gray and wan (in summer and winter). Returning to the metaphor of flor as flower, it "blooms" in spring and autumn, when the temperatures in the bodegas are optimal for growth. And while a similar veil forms naturally on wines in other parts of the world, notably France's Jura region, there is no other place in the world where it grows more intensely than here.

In fact, flor, ruthless omnivore that it is, even impacts the wine after it has died off. As fino and manzanilla age under flor, constantly refreshed with new wine to promote growth, yeast cells die and fall to the bottom of the barrel to form the *cabezuela* (fine lees). As with any wine aged for a long period on the lees (Champagne and Muscadet being two of the more famous examples), contact with the fine lees lends a sort of savory, mushroomy character to the wine. This becomes particularly evident in older finos and manzanillas, like Emilio Hidalgo's Fino Especial La Panesa, which averages around fifteen years of age at bottling.

As fino and manzanilla age, particularities began to emerge between barrels. Thus, one of the more difficult tasks of the *capataz* is managing the growth of flor across hundreds, often thousands, of different barrels of varying ages. Fernando Hidalgo of Bodegas Emilio Hidalgo explains the job as akin to raising children of the same blood with very different personalities; Eduardo Ojeda of Valdespino and Equipo Navazos calls it "steering a carriage pulled by many animals, with different dispositions." Both are referring not so much to the young wine that enters the solera as to the remarkable differences that emerge among barrels as they age. Much of this has to do with the unpredictable nature of flor and the individual character of each supremely old barrel.

Navigating the personalities of entire solera systems down to each barrel is what makes the job of the *capataz* quite different than that of a traditional winemaker. And while technology and laboratory testing has made managing these systems much easier, the best *capataz* in the region still rely more on intuition and experience, as they are not so much scientists as they are, in Ojeda's words, "[people] who manage the evolution of a family," and, more importantly, "create balance."

OLD BARRELS AND INTUITION

While the job of the *capataz* is taxing, the *tonelero*, or cooper, wins the Sherry Triangle's painstaking award. Although the wines now typically undergo their primary fermentation in stainless steel, aging is always conducted in old barrels, which, as they age, require a ton of expertise to maintain. The typical

sherry *bota* (barrel or cask) is made of American oak, and barrels most suitable for the aging of sherry generally range between fifty and eighty years of age, with some eclipsing the century mark. There are three main reasons for the use of old American oak: First, American oak provides an optimal amount of breathability. Second, the neutrality of old wood ensures that very minimal tannin or wood flavor will be imparted to the wine. And third, the barrels each have their own colonies of yeast and bacteria that help determine the character of the wine aged within them. Preserving their integrity is paramount.

As such, almost every bodega has a sort of cooper's corner—an area of the cellar littered with a tangle of old barrel staves and rusted metal hoops. What might look to most like a primitive trash heap is a sherry bodega's goldmine. Typically, the barrels within sherry bodegas are painted black, which—while also visually appealing—is done to highlight leaks and defects. Often these issues can be dealt with via the Band-Aid approach; at other times a stave must be replaced, a time-consuming process that requires that the contents of the defective barrel be siphoned out, the surrounding barrels supported (to prevent a catastrophic Jenga-style collapse), and the barrel removed. The barrel is repaired with a stave of similar age and set back into its place, secured, and refilled.

The skill set required to maintain these barrels is one of the many requirements of winemaking in the Sherry Triangle that differentiate it from other winemaking regions, showing that despite the creep of modernization, this is a region still bound by tradition.

Of course, many of the improvements of modern winemaking have helped sherry. But often the changes have only helped illustrate the everlasting importance of intuition and experience. The specialized skills of the *capataz* and the *tonelero*—these cannot be replaced by a machine or controlled in a lab. But there's something deeper. Javier Hidalgo of Bodegas Hidalgo–La Gitana once said that sherry is in his "genetic information," and this rings true, not just for him, but also for the region itself. The vineyards and the grapes, the unique production processes, the long and colorful history of the industry, bodega architecture, the specifics of climate and geography: everything about sherry has been built into the DNA of the region, and its people, over centuries. That is the part of the winemaking process in the Sherry Triangle that I cannot possibly quantify, but it is here and it is palpable. And if sherry can teach us anything about wine in a grander sense it's that there is no tool or technique greater than experience.

SHERRY AND FLAMENCO: ANDALUSIA'S EXPRESSION OF EXTREMES

SHERRY AND FLAMENCO SHARE MANY things in common. But perhaps most striking is the fact that both have proven, more than once over the last two centuries, that they cannot be commercialized without losing the soul of what they are—which is, by extension, the very soul of their birthplace: Andalusia.

This is a region that has, at almost every turn, found poetic ways to express the dualism that has defined it for hundreds of years. Here *allegria* ("joy") and *peña* ("suffering") are inextricable. History has reminded the region that no momentous occasion or achievement is complete without recognition of how fleeting these moments can be. From this inner conflict, the foundation of flamenco, the *cante jondo*, "deep song"—a primitive expression of emotion and spirituality "imbued with the mysterious color of primordial ages," as the poet Federico García Lorca described it—was born.

At the heart of it is one somewhat intangible force: *duende*.

The *duende*, which Lorca described in many ways but perhaps most elegantly as "a momentary burst of inspiration, the blush of all that is truly alive," is born out of the constant awareness of death, of finiteness, and the deep sense of urgency and heartbreak it breeds. It is no wonder, then, that this word has come to describe not only the great flamenco singers but also the great bullfighters.

There is debate around whether or not flamenco originated with the arrival of the gypsies in Andalusia—or if they simply built on what was already there—but few would debate the fact that it is to the gypsies that Andalusia owes, says Lorca, "the building of these channels through which all the pain, all ritual gestures of race can escape."

In America, the closest thing we have to flamenco is the foundation of the blues: the chants and shouts of enslaved field workers before the Civil War. Flamenco remains, in its pure form, as raw as these early field hollers.

And it's through flamenco's wild, possessed form of dance and the cry of the flamenco singer—that "marvelous buccal undulation that smashes the cells of our tempered scale," says Lorca—that I began to understand not only this place, but also its wines.

The ability to recognize *terroir*—the geologic and climactic factors that give a wine its essential character—teaches us, poetically, about wine's connection to the earth. But what about its connection to people?

What Andalusia has become for me is a striking lesson about the connection between wine and place——and not place in a geological sense, but the sort of "place" that is spiritually and psychologically ingrained in a people over centuries.

Sherry, like flamenco, is about extremes. From the skeletal delicacy and intense dryness of fino and manzanilla to the tooth-achingly sweet, crude-oil black of PX—it is a full embrace of opposites, of sweetest and driest. And, like *peña* and *allegria*, they are inextricable. It is a wine that poses the question, in the words of Fernando Valencia of Pedro Romero, "What sort of people live here?!" But it also prompts you find the answer.

"If you are not used to drinking an old amontillado, for example, it's hard to understand; you may not appreciate it," says Jaime Gil, who works at the sherry producer Valdespino and is a devoted lover of flamenco. "Same with flamenco, if you aren't used to seeing it, you might just dismiss it as some guy crying and shouting. But if you go deep, you feel it. And like pure sherry, pure flamenco—if you feel it—can become something so good it hurts."

Efforts to make pure sherry and pure flamenco more appealing to a wider audience have damaged both. In the case of the former, commercialization meant—in the late-nineteenth century—a proliferation of low-quality blended sherry (the classic dry styles made sweet by the addition of PX or other, less desirable, sweeteners). Sherry spent nearly one hundred years clawing its way out of the mess it'd created and then, in the 1960s and 1970s, did it all over again. These efforts to mass-produce wines that appealed to a larger audience resulted in a whole laundry list of misconceptions about sherry.

In the early twentieth century, following flamenco's Golden Age— between 1869 and 1910—it began being exported and modified to suit public tastes. The period wherein true *cantaores* and *bailaores*, or flamenco singers and dancers, could make money performing flamenco in its pure form, gave way to a form of flamenco repurposed for a larger audience—stripped of its raw intensity in favor of a softened, controlled, more sentimental form of song and dance.

Marion Papenbrok writes in *Flamenco* that, "The atmosphere of the theater completed the transformation that for decades fashioned the inaccurate picture the majority of people have of flamenco."

Sherry and flamenco's plots are oddly parallel, two expressions of Andalusia so deeply tied to its history and identity that they have—in a new world where art, wine, food, music increasingly fall prey to globalization—through ups and downs, managed to preserve their integrity.

The flamenco guitarist Tiago della Vega said to me, "Flamenco is one of the rare things that wants to go backwards." In a sense, sherry, too, is at its best when it strives for the same.

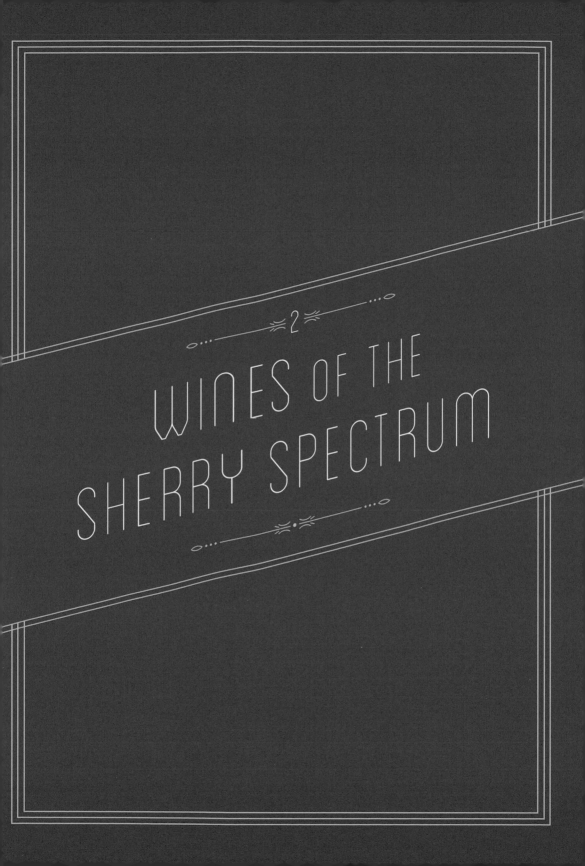

2

WINES OF THE
SHERRY SPECTRUM

y early initiation into the range of sherry styles went a lot like this: confusion; momentary enlightenment; more confusion. So, by the time I visited the Sherry Triangle for the first time I was determined—like so many who have come before me—to get some straight answers to some pressing questions. When does a fino become an amontillado? What, exactly, is palo cortado? And why in hell are there so many names for blended sherries that are made more or less in the same way?

One thing I found out is that organizing logical and internally coherent systems is not of the great strengths of the Spanish. (The Germans, on the other hand, with their even more perplexing classification of Riesling—well, I'm not sure what their excuse is.) Yet I think it's fair to say that the variety of wines available in the Sherry Triangle originated less out of the industry's apparent disregard for—or even suspicion of—a clearly defined system than out of various attempts to please the market and help it appreciate what has always been an idiosyncratic wine. In short, it was a way to create something for everyone. Such flexibility has led to a lot of unfortunate developments (the focus on cheap, blended sherry not least among them), but this willingness to please, and the talent for hospitality it represents, is quintessentially Spanish.

The sherry expert and historian Álvaro Girón Sierra once said to me, on the topic of palo cortado (the most ambiguous, fuzzily defined style of sherry), "Sometimes I think there is too much romance in Jerez; we need more knowledge." But I have a feeling that, however frustrating it is, he appreciates how deeply Spanish—and deeply *Andaluz*, for that matter—the romance is.

"In the nineteenth century," says Girón Sierra, "it was just a lot of chalk and the *capataz*, making marks, and trying to convey all of this complexity in the solera system and address things that were mainly unpredictable." ("Chalk" refers to the marks the *capataz* used to label and classify each barrel; see page 25.)

Throughout sherry's history, a variety of these chalk symbols—most of them resembling hieroglyphics—were used to try and keep track of variation from barrel to barrel. But it wasn't until well into the twentieth century, when winemaking became more predictive in general, that this actually resulted in wines that neatly fell into one consistent category or another like they do today. Diego Ignacio Parada y Barreto, writing in 1868 (and in terrific detail), describes only two main types of sherry: amontillado and palo cortado. Fino, though defined as early as 1846 in Richard Ford's *Gatherings from Spain* as a designation of the finest base wine (fino, after all, translates to "fine"), had not yet been widely established as its own style of sherry. Palo cortado was, at that time, essentially described as basic dry sherry. And amontillado was defined as finer, more delicate, more rare—and as made by accident, not design. (Today, it's palo cortado that is defined as a wine that cannot be "made," but is a product of an uncontrollable natural occurrence.)

By the time Henry Vizetelly released *Facts About Sherry* in 1875, the word "fino" had begun to appear in the press with greater frequency—and not just as an adjective describing the base wine, but in reference to a separate style of sherry. Although Vizetelly clearly defined fino as a wine distinct from amontillado, throughout the latter part of the nineteenth century the division between the two styles wasn't always precise; they were both described as "very fine, pale" wines, and what distinguished one from the other wasn't always clear. Part of this was because, as Girón Sierra points out, "there was not a developed way of managing the solera system, and keeping the wine aging biologically for any extended period wasn't easy." The result was that the finos of the time were, stylistically, closer to what we'd now call amontillado—likely showing more oxidation than the style that has defined the finos made since the 1970s, when changing preferences led to wines bottled younger and with heavier filtration.

Confused? Good. It will make the classification system of the twenty-first century seem remarkably lucid in comparison.

Dry Sherries

Sherry's regulatory council, the Consejo Regulador, defines what we call "dry sherry" (which they refer to as *vinos generosos*, or "generous wines") as wines with a maximum of five grams of residual sugar per liter produced from grape juice that has been fermented to complete dryness. According to regulations, there are four main styles of dry sherry, all with differing modes of production: manzanilla and fino (which, again, differ in character, but are made the same way), amontillado, palo cortado, and oloroso. These styles fit nicely, in this order, along a spectrum from lightest to fullest, and from purely biological (that is, aged under flor) to purely oxidative (aged sans flor).

Finos and manzanillas form the spectrum's starting point. They are aged biologically under flor for the entirety of their lives and are the leanest and palest sherries. As we continue along the spectrum, the wines start showing signs of oxidative aging. This happens because either the wines are allowed to age long enough for the flor to slowly die *or* additional alcohol is added to intentionally kill off the flor. Without flor's protective vacuum seal, oxygen begins to impact the wines. Older finos and manzanillas (those that start creeping into the double

digits) still show a dominant biological impact, but also some signs of oxidation due to the weakness of the flor. These are often referred to as "manzanilla pasada" or "fino-amontillado" even though the latter is no longer a legal classification.

If a fino or manzanilla is left to age to the point that *all* the flor dies (or is killed off), it begins its journey to becoming an amontillado—a style that combines the nutty, savory character born from longer oxidation with a very strong flor character from earlier in the wine's life. Even when a sherry has spent decades in a solera system, its time spent under flor still lives on inside the wine like a faded Polaroid.

Next stop: palo cortado. Despite all the modern mystery surrounding its production (which I'll touch on in more detail later), palo cortado is really just a halfway point between amontillado and oloroso. The wine generally sees some time under flor, but not nearly as much as amontillado. As such, the flor does not live long enough to consume all of the wine's flesh, and the result is a style that is rounder and richer on the palate than amontillado.

Yet palo cortado is still lighter and more elegant than oloroso, which forms the spectrum's other bookend. Oloroso is the only dry style that is a completely oxidative wine, never aged under flor. Classic examples are dry; however, the higher level of glycerol (the chemical compound that gives wine its viscosity) gives an impression of sweetness in the mouth. This is a wine built for beef, and in Andalusia that is exactly what you drink it with.

Sweet (and Sweetened) Sherries

Beyond the spectrum of dry wines there are two additional categories: sweet and sweetened. The distinction is important. The former category includes the naturally sweet wines pedro ximénez or PX, which is made from dried grapes of the same name, and moscatel, which is made in much the same way from dried Moscatel (Muscat) grapes. Though these sweet wines form a comparatively small part of total sherry production, they are still an important part of almost every bodega's range.

Sweetened or "blended" sherries form a separate category that includes pale creams, creams, amorosos, mediums, browns, and East Indias—effectively, the grab bag from which much of the confusion about sherry has originated. These wines are sweet and cheap, historically produced for export markets. They have their place, of course, and there are a handful of terrific blended sherries made in the region (like Emilio Hidalgo's Cream Morenita and Hidalgo– La Gitana's Cream Alameda), but they form a category whose separateness from both dry and naturally sweet sherry is important to reinforce.

Fino and Manzanilla

What distinguishes fino from manzanilla is really a matter of geography. Both are aged purely biologically. And for both wines, the Consejo Regulador rules state that each must spend a minimum of two years under flor (recently reduced from three years) before being bottled, but most producers continue to age their finos and manzanillas for four or more years, with some, like Valdespino's Fino Inocente, spending as many as ten years under flor.

Together fino and manzanilla make up about 40 percent of all wines officially labeled sherry. They are also the driest wines in the world, which is just one of the reasons sherry lovers see red when the topic of sherry comes up and someone says, "Sherry? I don't like sweet wine." These wines achieve their extreme level of dryness thanks to flor, which feeds off of glycerol, plucking the meat off the base wine's bones until all that's left is a structural skeleton so delicate it's as if it were woven together with fishing line. This dryness gives the impression of both salinity and acidity on the palate. It also masks the wine's alcohol content—which is at least 15 percent at bottling— endowing it with a sort of ethereal lightness not often associated with wines above 14 percent.

The impact of flor on the texture of the wine—the way it strips it down to its essentials—is one of the more fascinating outcomes of biological aging. But flor also imparts a very specific aroma and flavor to the wine, which is most pronounced in fino and manzanilla. Some describe it as a combination of herbal and yeasty, others call it steely and pungent, but once you become acquainted with how flor leaves its mark on a wine, its impression is as recognizable as a Warhol print.

As a style of sherry, fino as we know it today is a truly modern invention. Prior to the 1970s, wines labeled "fino" or "manzanilla" were not as aggressively filtered as many are today, resulting in wines that were not only darker in color but also fuller bodied. They were also typically released with a higher average age, making them stylistically closer to what we might today call a fino-amontillado or a manzanilla pasada—wines that are often starting to show slight notes of oxidation due to the weakening of flor with age.

There is also evidence that after fino began gaining momentum as a commercial product in the last decades of the nineteenth century and on through the beginning of the twentieth, many of the most esteemed finos and amontillados of the period were not fortified (and many were not fined—that is, clarified using things like clay or egg white or, believe it, animal blood— either). This was part of a (now eerily familiar) movement toward what the

press at the time dubbed "natural wine." These "natural" sherries, as they were called, often came from the best vineyard sites and were prized for their fineness and purity. And, even as early as the 1830s, fortification of the finest wines was eschewed, because, as Henry D. Inglis wrote in 1831 of a particularly delicate amontillado, "whatever is added to it, entirely spoils it." But these wines still constituted a very small portion of the total sherry market at the time. And with an ever-thirsty British market—and a sherry export business whose "bread and butter," as the historian Álvaro Girón Sierra points out, "has always been based on less virtuous blends"—wines that were more difficult to produce simply couldn't become the norm. They were, by nature, boutique.

So while Equipo Navazos has, in the spirit of these historic finos, released two unfiltered, 100 percent Palomino Fino wines aged under flor—Niepoort-Navazos and Florpower—today fino, and sherry in general, is synonymous with fortification.

In fact, before heavier carbon filtration of the wines started to become more commonplace in the 1970s and 1980s, finos were often stabilized by an extra fortification. The first fortification, to 15 percent, would come, as it does today, after primary fermentation and before the wines entered the solera system; a second fortification, to around 17 percent, would be conducted closer to bottling. In the absence of filtration, the higher alcohol level ensured that any solids left in the wine would not referment in bottle.

Today, Fernando de Castilla's Fino Antique and Osborne's Fino Coquinero, which are both fortified to 17 percent alcohol, are different interpretations of this old style, but they remain exceptions, as the demand for lighter, younger wines gave rise to the nearly crystal-clear finos that most of us are now well acquainted with.

But demand for very minimally (if at all) filtered finos and manzanillas, dubbed *en rama*, or raw, are shifting the style once again. *En rama* sherries are close approximations of what the wine tastes like from barrel sans filtration, which tends to mute aromas and fade the color of the wine from golden to almost clear in bottle. There is, of course, nothing wrong with more heavily filtered finos and manzanillas (in fact, there aren't many things that taste better cold on a hot day), but it's true that a good deal of complexity and character are lost as a result of heavy filtration—a realization that has fueled the *en rama* trend among sherry lovers both in and outside of Spain.

EN RAMA SHERRIES

WHILE PRODUCERS LIKE BARBADILLO have been bottling special, minimally filtered wines for more than a decade, the words *en rama* (raw) didn't really enter the American consumer's vocabulary until late 2011. Interest spread rapidly. At the time of writing, in late 2013, the list of producers releasing at least one *en rama* wine now includes Lustau (who, as of 2013, bottles one from each of the three sherry towns), Valdespino, Hidalgo–La Gitana, González Byass, Equipo Navazos, Delgado Zuleta, Gutiérrez Colosía, Tradición, Fernando de Castilla, Sánchez Romate, Alvear, Argüeso, Sacristía AB, and Alexander Jules, among others.

And while this trend feels novel, it's not the first time that sherry lovers have rattled the cages in a demand for less adulterated wines. During the nineteenth century the perceived negative impact of heavy fining was well documented and many lovers of sherry argued for more "natural" wines. The most outspoken advocate of these wines during this period was Walter McGee, writing under the nom de plume Don Pedro Verdad (Sir Peter Truth). "So long as English people expect their wines to look bright, natural wines must be fined repeatedly in order to make them clear," he said. "The result being that they lose a great deal of *finura* (delicacy)." He was writing, mind you, in 1876.

These unfortified, unfiltered, and unsweetened finos and amontillados of the nineteenth century found favor within a niche group of connoisseurs in England. A similar demand for purer, unfiltered sherries is capturing, nearly 150 years later, the attention of wine lovers and bartenders from London to New York to San Francisco.

8 *En Rama* Wines to Try

Unless otherwise indicated, prices refer to 375-milliliter bottlings.

- Valdespino Manzanilla Deliciosa En Rama ($15)
- Lustau Puerto Fino En Rama ($22, 500ml)
- Hidalgo–La Gitana Manzanilla En Rama ($30, 750ml)
- González Byass Tío Pepe En Rama ($22, 750ml)
- Equipo Navazos Manzanilla "I Think" En Rama ($15)
- Barbadillo Manzanilla Solear En Rama (seasonal, $15)
- Fernando de Castilla Fino En Rama ($20)
- Bodegas Tradición Fino Tradición ($50, 750ml)

MANZANILLA: FINO'S BROTHER FROM ANOTHER MOTHER

The origin of the name "manzanilla" has long been a subject of debate. To this day, depending on whom you ask, you'll get one of three theories. The first suggests that the name derives from the Spanish word for apple, *manzana*, because the wine's aromas are said to recall that of small, pungent apples, or *manzanillas*. A second theory, and the one most often repeated by Jerezanos with a bone to pick, is that it is named for the town of Manzanilla, west of Sevilla in the province of Huelva, and that the wine actually originated there and not in Sanlúcar de Barrameda (where modern-day manzanilla is aged). The third, and most widely accepted theory, is that wine was named for its aromatic resemblance to chamomile, also called *manzanilla* in Spanish.

Whatever the truth of its name's origin, the distinction of manzanilla from fino was originally born of exclusion. Despite the fact that intentional flor aging and the use of the solera system are said to have originated in Sanlúcar, the wines produced there were not always considered "sherry." This is not to say that Sanlúcar wasn't making wonderful, sherrylike wines at this time—quite the contrary. In fact, in the mid-nineteenth century the wines became known as a lighter alternative to sherry and as its popularity in Victorian England grew, manzanilla's presence in the press increased. Depending on who was writing (and likely how much they'd had to drink) its pedigree ranged from "delicious, but simple" to "exquisite." Invariably, words like "pale," "delicate," and "pure" were used and writers repeatedly drew parallels between manzanilla and both Rhine wine (which generally referred to Riesling) and Chablis.

Today, of course, the wines of Sanlúcar de Barrameda are an inextricable part of what we define as sherry. Still, manzanilla has always been a wine whose character is unique enough that it merits distinction from fino—it does, after all, have its own DO, Manzanilla-Sanlúcar de Barrameda—despite the fact that production methods in Jerez, Sanlúcar, and El Puerto de Santa María are virtually the same. Grapes for the production of wine in all three towns can also come from anywhere within the Jerez-Xérès-Sherry DO.

The difference in the wine's character, then, is the result of its being aged in Sanlúcar de Barrameda rather than say, Jerez. There are significant variations in climate between the two places—notably the more powerful Atlantic influence in Sanlúcar, whose temperatures are more moderate and humidity levels higher. In terms of yeast strains, the flor here also tends to be compositionally different.

There are also cultural differences. If you spend more than an afternoon in each place you'll notice a healthy amount of ribbing, arising from Jerez's perceived superiority and Sanlúcar's defiance of that perception. It's mostly framed as friendly competition, but it goes a bit deeper. They are different in much the same way that Napa, with its reputation as the playground of the rich, has, despite proximity, a different vibe from Sonoma, which still maintains more of a "screw-the-man" mentality. In more ways than one, Jerez is the Napa to Sanlúcar's Sonoma.

What Jerez and Sanlúcar, as well as El Puerto know, however, is that despite their differences they have to work together to turn around their shared fortunes. Over the last fifty years the wines, specifically manzanilla and fino, have been reduced to, as Peter Liem and Jesús Barquín astutely point out in *Sherry, Manzanilla & Montilla*, "a suitable accompaniment to tapas, but hardly something worthy of serious attention." Yet, these are not only some of the world's most unique wines, but in terms of quality, they are among the great white wines. Even the simplest finos and manzanillas, dangerously poundable as they may be, require an inordinate investment to produce, and their absurdly low price tag is one of the many reasons why sherry has long been the wine world's best-kept secret.

SERVING AND STORING SHERRY

IN THE LAND OF SHERRY THERE ARE VERY few hard-and-fast rules, but avoiding warm fino and manzanilla at all costs is certainly one of them. While this may seem obvious now, there was once a time not so long ago when most American sherry lovers were likely to watch a bottle of fino, situated on the back bar right next to a bottle of Jim Beam, come right off the shelf and into their glass. But times they are a-changin'.

Though there are a vast range of styles within the sherry spectrum that make it difficult to generalize, treating sherry like you would a table wine—whether white or red—is always better than treating it like a spirit. Beyond this, there are some basic ground rules that will help you experience each style at its prime.

Storage

As a general rule the wines should be stored at cellar temperature. That is, in the vicinity of 55°F and definitely not on a wine rack near your window or in your laundry room. The wine fridge is your friend.

While many believe that manzanilla and fino should be consumed as close to bottling as possible, this is not necessarily the case. The process of filtration and bottling can be traumatic for the wine, often leaving it less expressive and inte-grated for several months after bottling. This is true for most table wines as well.

Thus fino and manzanilla, like other wines, tend to show their best after they've had time to acclimate to their new environment. Now that bottling dates are routinely printed on the back of sherry labels (they begin with an L), it's possible to be mindful of this. Further, in *Sherry, Manzanilla & Montilla*, Peter Liem and Jesús Barquín suggest that—against popular opinion—biological sherries tend to show much better six months to a year after bottling. I agree: with proper storage, the wines do improve considerably. And while *en rama* wines tend to be more delicate than their more heavily filtered counter-parts, even they need time not only to recover from bottling but also to evolve.

Long aging is another subject entirely. Fino and manzanilla gain weight in the bottle, which can be jarring for someone used to the leanness of their younger state. That having been said, tasting fino or manzanilla that has been in bottle for half a decade or more can be a reminder of how much more we have to discover about these wines and what they are capable of. (Oxidative wines, by virtue of their aging process, are not impacted by bottle aging.)

Life After Opening

Once a bottle of fino or manzanilla is opened it will last about two to three days in the fridge before it starts to dull and lose its vibrancy. Some can keep longer, but as a general rule three days is the beginning of the end. Amontillado, because it undergoes oxidative aging, can last much longer—usually up to a few weeks—while oloroso and palo cortado can go even further, often up to a couple of months. The wines of advanced age can often keep for more than a year, while PX can last several years, properly stoppered.

Serving Temperature

Fino and manzanilla typically drink best, like any other white wine, somewhere in between refrigerator temp and cellar temp. To achieve this without a thermometer, I generally take the bottle out of the fridge and let it sit out for around ten minutes before serving. Not an exact science, but effective nonetheless.

Amontillado, palo cortado, and oloroso are best served slightly warmer—closer to cellar temperature—so that they can show their full range of aromas without getting so warm that their alcohols singe your nose hairs. PX is also best served in this temperature range.

Glassware

In the sherry region the *copita*—a small glass that would typically be used in America for sampling wine or spirits—is the dominant glassware for sherry. In fact, only the finest restaurants will serve sherry in anything else.

As of late, however, many producers are questioning how effective the glass is in expressing sherry's full range of aromas. Sherry is a wine, so why is it served in a glass that was historically used for sampling spirits? One producer, who will remain anonymous, joked that he wanted to stage a PR campaign against the *copita* by rounding up 12,000 of them, putting them in the street, and then bulldozing them.

While I wouldn't go quite that far, I will say that the glass tends to underserve the wines across the entire range. My preferred glassware for fino and manzanilla is a stemmed white wineglass—and while this also serves amontillado, palo cortado, and oloroso well, they fare equally well in a Bordeaux glass.

Sweet sherries are best consumed in a port or a small white-wineglass.

Pairing

Sherry has proven its merit and compatibility with a wide range of cuisines—from gastro pub food, to Italian, to Japanese—but when it comes to choosing which wines to go with a particular dish, I offer you this old Andalusian adage: fino and manzanilla if it swims, amontillado if it flies, and oloroso if it walks.

My advice is to keep this in the back of your mind, but don't consider it a rigid guideline. For one thing, amontillado with pork—whether braised, grilled, or in a stew—explodes the flies-walks notion. As does a good roast chicken, which begs for fino of advanced age. Sherry invites adventure, and that shouldn't end at the dinner table. So, go with what sounds good—sherry truly has a way of surprising more than it fails.

PARTY IN PURGATORY: "FINO-AMONTILLADO" AND "MANZANILLA PASADA"

Sometime in 2010, an earthly saint gave me a bottle of Equipo Navazos's La Bota de Manzanilla Pasada 20. I remember decanting it, drinking it over the course of several hours, and wondering just how it had taken us modern wine people so long to figure out how infinitely complex—on the level of great Burgundy, Riesling, Champagne—sherry can be.

To this day that wine remains one of the greatest wines I've ever tasted, and yet it doesn't exactly fit into one specific category, at least as we define them today. It was sourced from the best and oldest barrel, called the *bota punta*, within a very old solera of manzanilla housed in the cellars of La Guita. Averaging over fifteen years of age, the wine embodied a contrast between the beginnings of oxidation and the briny freshness of flor-aged manzanilla that made for a tension you could actually *feel*. In simple terms, manzanilla pasada is merely an old manzanilla, which represents a sort of stylistic purgatory between manzanilla and amontillado. This style used to be more prevalent in the market during the first three-quarters of the twentieth century than it is today, but there are several examples—like Hidalgo–La Gitana's Manzanilla Pasada Pastrana, Lustau's Almacenista Manuel Cuevas Jurado Manzanilla Pasada, La Cigarrera's Manzanilla Pasada, and periodic manzanilla pasada releases from Equipo Navazos, among several others—that continue to represent some of the most intriguing wines from Sanlúcar.

The same is true of Jerez and El Puerto, where the style was commonly bottled as "fino-amontillado"; that term has since been banned by the EU. But, like manzanilla pasada, the style still persists, as evidenced by Emilio Hidalgo's Fino La Panesa Especial, Valdespino's Inocente, Gutiérrez Colosía's Fino Amerigo, Fernando de Castilla's Fino Antique, and Equipo Navazos's numerous fino bottlings (not least among them the defiantly named La Bota de Fino Amontillado 45). At their best, these wines articulate the profound transition from biological to oxidative aging. And instead of answering the question of exactly when a fino or manzanilla becomes an amontillado, they embrace the period of delicious ambiguity in between.

Amontillado

The word *amontillado* is an adjective meaning "Montilla-like," referring to the wines produced in the town of Montilla, which is situated inland about a hundred miles east of Jerez, near the city of Córdoba. The dry wines of Montilla are produced in a similar fashion to those of the Sherry Triangle, but are instead made from the Pedro Ximénez grape and, in the case of the fino, are not fortified, given the greater ripening potential of the grape. The biological wines made there tended (and still tend) to be richer in flavor.

While we don't know if the wine first called amontillado in the Sherry Triangle actually came from Montilla or if the Jerezanos were simply trying to make wine *a la moda Montilla,* it's more likely that the latter is true. Certainly by the beginning of the nineteenth century wines called amontillado were made in Jerez, as evidenced by advertisements in the British press linking amontillado to specific Jerez *pagos* like Macharnudo.

As a style of wine from the Sherry Triangle, amontillado predates the arrival of fino in the market by more than a half century, and by the beginning of the nineteenth century it had already established itself as one of the world's most sought-after wines, due in large part to the mystery surrounding its production. At the time, amontillado was considered a "gift from nature"—a wine not produced by carefully regulated methods, but rather appearing by happy accident.

Sir Arthur de Capell Brooke, in his 1831 *Sketches in Spain and Morocco,* writes, "Amontillado is something like a phenomenon in winemaking, for no cultivator can be certain the grape will produce it." In *Gatherings from Spain* (1846), John Murray further links this phenomenon to the wine's prestige, saying, "This amontillado, when the genuine production of nature, is very valuable ... "

There are several hypotheses on how this "accidental" wine was really produced, including picking grapes earlier in the season, or vine age (it was believed that young vines could not produce amontillado). More likely what was happening was that flor was impacting some wines and not others, and cellar masters did not yet understand how to cultivate or maintain flor well enough to actually *produce* amontillado.

Today, of course, the production of amontillado is well understood. By modern definition it's a wine that is aged under flor as a fino or manzanilla until the flor has died off or is killed by fortifying the wine to at least 17 percent, at which point the wine continues aging oxdatively for a period before being bottled. In this sense it is a wine that lives two lives: a biological childhood and an oxidative adulthood.

The evolution of a fino or manzanilla to an amontillado brings us back to one of sherry's more vexed questions: If an amontillado is essentially a very old fino or manzanilla, when exactly does the wine stop being fino or manzanilla and become an amontillado? The answer is that there is no exact moment, and different tasters and producers might even categorize the same wine differently. What's more, much of the distinction is challenged by the variation of styles of amontillado among bodegas and the age of the amontillado at bottling. By regulation, amontillado must spend at least two years under flor, but many of the finest examples spend upward of eight to ten years aging biologically, giving them a stronger flor imprint that—even with amontillados of advanced age—lends an eternal sort of tension between the loud flavors of oxidation and the leanness and austerity that biological aging imparts. The yin and yang of these dueling identities—one shaped by its biological childhood and one by its oxidative adulthood—have inspired a sort of religious admiration of the wine for centuries.

Edgar Allan Poe, king of duality that he was, was also a well-documented lover of sherry. His famous short story "A Cask of Amontillado," written during amontillado's reign in 1846, attests to its international reach: it was written in Baltimore by an American about non-Spanish sherry lovers. The story follows Montresor, who lures his victim, Fortunato, to his death by promising a "pipe" (or large cask) of fine amontillado. "He had a weak point—this Fortunato—although in other regards he was a man to be respected and even feared. He prided himself on his connoisseurship in wine." Such good taste was the death of him.

Palo Cortado

For decades palo cortado has enjoyed the good press that accompanies a mysterious backstory and the perpetuation of myths Hefneresque in their ambiguity. (Are those *really* his girlfriends? Is this wine *really* an accident?) It is the only style of sherry that has an official classification but no real definition. The Consejo Regulador describes it only as a wine that combines the "delicate bouquet of an amontillado with the body and palate of an oloroso."

Because there is no concrete regulation on how the wine must be made in order to qualify as palo cortado, determining what it is remains approximate at best. While most can agree that true palo cortado should be a bridge between amontillado and oloroso, the interpretation of what that should taste like varies. Some, like Emilio Hidalgo's Marqués de Rodil, which spends an unusually long time under flor (around eight years), taste closer to amontillado. Others, like Lustau's Palo Cortado Península, show more of the round, roasted notes of oloroso. And still others, like Fernando de Castilla's Palo Cortado Antique, fall directly in the center. Thus, like all styles of sherry, palo cortado has a tiny spectrum within it—it's just more varied and far more vague than the others. But for all of its diversity of expressions, palo cortado's ambiguity is less a product of flavor profile than of process.

The name *palo cortado* means "cut stick," and refers to the chalk symbol (⌐) that the *capataz* marks on the wine barrel to identify the style. All wines destined to become a fino or manzanilla are marked with a "palo," represented with a slash (/). But if a barrel earmarked for biological aging deviates from its original path, becoming fuller (more *gordo*) on the palate over time, then the *capataz* will cross the *palo* symbol with a horizontal line called a *cortado*. He or she will then remove the barrel from the fino solera, fortify it to at least 17 percent, and move it to the palo cortado solera.

In a general sense, then, palo cortado is best understood as a wine that, containing the finest mosto, was once destined to become fino, and that for some reason—whether it be the specific bacterial and yeast colonies in a barrel or a weak layer of flor—shows characteristics that defy traditional categorization as fino. Thus, in the modern era it has been considered, as Antonio Flores of González Byass calls it, "the rebel wine."

Surely, some bodegas do leave this occurrence up to chance, even in an age where it would be just as simple to control the elements and steer a wine in the palo cortado direction. But the perpetuation of this element of mystery and the claim that palo cortado cannot be "made" has given the wine an air of luxury and rarity that has certainly helped it over the years.

Jesús Barquín, part-owner of Equipo Navazos and coauthor of *Sherry, Manzanilla & Montilla*, describes, in a 2007 article for *The World of Fine Wine*, the period in the 1970s when the story of palo cortado as "mystery wine" reached its height. A rumor started circulating that palo cortado was disappearing and, "little by little, the interest in this class of wine grew (even if it remained within a relatively small circle of devotees) and new brands began to appear."

It's logical to assume that, if it were left up to chance, the wine truly would be in danger of disappearing. But, as Barquín points out, this romantic notion "already belongs to history."

The truth is that one hundred or even just fifty years ago, wine from every region in the world was far more captive to chance. In fact, some of the greatest wines of the twentieth century were, in many ways, happy accidents. Take Bordeaux's now-legendary 1947 Cheval Blanc. By laboratory standards the wine is a complete mess—it contains not only high levels of volatile acidity, but also high alcohol for the time (14.4 percent) and relatively high levels of residual sugar, yet there are few wine connoisseurs who wouldn't call it a masterpiece;

some even consider it to be the greatest wine of the twentieth century. Today, technological advancements and precision in the cellar basically guarantee that Cheval Blanc will never ever again produce such a wine—after all, it's highly unlikely that one of the top châteaux in the world would let a wine so technically "flawed" touch glass again.

Of course, wine will always be a product of chance because it is a product of nature, but knowledge and technology have made it something far easier to control. Modern advancements in winemaking in the Sherry Triangle—most notably, the fermentation of large lots in stainless steel rather than barrel—have produced wines of greater consistency; the result is, naturally, that less is left up to chance.

While there certainly still are butts of fino that deviate enough to defy their original classification, it's easy to imagine how a palo cortado might be made by simply selecting fine musts destined for fino, allowing the wine to age under flor as a fino for a short period of time, and then fortifying it to at least 17 percent to let the wine age oxidatively. The result would be something a tad lighter and more finessed than oloroso and weightier than amontillado. Which, of course, sounds exactly like palo cortado.

Oloroso

Welcome to the dry sherry spectrum's other bookend—the bass to fino's treble.

Fino is shaped by its lifetime under flor, and by the end is long and lean, like a marathon runner. Oloroso, on the other hand, is built to throw discus: exposure to oxygen and evaporation bulks it up rather than strips it down. There is beauty in both styles, just of very different kinds.

Aside from that accidental encounter with Harvey's Bristol Cream in my teens, Lustau's Emperatriz Eugenia Oloroso was the first real sherry I ever tasted. The word *oloroso* means "fragrant" in Spanish and there's no word in the dictionary that could describe that wine better. It smelled like walnuts, figs, and tea and was round and viscous in the mouth, but dry and elegant on the finish. I remember thinking, "What the hell is this?"—and quickly ordering another. Sherry's lack of immediacy—its austerity, frankly—is part of its allure, but if there's any style that's keen on making a good impression, it's oloroso.

Because the wine is fortified to a level beyond which flor can thrive—and thus its whole life is oxidative, without any biological aging—the solera system's role in the production of oloroso is slightly different. Here the primary function of refreshing the wine is to make up for the percentage lost by both bottling and, more importantly, evaporation, which can amount to as much as 5 percent per year. Those familiar with the production of barrel-aged spirits will know this yearly loss as the "angel's share"—it's a little bit like the wine's way of pouring some out for the homies.

Regardless of how often the solera is refreshed, through evaporation the alcohol level in oloroso will inevitably rise as it ages and, at bottling, many olorosos will average around 20 percent alcohol, while those that have an average age of thirty years or more can often flirt with 25 percent alcohol, like El Maestro Sierra's Oloroso 1/7, which is bottled at 24 percent and is at least fifty years old. Olorosos that have a particularly high level of glycerol and, thus, body, are further classified as *pata de gallina*, or "hen's foot" (the name is derived from the chalk mark used to designate these barrels), while olorosos that are less fine and deemed too coarse to be bottled as oloroso are classified as *rayas* and are generally used in the production of blended sherry.

Though the best olorosos are completely dry, consumers often miss the mark and assume sweetness. This is often due to the fact that in oloroso's darker days in the 1970s and 1980s, many were sweetened and labeled "rich oloroso," "sweet oloroso," or "oloroso dulce." A 1978 article in the *Boston Globe* titled "Aperitifs Enhance Your Appetite" offers a prime example of how confused things had gotten: "For aperitifs stick to drier sherries designated 'fino,' 'manzanilla,' or 'amontillado,' and avoid the sweeter ones marked 'oloroso' or 'cream.'"

Beginning in 2012, the Consejo Regulador banned all of those "rich" and "sweet" olorosos from being labeled oloroso at all, though producers may still legally sweeten an oloroso with a very small addition of pedro ximénez (as long as the total residual sugar doesn't eclipse five grams per liter). However, the majority of the wines that now bear the oloroso name are completely dry.

But the misconception that oloroso is sweet isn't entirely the result of sweetened examples of the style entering the marketplace. Indeed, even oloroso that is bottled completely dry is often *perceived* as sweet by the taster. This is thanks to the chemical compound glycerol, a natural by-product of fermentation that gives texture and weight to wine—something like the same way cornstarch gives hot-and-sour soup its trademark goopiness. As glycerol combines with alcohol, and water evaporates from the wine during aging in barrel, it becomes even more concentrated and, after eight to ten years in a solera system, an oloroso might have a glycerol level six to eight times higher than an amontillado of a similar age. The effect is a wine that is rich and round and gives the impression of sweetness even though it's totally dry.

Despite all the confusion, though, dry oloroso remains the sort of marijuana of sherry styles. It's often the first sherry people try, and once they develop a taste for it, it becomes the gateway to the other styles—the "harder stuff." But oloroso remains addictive long after you've moved on to amontillado or fino.

VOS, VORS, and "Vintage" Sherry

Most of the bodegas in the sherry region have a place within them called a *sacristía*, where wines of significant age are kept. In these nooks one is reminded quite viscerally that the Sherry Triangle is one of the world's most storied wine regions.

A *sacristía* in a church is the place where the priest and other celebrants prepare for service, and where the sacred vessels, garments, and documents are kept. It's a similarly sacred room in the bodega, often kept locked, with low ceilings, dim lighting, and a palpable silence. There is a religious sort of devotion in the way the old wines are kept here, as if the hundred-year-old barrel of pedro ximénez barely the size of a newborn at Bodegas La Cigarrera were the body of a saint or some petrified piece of manna. These nooks, and the wines within them, provoke an odd urge to find a statue of Saint Francis, light a candle, and drop to both knees—because, well, it's not all that often that you're offered a wine that predates the invention of the telegraph, or a pull from a solera system started four years before America declared independence.

These old wines are housed in solera systems that can be as small as a single barrel, and were, up until recently, rarely available in the market. Many of them were reserved for consumption by family and special guests, which is why many have been able to survive with such a high average age for so long.

In response to more and more bodegas bottling these older wines, in 2000 the Consejo Regulador created a system of classification for old wines. Old sherries are now categorized as either VOS (Vinum Optimum Signatum, or Very Old Sherry) for wines over twenty years old or VORS (Vinum Optimum Rare Signatum, or Very Old Rare Sherry) for wines over thirty years of average age. Sherries must pass through a committee to be certified as such.

At twenty, thirty, or fifty years of age, sherry, particularly dry sherry, is especially idiosyncratic. Extended contact with the barrel combined with evaporation—which leads to the wine's becoming more concentrated—can lead to intense savory flavors, breeding wines that are truly anthems to umami. And while at advanced ages the wines often maintain aromas and flavors of dried fruits, it's their ability to express the extreme opposite of fruit—delivered with the potency of a belty Whitney Houston ballad or a sweaty Mission of Burma rant—that make them unique.

But not all VOS or VORS sherries are so loud. Ashley Santoro, the former wine director at New York's longtime sherry haven, Casa Mono, once described Valdespino's incredible, roughly eighty-year-old Palo Cortado Cardenal as smelling like dark alleys and crime. "This wine," she said, "is actually terrifying." And it's true that there's a depth and intensity to the wine that is almost sinister.

The collection of emotions I've experienced tasting old sherry is unlike any other I've experienced in my wine career. Having had the opportunity to taste many of the world's great wines before I experienced some of the great wines of the Sherry Triangle helped me understand the significance of these wines and the magnitude of their uniqueness.

"This is not a shoe factory," says Mari Carmen Borrego Plá of Bodegas El Maestro Sierra. "This is an artisanal process; what we are selling is the legacy of our ancestors." This legacy is comprised of three thousand years of wine history, culminating in what is, today, a completely singular and complex region with a dizzying array of wines. But it's also more literal: these producers are actually bottling their own ancestors' wines, sourced from solera systems that have been kept and refreshed for decades—even centuries.

Vintage-Dated Sherry

From the rise of solera system as a widespread method of producing sherry in the early nineteenth century to sherry's Golden Age at the end of it, the solera system of fractional blending existed alongside the *añada* system, or the practice of bottling sherry from one single vintage in the same way that most of the world's wine is produced.

But by the late nineteenth century the *añada* system began to slowly fall out of favor. This happened for a few reasons, not least among them money. The amount of wine lost in this process is higher than it is with the solera system. Because the wines cannot be refreshed with younger wine, oxidation rates in *añada* wine are much higher and the evaporation rate will shrink the vintage holdings much faster.

Second, the *añada* system is captive to the vintage; if the quality of a vintage is low, the quality of the wine will suffer. By blending via the solera system, these variations are mitigated and thus the value of the wine does not fluctuate annually. And third, while it's possible to make vintage-dated fino or manzanilla (Bodegas Alvear in Montilla still does), it's difficult to maintain flor without being able to add younger wine to feed it.

So, as demand for sherry continued to grow, the solera system provided an organized way to produce consistent wines of all styles in larger quantities and reduce the deterioration of stocks if sales slowed down.

Today, larger producers like Lustau, González Byass, and Williams & Humbert continue to make small amounts of *añada* sherry, as does Bodegas Tradición—a small bodega founded in 1998 that specializes in VOS and VORS sherry, several of them vintage-dated.

While it's hard to neatly summarize the flavor profile of *añada* wines compared to those aged in the solera system, in general the wines tend to be more concentrated, showing a greater influence of wood due to the more rapid evaporation, and the fact that they cannot be refreshed with younger wine. Yet many examples—depending, like most wines, on the quality of the harvest—can show incredible finesse and delicacy.

These *añada* wines will likely never be a major part of sherry production again, but they are fascinating wines that offer glimpses of a particular moment in time in a way that the solera system cannot.

Sweet Sherry

The concentrated VOS and VORS sherries are certainly polarizing in their intensity, but the region's two sweet wines, pedro ximénez and moscatel, are unmatched in their ability to carve a clear divide. You either love them or you hate them, but no one can argue that they aren't utterly unique.

PEDRO XIMÉNEZ

Pedro ximénez, the principal sweet wine of the Sherry Triangle, isn't exactly built for mass appeal. Bodega owners seem well aware of this, having watched plenty of visitors swirl glasses of PX, confounded by its color (nearly black) and the way it clings to the inside of the glass like crude oil. The uninitiated always take to the glass with trepidation, stealing glances from side to side as if trying to determine whether or not they're being poisoned. Yet PX wines, however intensely sweet and visually jarring they may be, are not only some of the oldest, but often among the most distinctive in the region.

The grape Pedro Ximénez finds its spiritual home in Montilla-Moriles, located about a hundred miles northeast of Jerez. Here, both sweet and dry wines from PX are made in the image of the Sherry Triangle, and while the biologically aged dry wines from this region—which are covered in more detail in Chapter 5—often equal the quality of fino and amontillado from the Sherry Triangle, the region is still best known for the production of sweet PX.

Grapes destined for PX are harvested at high levels of sugar in comparison to Palomino Fino—usually between 13.5 and 14.5 percent—and are laid out to dry in the sun for around two weeks or more to rasinate, further concentrating their sugars, which can spike to over 450 grams of residual sugar per liter (which is nearly twice as sweet as Aunt Jemima pancake syrup, to give you an idea) at pressing. Fermentation of this juice is nearly impossible, given that sugar levels are too high for the yeasts to do their work. Thus the alcoholic strength of the wine largely depends on the amount of alcohol added to it, which can push the total level to around 17 to 18 percent in Jerez and 15 percent for those PXs destined to age in Montilla.

In the Sherry Triangle the barrels are filled to the same capacity as they would be for dry sherry—five-sixths full—while in Montilla the barrels are filled to capacity. As a result of less exposure to oxygen and lower alcohol, PX from Montilla tends to be slightly lighter and fresher than those produced in the Sherry Triangle.

Like oloroso, pedro ximénez is aged via the solera system; refreshing the wine replaces that which has evaporated during the aging process. But unlike oloroso, the alcohol content of PX actually decreases with age, its weight and sweetness making it less susceptible to absorption into the wood, resulting in a higher rate of evaporation for alcohol in relation to water. Thus, by the time many of the wines are bottled they often have to be fortified again in order to meet the minimum 15 percent alcohol required by the Consejo Regulador.

Historically, Pedro Ximénez shared a larger percentage of vineyard area within the Sherry Triangle, but the climate—which is generally cooler and considerably more humid than in Montilla—made the grapes more susceptible to rot, both on the vine and during the drying period. As a result, PX plantings began to shrink and, today, almost all of the PX that is aged in the Sherry Triangle originates from Montilla-Moriles.

MOSCATEL

Moscatel is basically the redheaded stepchild of the Sherry Triangle. The grape, which is the Spanish name for Muscat of Alexandria (or, as it's called in Italy, Zibibbo), is a specific clone of Muscat that has, for centuries, been primarily responsible for copper-colored, highly aromatic sweet wines produced primarily in southern Italy, southern Spain, and southern France. Here in the Sherry Triangle Moscatel vines make up a mere 2 percent of total plantings, limited to the sandy *arenas* soils around Chipiona—a seaside town between Sanlúcar de Barrameda and Rota. Moscatel's production method is similar to that of PX, save for a slightly shorter drying period, but the wines, by contrast, aren't nearly as sweet, trading PX's dark tones and high levels of sugar for a lighter, floral touch.

While PX dominates the top tier of sweet wine production in the Sherry Triangle, there are a handful of moscatel bottlings that rank among the best—and certainly the most underappreciated—sweet wines in the region. Not least among them is Valdespino's Moscatel Viejísimo Toneles, a wine that is over eighty years old and sourced from solera comprised of *toneles*, or 1,000-liter barrels, rather than the usual 600 liters. The solera (that is, the oldest level) of the *toneles* solera system contains just one *tonel*, which is kept under padlock in the bodega, and from which only 250 liters, or just over 650 half bottles, are drawn each year.

BLENDED SHERRIES

Like many Americans, I've filed most of my blended sherry experiences away in my Mistakes in Alcohol Consumption folder, right next to Limoncello and Coke, Long Island Iced Tea, and anything involving coconut rum.

This group of sherries—which includes wines labeled pale cream, cream, brown, and East India—does include some terrific sweetened wines, like Emilio Hidalgo's Cream Morenita, Hidalgo–La Gitana's Cream Alameda, and Equipo Navazos' La Bota de Viejo Cream 19 and 38, among others. But, unfortunately, the blended category has been responsible for quite a bit of confusion and a fair amount of variation in quality. Let's break it down.

Blended sherries are finos, manzanillas, amontillados, or olorosos that have had sweetness added to them. Pale cream sherry, for example, is a blend of either fino or manzanilla and concentrated, unfermented grape must. Pale creams are generally slightly less sweet than amorosos, which are typically blends of oloroso and PX and are today mostly referred to as cream sherries. Brown sherry is also made from an oloroso base, but is blended with a combination of PX and *vino de color*—which is essentially sherry that has been boiled down to a syrup that can cheaply add color and sweetness to the wine. "Medium" is a blanket name given to a medium-sweet sherry (essentially a cream), and *vino de pasto*, though rarely seen anymore, is the name given to an amontillado sweetened with PX. Today cream sherry dominates the category, while many of the other styles have disappeared back into the grab bag from which they originated.

Another category that was a fixture during the nineteenth century but has all but disappeared is East India. Like madeira, it was aged on ships—in this case, ships destined for the East Indies—a process that was thought to improve the wine via the motion of the ship and the stifling heat the wines were subjected to as the boats passed through the tropics. Today, Lustau is one of the few producers that still bottles this style of blended sherry, though they've found a way to mimic the style sans the sea voyage.

Blended sherry has, since the late eighteenth century, been an important part of the export market for sherry and was, as Javier Maldonado Rosso explains in his 1998 book, *The Formation of Capitalism in the Sherry Triangle*, part of the transformation of industry brought on in part by adjusting wines to changes in the British palate. Henry Vizetelly, writing in 1875, provides some insight into where things stood a century later. "English correspondents often write for the driest varieties, still they rarely, if ever, get them. 'Whenever we receive an order for the driest amontillado I have,' remarked the principal shipper of this wine, 'I always put a gallon or more of *dulce* into it before shipping it, because I know that if I shipped the wine in its natural state I should be certain to have it returned upon my hands.'"

This divide, as Álvaro Girón Sierra describes it, "between 'jerez' and 'sherry,'" or rather between the pure styles of sherry (*jerez*), as the Spaniards have always consumed them, and the sweetened sherries (which, to Jerezanos, represents the Anglicization of both the word and the wine) that have traditionally been produced for the export markets, has been an issue for the industry for over a century.

In 1902, Pedro Domecq, writing in the political and literary journal *El Guadelete* on the current status of the sherry wine business, includes suggestions on how to improve it. His primary plea: hedge on "sherry wines that represent the Jerez de la Frontera in its various natural types without being combined to the taste of each market." At the time, blended wines often bore the same classification (for example, amontillado, oloroso) as the unblended, classic styles, and this led to a wealth of confusion and, ultimately, damage to the reputation of classic sherry styles (sound familiar?).

Domecq's pleas ended up falling on deaf ears and now, over a century after he published his article, many sherry lovers are still voicing the same concerns. The blended wines can be supremely delicious—and are particularly well suited to cocktails—but rarely do they compare to the pure styles of sherry, and they remain, in many markets, a distraction from what Jerez does best.

"Throw a line that independently and energetically frees wines of Jerez from the confinement and routines that blur it," pleaded Domecq. "This line should divide the sherry classified by the whims of the market and of man, from sherry how God made it and named it for the loyal and faithful city that produces it, ages it, and conserves it with unwavering faith, in all of its unique and nearly ignored virtues."

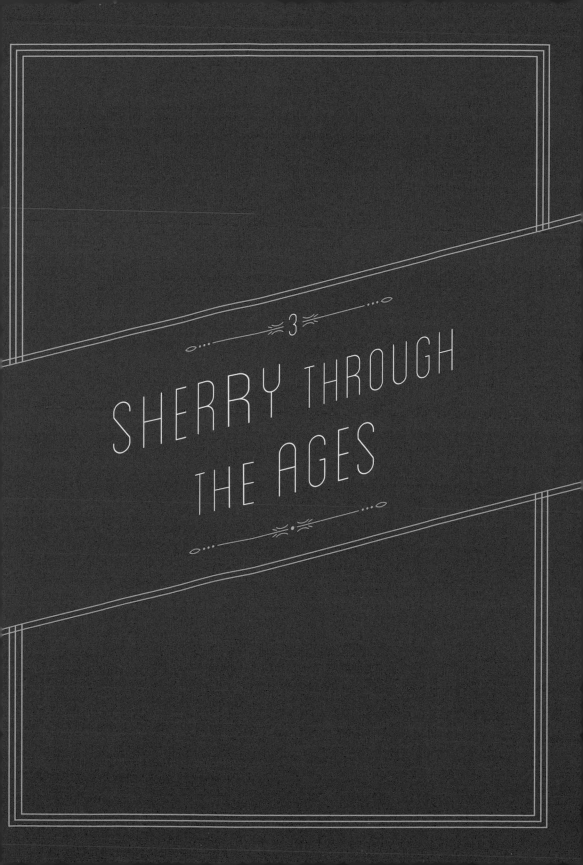

3

SHERRY THROUGH THE AGES

Summing up sherry's history—with its veritable conga line of characters, ranging from conquerors to world explorers, drunken sailors, writers, poets, cocktail-slinging Americans, Californian imitators, and new-school evangelists—is about as easy as defining the wine itself. Which is to say, not easy at all.

Even the name requires an explanation.

The word "sherry" is an Anglicization of Xérès or Jerez, both themselves corruptions of Šerīš or Scheris, the name given to modern Jerez during the Moorish domination of Andalusia, from the eighth through the first half of the thirteenth century CE. And these are but a few of the many aliases that have been given to this city that has long been the capital of sherry production.

Though the history is sketchy, we do know that around 1100 BCE the Phoenicians founded the city of Gadir (modern Cádiz) and then moved north and inland to settle the historic city of Xera, which some historians place smack-dab on the site of modern Jerez, while others insist its location was further inland by as much as ten miles. Whether the Phoenicians discovered a region where winemaking already existed or winemaking originated with them is also unknown, but what we know for sure is that it flourished during their centuries-long rule. By the eighth century BCE the Phoenicians had fled the region because, as local legend has it, after nearly four hundred years they'd finally had it up to here with the levante, the hellishly hot wind that blows from the southeast through the Strait of Gibraltar. They were soon replaced by the Carthaginians (Roman-hating, Punic War–fighting people from Carthage in modern-day Tunisia), who established themselves in the region for three hundred years until the Romans kicked them out, seizing Cádiz in 206 BCE and casually going on to conquer most of Western Europe.

Judging by archeological evidence and surviving texts, winegrowing remained constant in the Sherry Triangle through the occupation of the Carthaginians and flourished, as so many modern European wine regions did, during Roman times. The writings of everyone from Pliny the Elder to Columella, an agricultural expert who was born in Gādēs (the Roman name for Cádiz), evidence not only the sophistication of farming in Roman times, but also the truth that—save, perhaps, for the practice of sprinkling aged human urine on young vines to promote growth—viticulture really hasn't changed all that much since then. Archaeological excavations within the Sherry Triangle have unearthed coins from the period with bunches of grapes on their reverse, further proof that this part of the Baetic province was well known for its wine production.

The Roman domination of Spain effectively came to a halt in 409 CE, when the Vandals (ruthlessly violent and aptly named Germanic barbarians) crossed the Pyrenees from modern-day France into Spain, traipsed across the Iberian Peninsula, and settled in the wealthy southernmost province of Baetica. They renamed it Vandalusia, or, in Latin, "Land of the Vandals," which remains the name of the region (sans V) to this day.

The Vandals stayed less than twenty years before packing up the entire tribe and moving on to wreak havoc on North Africa. They were replaced by the Visigoths (a tribe of Goths), who held court for just under three centuries, their rule plagued by war, economic inequality, and a powerful (and particularly gauche) ruling class with little interest in cultural or intellectual advancement. They were, as such, very little contest for the Moors, who arrived from North Africa and the Middle East in the beginning of the eighth century and conquered most of the Iberian Peninsula in a decade's time. It's during the four hundred years that followed that Jerez (then Šerīš) became one the great cities in the history of Europe, leaving an enduring cultural and intellectual mark on the region through music, art, food, and architecture.

Despite the Moors' practice of abstaining from alcohol, winegrowing in the region did not cease during this period. In fact, many accounts show that it thrived through the two hundred years of Moorish-Christian conflict. (During this period, which ended in the Christian Reconquest in 1264, Jerez was such a constant battleground that it became known as Jerez de la Frontera, in reference to its role as a "frontier" between the Moors and the Christians.)

The Heady Days of World Exploration

While the establishment of the sherry trade with England began in earnest at least as early as the fourteenth century (some place it as far back as the twelfth century) under the medieval king-entrepreneur, Edward III—known as "The King of the Sea" for his expansion of commercial trade—it wasn't until the age of world exploration that the sherry region expanded in both wealth and importance.

By the early 1500s, Sanlúcar de Barrameda and El Puerto de Santa María had become popular port towns for world explorers and hubs for much of the action surrounding the discovery of new lands. In fact, it was here, in El Puerto de Santa María, that the first map of America was drawn—by Juan de la Cosa, the owner of Columbus's flagship *Santa María*—in 1500.

Eight years earlier, when Columbus bumped into the Caribbean for the first time, it's possible that he and his crew had spent the length of the Atlantic journey on a sherry bender. Like many of the A-list explorers of the late fifteenth and early sixteenth centuries, he had a thing for it. So did Magellan. Just twenty-seven years later, in 1519, when he set off from Sanlúcar de Barrameda on a whirlwind tour of Earth's virgin corners he is said to have spent more money on sherry than he did on weapons—which might explain why he lost 242 men and fourteen ships.

By the reign of Elizabeth I of England during the second half of the sixteenth century, sherry had become the wine of choice among the English. Pedro de Medina, the leading Spanish cosmographer of the time and a former librarian to the Duke of Medina Sidonia, wrote in 1548 that during the mid-sixteenth century more than 60,000 barrels of wine were being produced in the Sherry Triangle each year, 40,000 of which were being exported, primarily to England. (Assuming that the barrels exported are the same size as today's and filled to 500-liter capacity, that would work out to more than 26 million 750-milliter bottles.)

As the sherry trade with Britain expanded and the exploration of the West became big business, the wealth of the sherry towns grew exponentially.

El Puerto de Santa María became the home of many wealthy merchants and traders (not least among them Christopher Columbus), eventually earning its nickname La Cuidad de los Cien Palacios (City of a Hundred Palaces).

While the sherry towns continued to prosper during the sixteenth century, tensions began to build between the Spanish and the English—and by 1587, when Sir Francis Drake decided to sack the city of Cádiz and run off with nearly 3,000 barrels of sherry, things had pretty much soured. In the years leading up to the sack, the war had drastically cut wine imports from Spain and, ironically, the return of Drake's booty to England turned out to be terrific PR for the wines. Many historians claim that Drake's love for sherry and his famous sacking helped introduce sherry drinking to a far wider audience and no doubt contributed to the enduring English enthusiasm that almost single-handedly made sherry one of the world's most revered wines.

With their persistent interest and growing demand, the English couldn't be kept out of the sherry market for too long. By the end of the Anglo-Spanish War in 1604, English merchants began to trickle back into the Sherry Triangle and boats carrying sherry between the port towns of El Puerto de Santa María and Sanlúcar and England resumed their constant loop.

Throughout the rest of the seventeenth century, sherry continued to be a major export to England despite the fact that the two countries continued their bickering and reciprocal sacking and killing. However, by the middle of the eighteenth century sales had sagged as sherry struggled to pull its weight against an increasingly prosperous port wine industry, as well as the rising interest in both madeira and the wines of Málaga.

As trade with England suffered, trade with the Americas became more important. Several bodegas that still exist today were founded in the eighteenth century and some, like Delgado Zuleta—the oldest bodega still in existence in the Sherry Triangle, founded in 1719 and officially registered in 1744—were established for the express purpose of trading with the Americas. Other bodegas founded during this period that remain important players today include La Cigarrera (1758), Osborne (1768), Sánchez Romate (1781), and Hidalgo–La Gitana (1792).

By the sunset of the eighteenth century things had begun to pick up again, thanks in large part to a loosening of regulations by the Spanish Crown—which historically favored a select group of established shippers—in the 1770s. This prompted an influx of Spanish entrepreneurs during the latter part of the century, followed by English capital well into the next, inspiring, as David Ringrose puts it, "a century-long expansion." Sherry exports rose 150 percent between 1773 and 1802 and then doubled again by the mid-1800s.

The rapid growth of the industry during the nineteenth century turned the Sherry Triangle back into the playground for the aristocracy it'd once been during the early days of world exploration. Rich sherry shippers had expansive mansions with manicured lawns, and the bodegas of the day were built in the "cathedral style," with soaring ceilings and lavish décor. Much of the grandeur of the time was modeled on the English idea of decadence, and Jerez, specifically, had the feel of a foreign colony: there were French chefs, English suits, white-gloved servants, and everyone was, as Julian Jeffs put it, "gay and carefree. Money was no object."

A New (and Very Drunken) America

On the other side of the pond, a newly independent America was thriving. By the end of the eighteenth century nearly every watering hole up and down the eastern seaboard offered not only a collection of port, sherry, madeira, Champagne, claret, and the like, but also dozens of punches, flips, and sangarees—the sorts of drinks that defined American mixology's formative days.

Early America, it turns out, was a remarkably drunken place, with the tavern—often credited as the birthplace of the Revolution—serving as a nucleus of American social life. Here ideas were shared, politics discussed, billiards played, traveling sideshows performed, and brawls lost and won. And here the early forebears of the cocktail were concocted.

Sherry, during this time, was still a luxury, a drink reserved for the prosperous; the humbler classes were mostly interested in rum and rye whiskey. But by the middle of the nineteenth century, sherry began to boom in America, its popularity trickling down from the upper classes to, really, every man, woman, and college student, thanks primarily to one drink: the Sherry Cobbler. Simply sugar, sherry, a bit of citrus, and a lot of crushed ice, the cobbler not only became the most popular drink in America, but its influence also spread back across the pond to London and Paris. By the 1860s its popularity had reached a fever pitch. During the Exhibition Universelle in Paris in 1867 the French couldn't have cared less about our art on display, but, as David Wondrich points out, they couldn't get enough of our Sherry Cobblers: the exposition's American bar was going through roughly five hundred bottles of sherry per day serving up cobblers to a mostly French crowd.

As America continued to prosper, the tavern as the center of social life was soon replaced by the grand hotel bars and the restaurants connected to them. The cocktail surely helped to democratize sherry, but as the century progressed the wine itself became an integral part of the American table as well. If you rummage through stacks of nineteenth-century menus, it's clear that if you weren't drinking amontillado with your turtle soup you weren't with the program. One list, from Boston's famed Revere House and dated May 18, 1851, offers sixteen sherries, five of them vintage-dated, alongside a special three-course dinner: turkey and oysters and mock turtle soup—which, of course, was served with amontillado.

But back in the Sherry Triangle, the increased worldwide demand for sherry during the mid-nineteenth century was producing problems that still plague the industry. The word "sherry" was never protected by law and, as a result, less worthy wine-producing regions took the opportunity to make grim, approximate versions of the original, which often contained mixtures of anything from potato spirits (vodka) to Marsala wine to cider. On top of that, the Spanish, in trying to keep up with the demand while making a wine that is one of the world's most resistant to efficient production, began cutting corners and themselves making inferior wine.

Added to that, a gaggle of well-known doctors—most notable among them, Doctor J. L. W. Thudichum—began claiming in the press that the addition of gypsum (calcium sulfate, used to acidify and stabilize) to the wines made them dangerously unhealthy. Newspapers printed it as fact, causing droves of English sherry drinkers to refuse their regular pint. By the late 1880s, sherry had fallen out of favor in Great Britain, and when the doctors finally came around to admitting they were wrong to condemn it in the first place, it was too late. Finally, to add insult to injury, phylloxera—the grape louse that destroyed most of Europe's vineyards at the end of the nineteenth century—reached the Sherry Triangle in 1894 and sent the industry into unavoidable decline. By the early twentieth century, sherry consumption had practically skipped a full generation in England.

In America, the reign of the cocktail kept sherry within reach and relevant. And when Prohibition turned the lights out on Broadway, many American bartenders fled to London and Paris, exciting European crowds with the very American penchant for mixing wines and spirits, throwing them in a glass, and calling it entertainment. Places like the American Bar at the Savoy in London and the Artist's Bar (aka Fred Payne's Bar) in Paris became new incubators for the American cocktail. In London, the rise of the cocktail—and the accompanying cocktail party—helped revive sherry in the 1920s, eventually leading it back to English tables and pubs. In a special cable to the *New York Times* in 1931, the correspondent declared that the opening of a new sherry bar in the Dorchester House in London "gave proof that England was abandoning cocktails and returning to her old time allegiance, sherry."

After Repeal in America, the cultural fallout from the temperance movement lingered deep and long, and this had an impact on how sherry was now perceived. Cocktails, and spirits in general, were framed as vulgar, and the virtue of drinking sherry on its own was promoted by opportunistic wine merchants. Lucius Beebe, the writer and author of *The Stork Club Bar Book*, sarcastically pointed out in a piece for the *Daily Boston Globe*, in 1934, that "nice people drink sherry before dinners, while all who hoist a Martini are at best vulgarians and probably secret wife beaters."

California "Sherry," on the Rocks

In America, sherry remained relevant enough that over the next few decades winemakers in California began imitating the wines of the Sherry Triangle. By 1948, the first "commercially available sherry to be made in this country by the same methods followed in Spain," popped up, according to Jane Nickerson in an article for the *New York Times*.

Four years later, in another piece for the *New York Times*, Nickerson provided a clear view of just how popular California sherry had become. "In this category of wines fortified with brandy, by far and away the most popular in this country is sherry. It is, as it develops, the most popular of all American wines," she wrote. "Wineman Frank Schoonmaker recently pointed out that Spain, originator of sherry, produced three times as much wine of all types as the entire United States, but that California produced eight times as much sherry as Spain." Imagine if California would've stayed on this path—Napa might have been imagined in the mold of Jerez instead of Bordeaux.

Nickerson also revealed that in the four years since the first commercial sherry was released, Californian production had advanced quickly, employing the solera system and even aging dry sherries under flor. In fact, some of the most detailed and progressive studies on flor growth and management during the 1940s and 1950s originated from the University of California at Davis and the University of California at Berkeley. But the wines—which were generally labeled Golden Sherry, California Sherry, or, simply, Cocktail Sherry—weren't exactly doing Spain any favors.

In a 1952 interview with Nickerson for the *New York Times*, Richard Bett, then the director of Williams & Humbert in Jerez, hypothesized that consumption of imported sherry was being discouraged because of price. "One could get a California sherry for 80 cents a bottle, Mr. Bett explained, whereas the least sound import sold for was $2.50." Bett also chalked up the trouble with sherry in the U.S. market to the American inclination to think of sherry as a substitute for spirits rather than a versatile wine suitable for a number of occasions. This, he suggested, was a product of the post-Prohibition state of American consumption:

"Drinking was all rather mad, wasn't it, and Americans were grabbing a bottle with two hands." Apparently we were acting like a bunch of uncivilized drunks, more likely to brown-bag sherry than drink it with dinner. He thought, however, that our attitude toward wine and spirits had become, since then, "more rational."

Throughout the 1950s and into the 1960s a growing preference in both the American and the English markets for dry wine is well documented. Mr. Bett, in a 1960 interview with the *New York Times*, stated that "a preference for dry drinks has become a symbol of status. If you like your drinks dry, the assumption seems to be, that it is an indication of a cultivated palate and savoir-faire."

This rise in demand for lighter, drier wines—which was also evident in countries like Holland and Sweden—gave rise to a shift in the style and production methods of the wines coming out of the Sherry Triangle. The light, almost clear style of modern-day fino and manzanilla is a product of this change in demand, facilitated by the rise of carbon filtration, which yields lighter-bodied and lighter-colored wines. The rising demand prompted a swift expansion of the sherry industry (vineyard acreage reached its twentieth-century high of 54,000 acres by the 1980s), marking the last great boom in worldwide sherry sales.

But in America, the preference for dry drinks never extended to dry sherry. Instead, wines like Pinot Grigio rose to prominence and sherry consumption in America remained flat, mostly as a result of sherry's inability to break through and establish itself as a dry wine and not something fundamentally different, which it had become in the American consciousness.

By the mid-1970s consumption rates were rising for table wine in America, but dialogue around sherry as a wine had been reduced to a whimper. During this period there were tips on lightly flavoring your Mornay sauce with sherry, whipping up a great veal scaloppine recipe for the weekend, or adding a dash of nutty intrigue to your creamed crab, but when sherry met glass in America it was often on ice and poured from bottles labeled Harvey's Bristol Cream or Williams & Humbert Dry Sack (which is, of course, not dry at all). At best, sherry was considered an aperitif, like Dubonnet, and sipped the same way.

In 1981, Terry Robards wrote in the *New York Times* that while "no properly British social function could survive for long without the presence of Sherry of some kind or other . . . the same cannot be said of the United States, where the exquisite finos remain largely undiscovered and the dominant Sherry is sweet and consumers are encouraged to drink it on the rocks."

Well, not anymore. Forget the rocks glasses and warm decanters of cream sherry, because there has never been a better time to be an American sherry lover.

4

THE MODERN SHERRY RENAISSANCE

"**S**herry is one of the greatest of all misunderstood wines," writes William Grimes in a 1999 article for the *New York Times* titled "The Trouble with Sherry." "Actually, the case is worse than that. Most diners pay so little attention to it that misunderstanding would represent a rise in status for this most unfortunate beverage."

A lot has changed.

What's fueled sherry's seemingly unlikely rise is really the confluence of many factors—the tireless evangelism of an influential few, the growing availability of high-quality sherries in the market, the return of sherry to the barman's repertoire—but none has been more important than a general revolution in taste, both literally and culturally. Sounds heady, but it's pretty basic: what we want from what we eat has changed, and the same is true for what we drink.

"Food changed," says Levi Dalton, a longtime sommelier and the host of the popular wine podcast *I'll Drink to That!*, who began pushing sherry as early as the late 1990s. The focus began to shift from classic French cooking to chefs who were interested in borrowing from all over the world. Gone were rich sauces and in their place were proteins paired with spice and higher acid components, like citrus, vinegar, and fermentation. "What goes well with high acid food? *Not* Bordeaux—and I watched it go out," says Dalton. "People started looking for different wines to complement the food they were having and it's no mystery that as people became more accustomed to higher acid food they became interested in leaner wines."

American tastes in wine—and American wine production—illustrate this shift quite dramatically. In the course of twenty years we've gone from an overwhelming preference for fruit, ripeness, and youth to a slowly but steadily increasing taste for higher acid, savory, and even bitter flavors. In urban America, Cosmos are being unseated by Negronis, and bitters, amaro, and orange wine are all having a moment. And again, I pity the head of iceberg that gets wedged between the endive and the radicchio at Whole Foods. In wine, a growing preference for minerality over ripe fruit and acid over alcohol is driving avant-garde production from California to the Coteaux du Loir.

Such a change would've been hard to predict twenty-five years ago, yet in looking back at wine writing over the last 150 years—particularly in Britain—it's clear that this is nothing more than history repeating itself. In the late nineteenth and early twentieth centuries, the rise of dry sherry coincided with the ascent of nondosage (very dry) Champagne. George Saintsbury, in his 1920 work, *Notes on a Cellar-Book*, writes, "Perhaps some people have forgotten, or never knew, how comparatively recent the taste for dry sherries is. It preceded, indeed, for a fairly long time that for dry champagne, but in both cases the 'dry' is evidence of a general revolution in taste." Such a sentence would be remarkably accurate if written today, as the rise of nondosage Champagne and dry sherry are, once again, running tandem.

But the changes that have paved the way for sherry's ascent are about more than taste. They're about what we are asking of what we drink. "When you think about the worthwhile things you've fallen in love with, it probably wasn't immediate," says Derek Brown, the owner of Mockingbird Hill, a sherry bar in Washington, D.C. "But people tend to suspend that with drinking; they feel like they immediately have to connect to something." During the 1980s and 1990s what we asked of wine was immediacy—it had to make a good first impression or it didn't have a chance in hell of making it to the second date. The style of wines being produced in many of the world's top regions reflected this. New was also in: the gloss of the American wine was appealing; the farmer toiling in the Loire Valley was less relevant, if we thought of him at all. But an increase in the quality of wine production all over the world, the flood of new wines to the American market, and the rise of America as the world's number one wine-consuming nation combined to give this country an opportunity to be adventurous. And America is nothing if not curious.

As the organic and local food movement spread beyond California to become the concern of the entire country, people began asking different questions. Authenticity, origin, farming, and history became more a part of the greater conversation about wine. And virtue was not simply being determined by ratings or prestige, but by methods and uniqueness.

Sherry, it turns out, is not a wine that is about immediacy, nor is it about fruit. It does not have the patina of Napa or Bordeaux or the modern prestige of Burgundy. But there is no other wine in the world like it, and very few so married to tradition. "Sherry is like the Galápagos Islands of wine," says Dalton. "It's totally different than anything else and it's special because of that."

Sommeliers, bartenders, retailers, and importers all of a sudden wanted to claim it and support it in all of its mystery and idiosyncrasy. "For many years I was just trying to get the liquid into someone's glass," says Dalton. "And then there was this moment when things changed. Everyone wanted some."

Sherry and the Sommelier Underground

Twenty or thirty years ago, hedging on wines no one had heard of and getting people excited about them didn't define sommelier culture the way it does now. No longer is the American sommelier built in the image of the stoic, *tastevin*-wielding Frenchman; today they are ever more vocal, varied, and open—an evolution that has helped them connect in a meaningful way with consumers and become ever more powerful arbiters of taste. Thus, underdog regions that have long been objects of affection in the sommelier community—like the Sherry Triangle, Beaujolais, Muscadet, the Jura, and the Mosel—have earned greater exposure.

Paul Grieco's rabble-rousing wine bar, Terroir, opened its first location in New York's East Village in 2008, specializing in precisely these regions. From the day he opened the doors he's been giving away free glasses of sherry to anyone who crossed the threshold before 7 p.m. Grieco's penchant for foisting sherry on unsuspecting patrons—coupled with the sherry manifestos that have periodically littered his psychedelic wine lists—foreshadowed the sort of countercultural bent that has been an important, and somewhat improbable, factor in sherry's revival.

"In America sherry has this element of cutting-edge appeal that ties in to the same Jura-loving, Brooklyn-living image," says Francis Percival, the London-based food editor and columnist for *The World of Fine Wine*. "But in London you'll notice that when sherry is written about it's entirely around sherry as part of this tapas dining boom over the last three or four years; that's been the primary entry point and part of a very specific cultural experience."

In this sense, in America sherry has not only "sidled out of the drawing room," as the title of a 2012 *New York Times* article by Eric Asimov proclaims, but, perhaps more importantly, it's sidled out of the tapas bar as well, finding a home on wine lists attached to kitchens built around a variety of different cuisines, as well as craft cocktail bars around the country (see "The Cocktail Effect," below). This combination formed a sort of collective unconscious shared by the wine and cocktail worlds during a time when, culturally, they were realizing what they had in common—most notably, a respect and curiosity about the connection of the beverage to history, tradition, and place. Sherry merely highlighted their shared values.

By 2006, interindustry chatter about sherry had already begun, but it was still underground. "There was really no real belief at that point that sherry would amount to anything [in America]," says André Tamers, the owner of DeMaison Selections and one of the first modern American importers to hedge on sherry in a major way. "There was a lot of poking fun among some pretty important distributors at the time; no one really took it seriously, because no one was buying it."

Tamers was, at the time, importing sherries from Bodegas La Cigarrera in Sanlúcar de Barrameda and Bodegas El Maestro Sierra in Jerez, both of them little more than *almacenistas*, selling small amounts of their wine locally and in other markets within Spain. Shortly after, he began bringing in the sherries of Bodegas Gutiérrez Colosía and Bodegas Grant in El Puerto de Santa María and, as of 2011, the sherries of César Florido in Chipiona. "I remember going to Ignacio Hidalgo [of La Cigarrera] early on when the numbers were really, really low and saying, 'Look, we've got to keep trying.'" Tamers promised himself that he'd give it ten years and if it didn't catch on, then he'd be able to say he gave it a college try.

He remembers watching the orange wine trend start to take off around the same time, in 2006 and 2007, and thought that if sommeliers were willing to get behind these esoteric wines from northern Italy then there was no reason why sherry couldn't make inroads. But he can't help but giggle when he recalls meeting with sommeliers in New York who'd dedicated half their white wine section to skin-fermented orange wine and listening to them complain that they couldn't sell sherry. "I used to say, 'Look, the reason you can't sell sherry is because your manzanilla is in the dessert section of the wine list.'" It's true. Sherry's afterthought status had reached such depths that manzanilla and fino, the driest wines in the world, were (and sometimes still are in places that haven't gotten the memo) left, disoriented, in the dessert section. But once Tamers got buyers to actually taste the wines, things began to change.

"In a way a lot of these sommeliers had their palates primed by the Italians," says Tamers referring to the growing trend in Italy of producing orange wines. "And at a certain point when we started going out, we found buyers were ready and accepting of this very savory flavor profile and, all of a sudden, you started seeing people not only grow their sherry cocktail list, but develop sherry programs at restaurants."

It wasn't just the Italians, either. The rise of dry Riesling and the wines of the Jura, among other intensely savory wines, readied the trade for sherry. Thanks to the work of importers like Tamers and many others, like Michael Skurnik, the longtime importer for Lustau and Stephen Meltzer of Classical Wines—a certain evangelism began brewing within the "international sommelier mafia," as Jancis Robinson calls them. Word of deliciousness spread quickly.

On the retail side, the same fanaticism was being bred, but the task was much more difficult: getting people to taste sherry is one thing; inspiring them to buy it is another. But early adopters like Kerin Auth of Tinto Fino in New York, Andy Booth of the Spanish Table in the Bay Area, Joe Salamone of Crush Wine & Spirits in New York, and Justin Berlin, formerly of PJ's in New York, among others, quickly became the ground troops within this growing sherry movement.

The Cocktail Effect

Despite the efforts of everyone from Tamers to Grieco to a handful of retailers, the early momentum behind sherry might owe more to the classic cocktail revival than to any particular push within the wine community. "I remember going to a sherry event in San Francisco back in 2008," says Andy Booth, who began working with sherry at the Spanish Table in Berkeley in the early 2000s. "And literally the entire room was bartenders; there was not one other wine person there."

The rediscovery of sherry as a major ingredient in nineteenth-century cocktailing captured the imagination of a very influential crop of bartenders earlier than it caught on in the wine world, inspiring a sort of geeky dedication. "Of all the things I've come across in all of my experience in spirits and wine, sherry and mezcal are the two things people are most fanatical about," says Phil Ward, the owner of New York's Mayahuel. Ward, like so many of sherry's advocates within the cocktail community, discovered sherry through the help of Steve Olson, a wine and spirits educator who, by the mid-2000s, had already been working to bring sherry back from the dead for half a decade. His event, the Vinos de Jerez Cocktail Competition, which he founded in 2005, coupled with the yearly trips to Jerez he'd been organizing since 2002, became the blue flame for the return of sherry to the barman's repertoire.

"America being a cocktail culture and sherry being a major component in cocktails in America's early days, it seemed like a no-brainer," says Andy Seymour, who started working with Olson to educate the trade about sherry in the late 1990s. "We said to ourselves: let's try and take something that Americans like and a product that we think is amazing and offer it in a form [the cocktail] that they can understand." It worked. The cocktail became sherry's gateway to an audience that might have otherwise dismissed it as geriatric jungle juice.

"I think who's carried sherry and will continue to carry sherry—at least the level below the high end—are the mixologists," says Levi Dalton of *I'll Drink to That!* "I think they carried amaro [the often polarizing category of Italian bitter liqueurs] by bringing it through the market and the same is true for sherry."

The Boutique Boom

By 2009, sherry was beginning to walk on its own, yet for a lot of buyers it was still incorrectly seen as a mass-market, almost antiartisanal product. But high-quality, boutique bottlings from the likes of Lustau, Hidalgo–La Gitana, Emilio Hidalgo, El Maestro Sierra, and Equipo Navazos started popping up on wine store shelves and in restaurants with greater frequency.

"I remember, in the summer of 2008, tasting the first Equipo Navazos bottling that actually had a notable presence in the market—La Bota de Amontillado 9," says Ashley Santoro, the former wine director for Casa Mono and Bar Jamón. "It was allocated [not for open sale, but rationed in small quantities to top restaurants] and I was told it was this club of around two hundred members, all sherry lovers, that were supporting this project to find the best botas in the region. The first thing that came to my mind was, 'There are two hundred people who love sherry?' and the second was, 'Who is buying this that it's so limited?'"

The buzz around the wines was immediate. Only 1,400 bottles (two barrels) were released and a fraction of them strategically placed all over New York City, from Per Se to Casa Mono to the now-defunct Convivio.

"I'd been drinking and buying sherry for several years at that point and I'd never tasted an amontillado like that," says Santoro. "I knew when I tasted the wine and when I saw where it was going that these guys were going to change things."

The wines not only captured the attention of influential buyers, but they also helped shift the image of sherry from a commercial product to a boutique wine worth wrangling for. They weren't the only ones, though, and that became apparent as soon as buyers began looking around. What Equipo Navazos proved—beyond the skill of founders Eduardo Ojeda and Jesús Barquín in selecting and blending exceptional lots of sherry—was just how much we'd been missing. "We are inventing almost nothing," says Barquín. "If what we are doing is interesting, it's because the wines that are produced in the sherry region are interesting."

Lustau, for example, had been bottling tiny quantities of exceptional wines sourced from almacenistas, small producers of sherry who sold their wines to larger producers, since the 1980s. Hidalgo–La Gitana's incredible Manzanilla Pasada Pastrana, which is bottled with minimal clarification from a single vineyard, had been under our noses since the 1990s. And André Tamers, we'd realize, was peddling some of the greatest small-production wines in the region.

In 2006 there were fewer than ten bodegas with any notable presence in the East Coast market; today there are more than thirty, contributing to a growth in export numbers after nearly fifty years of stagnancy. According to export data published by the Consejo Regulador, sherry's regulatory council, exports to the United States are up 25 percent in 2013 over 2012. To boot, sherry has been written about in almost every major newspaper and drinks- or food-related magazine over the last few years, which, for most of these publications, is about 100 percent more space than they've given sherry in the last twenty years.

RETRETE

Sidling Out of the Tapas Bar

Sherry's ascent has certainly benefited from the foolproof marriage of things like *jamón*, almonds, olives, and sherry—and the popularity of places that peddle it. After all, the most powerful endorsement of sherry is a full embrace of Andalusian culture, which gave us sherry, yes, but it also gave us the tapa. Iberian-centric bars and restaurants like Bar Vivant in Portland, Oregon; Gitane in San Francisco; Duende in Oakland; Mockingbird Hill in Washington, D.C.; Casa Mono and Bar Jamón, El Quinto Pino, La Vara, and Tertulia in New York; Bar Mateo in Durham, North Carolina; Jamonera in Philadelphia; and Vera in Chicago, among others, have acted as hubs from which a throbbing love of sherry has radiated.

But perhaps more striking than the connection of sherry to Iberian restaurants and tapas bars are the restaurants without Spanish roots that have made sherry a major part of their beverage programs—and, even more importantly, the sheer number of restaurants and retailers who now feel compelled to carry it at all.

In America, the fact that sherry had been nearly erased from the consciousness of the current generation has been an asset. There are no rules or barriers, no particular allegiances. This has allowed sherry to slip into wine lists connected to kitchens specializing in everything from gastropub fare (the Breslin, New York) to modern Italian (Marea, New York) to American (Nopa, San Francisco). Much of this is connected to changes in the kinds of wine lists that are proliferating in cities around the country. They've gotten shorter and increasingly eclectic, and they're less bound to the ethnic persuasion of the chef. It's on these lists that sherry's finding a comfortable home.

"Just to have it on your list gets you a little gold star you can put on your geek squad passport," says Carla Rseszewski, who built the sherry programs at the John Dory, the Breslin, and the Spotted Pig in New York. "But you have to still keep giving blood to it."

No matter how popular sherry becomes over the next few years it will always need the evangelism of the industry—because, well, sherry is not Pinot Grigio. It may never reach and saturate the mass market in such a way that you might run into it on a list at a country club in Tucson. (And if you do, I encourage you to use caution.)

But sherry is achieving something greater than mass-market appeal: it has inspired and enchanted a large group of consumers, sommeliers, bartenders, and writers who are now determined to make sure that there's enough blood (or *jamón*) that we all keep discovering it.

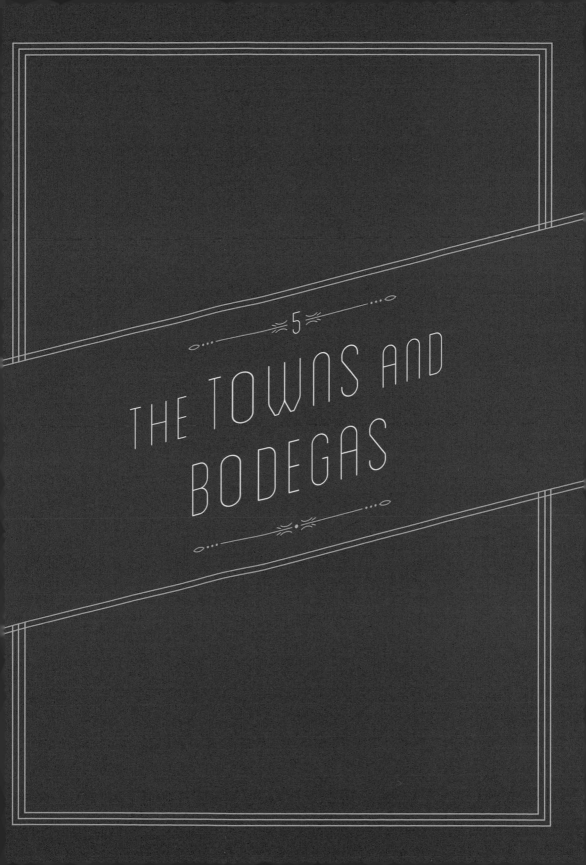

5

THE TOWNS AND
BODEGAS

milio Hidalgo's bodega, located near the center of Jerez on Calle Clavel, was the first I visited in the Sherry Triangle. Built in the classical style with thick, mold-covered walls, high ceilings, and film noir lighting, it was the perfect introduction to the sherry bodega's brooding calm—the sort of atmosphere that makes you yearn for a time when grand things were still built by hand, and by generations over centuries.

I arrived at ten o'clock on a January morning, the sun still on its first cup of coffee, gentle as it filtered through the esparto grass window shades, catching the dust kicked up from the dirt floors like gold dust. Admittedly, my first inclination was to Instagram the impossible lighting and the way it seemed to cinematically hug every angle. But my second inclination was to stop, and allow myself the feeling of overwhelming sadness that comes from knowing that we all nearly forgot about this place and its wines.

Almost anyone you speak to who's been to the Sherry Triangle will want to tell you how they felt when they walked into a sherry bodega for the first time— the lighting, the smell, the century-old barrels, the palpable silence. It's impossible to leave without vowing to make sure that we do not forget this place again.

Each bodega is different, but they offer variations on the same unforgettable impression. What truly sets them apart, however, is the people who run them, the legacy they're charged with preserving, and the towns that they are housed in.

While each of the three sherry towns and Montilla-Moriles (their sister from another mister, see page 153) share much in common, the distance between them is far wider than the road suggests. In fact, in the case of the Sherry Triangle, one might find it hard to imagine that there could be such vast cultural differences among three towns less than thirty minutes from each other—unless, of course, you've ever driven from New York's Lower East Side to Greenwich, Connecticut. The road dividing dive-bar patrons and country club dues–paying WASPs might as well be a land bridge between two different continents.

While the differences between Jerez de la Frontera and Sanlúcar de Barrameda, for example, are not quite as drastic, the more time I spent in the region the more I realized how tribal it is—each town with its own set of ingrained mores and customs. Identifying as "Jerezano" means something very different than feeling "Sanluqueño." The words have become adjectives in their own right, describing not just the inhabitants of each place, but different cultural inclinations and sentiments.

The connection to wine also varies by town, much of it the product of divergent histories and socioeconomic structures. Jerez de la Frontera has long been the foundation: the home of the sherry royalty and the town that has reaped the greatest benefits of the industry's prosperity. As such, it has also shouldered the industry's greatest disappointments. El Puerto de Santa María is the escapist's Jerez—beachier, more laid-back, and prized for both its location and its lean, flor-driven finos. For more than a century, it has operated as a satellite of Jerez, the place where many of the town's large shippers aged their finos. It's also the town whose landscape has changed the most in the last thirty years.

Sanlúcar, by contrast, has always been an island unto itself. The town's signature wine, manzanilla, has for most of its history been the wine of the people—a popular, democratic beverage that lacked the aristocratic status of the wines of Jerez and El Puerto. If you recall, in the early days of sherry's history, manzanilla wasn't even included in the concept of sherry. And perhaps because of this historically marginal status, a spirit of independence remains deep under the skin of the city, even today.

What all three towns (and Montilla-Moriles) share in common is that they are Andalusian. And while I wish I could neatly sum up what that means, translating a cultural identity shaped by more than three thousand years of ever-present history is best left to poets. This is, after all, a region and a people that, like their wines, do not lend themselves well to generalization. And that is part of the bond between the towns.

In the following pages you'll find a collection of the principal bodegas in the Sherry Triangle. This is not a comprehensive list; rather, I've based my selections on the following criteria: quality of the wines, historical importance of the bodega, and availability of the wines in export markets. For each bodega I offer a brief overview, a description of all the notable wines they produce, and an at-a-glance list of my favorite five (more or less) wines.

PRICE KEY

UNLESS OTHERWISE INDICATED, all prices refer to 375-milliliter bottlings.

$ = under 20
$$ = $20 to $35
$$$ = $35 to $50
$$$$ = $50+

Jerez de la Frontera

In the late afternoons I'd get lost in Jerez's narrow, winding streets, imagining the city as it was in its heyday. I'd repaint the abandoned bodegas in my mind and fill them back up with barrels so they would flood the streets with the smell of wine again. I'd indulge by adding a few horse-drawn carriages and impractically dressed women mincing about. In short, I'd imagine Jerez as *Downton Abbey*, but with tapas. And maybe that's what it was, once, when the rich built their mansions and villas here.

What's sure is that Jerez de la Frontera has never been a typical wine town. There are no vineyards within eyeshot; no winemakers milling about in muddy boots and faded blue jeans. Aside from the ubiquitous Tío Pepe swag and the fact that the locals seem unable to find a time of day in which it isn't appropriate to drink sherry, the fact that Jerez is a historic hub for wine production is not immediately obvious.

It used to be the smell that gave it away.

Jerezanos still talk about it—how when the bodegas used to ferment their wines in barrel, in the late summer months the entire city used to smell like wine. There are still faint traces of the city's aromatic past today, but only enough to remind you of what it must have once been like.

While glimmers of the patina and aristocratic conservatism that defined Jerez at its height still persist, it's impossible not to notice that Jerez de la Frontera is an economically depressed city in a part of Spain plagued with chronic unemployment. All of the *jamón* and fino in the world couldn't conceal its ache. Yet this city is as romantic as it is perpetually afflicted. And when I think about Jerez, it's wistfully, remembering the late spring lunches that often stretched into dinnertime, spent washing down plates of fried *cazón en adobo* with *copitas* of fino. Flipping over the check and thinking, *That's it?* truly never gets old. The Sherry Triangle is one of the few places in Spain where you can eat and drink this well for so little.

On weekend nights I'd tuck myself into one of the city's sherry bars, called *tabancos*, moving past the pack of locals that spilled out into the street, or I'd wander the gypsy quarters of the city, which always seem to echo with the sound of someone singing.

My fondest memories are of the nights spent at the various small flamenco clubs, called *peñas*, in those gypsy quarters. After the show (which, if you're at the right place, is devoid of most of the flourishes we Americans associate with flamenco), a small cash bar would generally stay open, serving fino and oloroso in plastic *copitas* to a swelling, almost exclusively gypsy crowd. I'll never forget one particularly wobbly walk home alone around 3:30 on an April morning, plastic *copita* in the back pocket of my jeans, the empty streets golden under the glow of the street lamps. Federico García Lorca didn't exactly write for moments as unpoetic as the drunk walk home, but his words kept playing in my head: "Oh, city of gypsies! Who could see you and forget?"

BODEGAS EL MAESTRO SIERRA

Doña Pilar Plá Pechovierto, the owner and matriarch of El Maestro Sierra, has the kind of smile that could make Vladimir Putin melt. Her conversation spills out an endless stream of parables, but she is her own best lesson: well into her nineties, she exudes the sort of vitality more often associated with someone in their young twenties with a backpack and a whim. Such joy, however, belies the history of her bodega's struggle.

Since its inception, El Maestro Sierra has challenged the established norms of Jerez de la Frontera's wine culture. It was founded in 1832 by José Antonio Sierra, a master cooper who was employed by many of the major sherry bodegas. During that time, Jerez de la Frontera was a firmly plutocratic city. The wine business was the hobby of the aristocracy—along with bull and horse breeding—and a clean line between bodega owners and bodega workers was very rarely crossed. Coopers fell squarely in the "worker" category, and as such, Sierra's quest to become a producer of sherry wasn't exactly welcomed. But after struggling for years, he established himself as a well-respected *almacenista*. Today, the El Maestro Sierra label pays tribute to his struggle with an allegorical illustration of a foxhunt, the fox representing Maestro Sierra and the hunters, the nobles.

When Doña Pilar's husband, a cousin of José Antonio Sierra, passed away in 1976, El Maestro Sierra became one of the few bodegas to be run by a woman— it still is, to this day. In 1992, under the direction of Pilar and her daughter Carmen, the bodega began bottling its own wines for export, eventually earning an international reputation as one of the finest boutique bodegas in the Sherry Triangle.

Today the cellar is under the careful watch of Ana Cabestrero who, in 2011, took over for longtime *capataz* Juan Clavijo, who'd spent nearly his entire life at the bodega. She joins Montse Molino of Barbadillo in Sanlúcar de Barrameda as one of the very few women *capataz* in the region.

NOTABLE WINES: The bodega enjoys a unique position atop a bluff within the town of Jerez de la Frontera, allowing for unobstructed exposure to the cooling

winds off the Atlantic Ocean. This exposure lends itself to cooler temperatures and more vigorous flor growth, resulting in the high-toned character that has come to define the house style. Ana and her team of four workers, including an inhouse cooper, still work entirely by hand, using the traditional *canoa* and *rocíador* to "run the scales" (see page 28).

The fino ($) is truly one of the best in Jerez. It averages around four years of age and is bottled straight off the lees with only minimal cold stabilization. The entry-level amontillado ($$) and oloroso ($) bottlings, aged twelve and fifteen years, respectively, are both terrific wines that offer a tremendous amount of value. The bodega's offerings reach their apogee, however, with the extremely limited stocks of old wines that form their Vinos Viejos range. The finest among them is the Amontillado 1830 VORS ($$$$), which is sourced from just two 2,000-liter barrels built by José Antonio Sierra in 1830. Though the average age of the wine at the time of bottling is tough to determine, it's at least fifty years old. Like the amontillado, the palo cortado ($$$$) in this range, bottled at around thirty years of age, shows a strong biological imprint despite its advanced age and limited time under flor.

The bodega also bottles a pair of exceptional olorosos from two separate soleras—the Oloroso 1/14 VORS ($$$$) and the Oloroso Extra Viejo 1/7 VORS ($$$$)—the "14" and "7" referring to the number of barrels in their respective solera systems. Both have an average age of around fifty years at bottling. In addition to the top-shelf dry sherries, the bodega releases small quantities of the roughly fifty-year-old Pedro Ximénez Viejísimo ($$$$), bottled at barrel strength, meaning that it is not refortified before bottling. Together these old wines constitute a total annual release of just four hundred 750-milliliter bottles and four hundred 375-milliliter bottles, each of them labeled by hand.

HOUSE STYLE: Lean, high-toned wines across the spectrum that are classic Jerez, sans flash.

TOP FIVE WINES: Fino ($), Amontillado ($$), Amontillado 1830 VORS ($$$$), Palo Cortado ($$$$), Oloroso 1/14 VORS ($$$$).

ESTABLISHED: 1830

BODEGAS EMILIO HIDALGO

While the name is not as immediately recognizable as those of some larger sherry bodegas, Emilio Hidalgo is one of the finest producers in Jerez. Today, the wines are housed in a classical bodega on Calle Clavel, several blocks from the center of Jerez, that has been in the family since the founding of the company, in 1874.

The bodega is currently under the direction of the fifth generation of Hidalgos, while wine production is overseen by second-generation *capataz* Manuel Jesús Nieves, whose father, Manuel Nieves, had been at Bodega Emilio Hidalgo since 1959. Manuel Jesús is one of the few young people who felt the generational pull toward sherry production, laments Fernando Hidalgo—one of two brothers, along with their cousin, who run the bodega. "The *capataz* used to be another member of the family, a person who is there at every christening and funeral, with succeeding generations from father to son," he says. "But that is changing; the generational succession is dying out."

At Emilio Hidalgo the tradition will live on for at least another generation. And the wines, which are truly some of the most refined and unique sherries on the market, remain committed to the house style, which favors elegance over girth.

NOTABLE WINES: While Hidalgo bottles a lovely entry-level fino for the local market, the crown jewel of the bodega is Fino Especial La Panesa ($$$, 750ml), which is bottled at an average age of at least fifteen years and only minimally filtered. It's easily one of the most complex, umami-forward finos on the market.

In this premium range, you'll also find Amontillado Viejo El Tresillo 1874 ($$$$, 750ml), an amontillado from a solera started in 1874 that averages around fifty years of age at bottling. It's an intense, complex wine worth seeking out. For those less inclined to go gumshoe, the house now bottles a younger version, Amontillado El Tresillo ($$$, 750ml), which averages around fifteen years of age at bottling and captures, as Fernando describes it, "the death of fino and the birth of an amontillado."

In the purely oxidative department, Hidalgo releases two separate bottlings, both drawn from the same solera system: Oloroso Seco Gobernador ($$, 750ml), which averages around twelve years of age at bottling and is sourced from a solera system whose solera (oldest) level is used to feed the youngest *criadera* of the Oloroso Viejo Villapanés ($$$, 750ml), which is bottled at an average age of around twenty years.

Perhaps the greatest value in this portfolio is the Palo Cortado Especial Marqués de Rodil ($$$, 750ml), which, for the style, spends an unusually long time under flor (eight years), combined with another eight years aging oxidatively. Lean, and almost amontillado-like texturally, it combines pungency with strong oxidative aromas of bergamot, tea, and nuts.

The house also bottles miniscule quantities of a few very old wines, including the Pedro Ximénez 1861 Santa Ana ($$$$, 750ml), an intense PX that the bodega estimates to be over one hundred years old. Most notable is the Palo Cortado Privilegio 1860 ($$$$, 750ml), which is a complex, expressive wine; an ounce is enough to flood the room with its aroma. It's arguably the finest wine in the cellar. Only around 150 bottles each of the Santa Ana and the Privilegio are released every year.

In addition to the dry and naturally sweet sherries, the house bottles a balanced, steely cream sherry called Cream Morenita ($, 750ml), which ranks among the region's best examples of the style.

HOUSE STYLE: The imprint of flor is strong here, as most of the wines—from fino to palo cortado—spend a longer than usual amount of time aging biologically. The resulting style is heavily flor-influenced, favoring leanness and finesse over power.

TOP FIVE WINES: Fino Especial La Panesa ($$$, 750ml), Amontillado El Tresillo ($$$, 750ml), Amontillado Viejo El Tresillo 1874 ($$$$, 750ml), Palo Cortado Especial Marqués de Rodil ($$$, 750ml), Palo Cortado Privilegio 1860 ($$$$, 750ml).

ESTABLISHED: 1874

BODEGAS GONZÁLEZ BYASS

It's impossible to look left or right in Jerez without seeing the Tío Pepe logo—that fino bottle dressed in a red hat and red bolero jacket complete with a flamenco guitar—emblazoned on an awning, a napkin canister, or an outdoor table. For decades, it has staked its claim as the most popular fino in the world and an indelible symbol of Spanish identity. In fact, Madrid's iconic neon Tío Pepe sign, which has shown on Puerta del Sol Square since 1936, is nothing short of a national landmark; the former mayor of Madrid, Alberto Ruiz-Gallardón, even went so far as to claim that the Tío Pepe signage is to Madrid as the Eiffel Tower is to Paris.

While Tío Pepe is its most well-known wine, Bodegas González Byass is one of the largest producers in Jerez, with more than thirty sherries as well as a number of other products, including gin, brandy, and table wine.

The bodega's story began with twenty-three-year-old Manuel María González, who, after witnessing the success of the sherry trade in England, bought a small bodega—now called La Sacristía—and shipped his first ten butts to England in 1835. The following year he took on two partners, Juan Bautista Dubosc and Francisco Gutiérrez de Agüera, who provided the capital necessary to expand.

As the company continued to thrive, González decided to continue this partnership with Dubosc and gave the company a new name, González & Dubosc, which remained on the labels until Dubosc's death, in 1863. Shortly after that, Robert Byass, the exclusive agent for the wines in England and a partner in the bodega (hence the name change to González, Dubosc & Co. by the mid-1800s), replaced Dubosc on the labels, and by the 1870s, González Byass was exporting more than 6,500 butts (which, if filled to capacity, translates to more than 5.2 million 750-milliliter bottles) of sherry to England per year.

Today the bodega remains one of the most important and prosperous names in the sherry region—their massive complex of bodegas in the center of Jerez, including one designed by Gustave Eiffel, standing as one of the few intact reminders of the grandeur that once defined the city.

NOTABLE WINES: Tío Pepe ($) remains the flagship, but the availability of finos that see less aggressive filtration has highlighted the relative shortcomings of the modern Tío Pepe style. Among these is the bodega's own Tío Pepe En Rama ($$, 750ml) bottling—a selection of some of the finest *botas* in the solera system bottled with minimal filtration. Originally intended as a one-off bottling to commemorate the 175th birthday of the bodega, it's now bottled once per year and is worth seeking out on release each spring. The most compelling wines in the fino category are contained in the bodega's Palmas line, an ode to the evolution of a fino to amontillado, represented in *palmas* (stages), each of the wines minimally filtered. Una Palma ($$, 500ml) is a wine of around six years of age bottled from just three casks (as of 2013); Dos Palmas ($$$, 500ml) is around eight years of age and is bottled from two casks; Tres Palmas ($$$$, 500ml) averages around ten years of age and is sourced from a single *bota*; and Cuatro Palmas ($$$$, 500ml), an amontillado that averages close to fifty years of age and is bottled from a single barrel from the Museo Solera, which is made up of just six barrels. These wines are all released in very small quantities, the Cuatro Palmas being the smallest, at just one hundred fifty 500-milliliter bottles released each year.

Another standout is Amontillado Seco Viña AB ($, 750ml). Originally bottled as a fino-amontillado, it began to be bottled as an amontillado in 2009 (though the aging and production methods remain unchanged) from a solera that is fed by Tío Pepe. It's delicate, with a pronounced flor character, and is easily one of the bodega's best values. Within this line there are a handful of other affordable wines, all falling at or under the $20 mark, but the Amontillado Viña AB is the standout.

The bodega's top shelf consists of a selection of four flashy VORS wines, beginning with the Del Duque Amontillado ($$$), a dry wine, but—as is characteristic of this line—a plusher take on the style. The second wine, Apóstoles ($$$), is a palo cortado that is aged for the last fifteen years of its life in PX casks, and thus, through absorption, ends up with around 45g/liter of residual sugar at bottling. Oloroso Dulce Matusalem ($$$), a blend of 75 percent oloroso and 25 percent PX, is essentially a very old cream sherry that, due to the extended time in barrel, is characterized by the comingling of sweet and bitter. The last of the line is Noe ($$$), an intense, spicy pedro ximénez that, while hefty, is supremely balanced.

Each year the bodega also sets aside around two hundred barrels' worth of their finest *mosto* to age as single-vintage *añada* wines, a rarity in the region. The *capataz* will then periodically pull from these stocks to bottle and release vintage sherries to the market. These *añada* bottlings, which so far have included ten olorosos and four palo cortados, often rank among the bodega's most compelling wines.

HOUSE STYLE: Varied. Stylistically, the house makes a wine for everyone. For those who favor minimal filtration and the savoriness of older fino, head for the Palmas wines or Tío Pepe En Rama. For sluggable young fino, there is, of course, Tío Pepe. And for those who love the bombast and richness often associated with the oxidative wines of Jerez, there is the VORS line.

TOP FIVE WINES: Tío Pepe En Rama ($$, 750ml), Palmas range ($$$–$$$$, 500ml), Amontillado Seca Viña AB ($, 750ml), añada range ($$$$, 750ml), Noe Pedro Ximénez Muy Viejo ($$$).

ESTABLISHED: 1835

BODEGAS REY FERNANDO DE CASTILLA

While the history of Bodegas Rey Fernando de Castilla as a bottler of sherry dates back to the 1960s—with the founding Andrade-Vanderwilde family's grape-growing activities dating back to as early as 1837—the bodega's establishment as one of the finest boutique sherry houses in the region really begins with its purchase by Jan Pettersen in 1999.

Pettersen, who is originally from Norway, had previously spent nearly sixteen years at Bodegas Osborne, first arriving in the early 1980s when the iconic bodega's focus was still firmly on sherry production. By the time he left, Osborne had, as the industry slumped, shifted its attention from sherry to a variety of other products with greater moneymaking potential, from *jamón* to bottled water to energy drinks. Pettersen became increasing disillusioned and yearned to be part of a company that, as he puts it, "fought for sherry."

That company ended up being his own. After taking complete control of the bodega in 2000, Pettersen expanded its sherry production via the purchase of a number of old soleras, many of them from the esteemed *almacenista* José Bustamante.

In just a decade's time Pettersen has turned Rey Fernando de Castilla into a model of what many, including myself, believe to be the future of Jerez: small production, high-quality wines made by bodegas willing to make changes to improve quality while still remaining dedicated to tradition. "We don't need to be revolutionary," says Pettersen. "We simply need to be *evolutionary*."

NOTABLE WINES: The Fernando de Castilla sherries are separated into two ranges: the high-end "Antique" and the entry-level "Classic," as well as, as of 2013, a limited-edition seasonal Fino En Rama ($$), which is around six years of age at bottling. The Fino Antique ($$, 500ml) is one of the most distinctive sherries bottled by the bodega, an homage to the old style of fino that Pettersen fell in love with when he first moved to Jerez in the early 1980s. These were "bigger, bolder finos" that were not only bottled at a higher average age (Fino Antique is around nine years of age at bottling), but were also not subject to the heavy filtration of the wines that became popular in the 1970s and nearly erased this style by the 1990s. In lieu of filtering, it's fortified twice, once before entering the solera and again before bottling, to kill all the flor and ensure that the wines are stable enough for shipment. The result is a 17 percent alcohol, unabashedly bold fino that is one of the only remaining examples of this old style.

The similarly forward Amontillado Antique ($$$, 500ml) is aged in the Fino Antique solera system for eight years and then enters its own solera system, aging for another twelve years, making it around twenty years of age at bottling. The Antique line reaches its apex with the Palo Cortado Antique ($$$, 500ml), which is not only one of the best examples of palo cortado, but one of the best wines in the Sherry Triangle. The line is rounded out by a bold, but detailed and steely Oloroso Antique ($$$, 500ml), which is aged in the solera for twenty years, and a superconcentrated thirty-year-old Pedro Ximénez Antique ($$$, 500ml), sourced from the oldest solera in the bodega.

The Classic line of sherries includes the bright, sluggable Fino Classic ($, 750ml) and Manzanilla Classic ($, 750ml), both bottled at around four to five years old, as well as the Amontillado Classic ($$, 750ml) aged around ten years, and easily the best value in this range. The line is rounded out with the Oloroso Classic ($$, 750ml) and the young Pedro Ximénez Classic ($$, 750ml), aged around nine years.

HOUSE STYLE: Bold, old-school Jerez-style sherries that are rich but balanced.

TOP SIX WINES: Fino En Rama ($$), Fino Antique ($$, 500ml), Amontillado Classic ($$, 750ml), Amontillado Antique ($$$, 500ml), Palo Cortado Antique ($$$, 500ml), Oloroso Antique ($$$, 500ml).

ESTABLISHED: 1964/1999

BODEGAS EMILIO LUSTAU

Like many of the great bodegas in the Sherry Triangle, Bodegas Emilio Lustau began as an *almacenista*. Its founder, Don José Ruiz-Berdejo, owned a small vineyard just outside of Jerez called Finca Nuestra Señora de la Esperanza, where he made a small amount of wine that he sold to larger bodegas for nearly fifty years before his son-in-law, Don Emilio Lustau Ortega, took over in 1931 and oversaw the expansion of the business.

Don Emilio moved to a bodega in the Santiago neighborhood in the center of Jerez and purchased several more vineyards in Balbaína and Raboatun, both *pagos* to the west and northwest of Jerez. By the 1950s he began bottling wines under the Emilio Lustau label for export.

His sons took over in the 1960s and continued to expand the bodega throughout the 1970s, but it wasn't until the 1980s, under the leadership of the late Rafael Balao, that Bodegas Emilio Lustau claimed its modern reputation as one of the most progressive and successful bodegas in the Sherry Triangle.

In 1983 Balao hired *capataz* Juan Fuentes Romero, who would guide the bodega through its purchase by Grupo Caballero—a large brandy and sherry producer located in El Puerto de Santa María—in 1990. The merger added 420 acres of vines to Lustau's holdings (they now total around 370, with the most important holdings located in the *pago* of Carrascal) and added the cash flow that allowed them to continue to expand.

In 2000, following the breakup of Bodegas Pedro Domecq under Beam Global and Pernod Ricard, Lustau purchased and restored six former Domecq bodegas, as well as the complete solera systems of four legendary Domecq brands: Fino La Ina, Amontillado Botaina, Oloroso Río Viejo, and Pedro Ximénez Viña 25. Lustau now bottles and markets around thirty different sherries.

NOTABLE WINES: Lustau's entire collection of sherries can be broken into four ranges: the classic line, known as the Solera Reserva range, which includes affordable wines like Manzanilla Papirusa and Amontillado Los Arcos; the Almacenista range (see box, pages 106–7); the Lustau Specialities range, which includes the En Rama line and all of the VORS wines; and the La Ina range, which includes the former Domecq brands, including Fino La Ina and Amontillado Botaina.

Of the Solera Reserva range, Puerto Fino ($, 750ml; aged in El Puerto) and the Fino Jarana ($, 750ml; aged in Jerez) are solid, value-driven wines that are representative of where they've been aged. The same is true for the bodega's entry-level Manzanilla Papirusa ($, 750ml). Both amontillados in the this range—Los Arcos ($$, 750ml) and Escuadrilla ($$, 750ml)—show a bit more girth than is typical of amontillado, but the Los Arcos, bottled at around twelve years of age, is the more chiseled of the two, offering a fine value and an ideal sherry for use in cocktails. The Oloroso Don Nuño ($$, 750ml) and the Palo Cortado Península ($$, 750ml) are also solid values in this range—rich and bold like the amontillados, but not without the sort of tension that keeps them balanced. Last but not least is the rich Gran Reserva Oloroso Emperatriz Eugenia ($$$, 750ml), bottled at over twenty years of age. The label, with its portrait of sweet-faced Eugenia, belies the contents—this is a dark, intense wine that has a tinge of sweetness via the concentration in cask.

The top of the range for both fino and manzanilla comes courtesy of Lustau's seasonal line of en rama sherries ($$, 500ml), bottled under the Specialities range, which includes finos from both Jerez and El Puerto as well as a manzanilla from Sanlúcar, each selected from a single barrel and released in small quantities. All three are compelling wines, but the Puerto Fino En Rama ($$, 500ml) is especially unique, showing that tension between creaminess and citric cut so characteristic of El Puerto. Also in this range are, since 2010, a line of VORS wines released in small quantities. Of the group, the VORS Oloroso ($$$$, 500ml)—a big, heady wine whose plushness adds harmony in combination with the astringency that long aging in wood tends to impart—is a standout. This line is also home to Lustau's East India Solera ($$, 750ml), the last remaining wine made in this style, which is produced to mimic the traditional method of aging via sea voyage. They do this by allowing the wine to age for three years in the *sacristía*, which is warmer and more humid than the rest of the bodega.

Since 2008, Lustau has also maintained and bottled the former Domecq brands Manzanilla Macarena ($, 750ml), Fino La Ina ($, 750ml), Amontillado Botaina ($$, 750ml), Oloroso Río Viejo ($$, 750ml), Cream Candela ($, 750ml), and Pedro Ximénez Viña 25 ($$$, 750ml). Outside of the En Rama range, La Ina ($, 750ml) is Lustau's most distinctive fino, showing more intense notes of acetaldehyde—a natural byproduct of biological aging that often lends an intense doughy aroma to finos with high levels of it—than most on the market.

THE ALMACENISTA BOTTLINGS OF LUSTAU

IN THE EARLY 1980S, WHEN EXPORT markets were dominated by mass-produced blended sherries and very young finos and manzanillas, then-director of Lustau Rafael Balao hedged on smaller production of quality dry sherry. As a nod to Lustau's past, he established the Solera Reserva range, first bottled from original stocks left over from Lustau's *almacenista* days. In 1981 he expanded this idea to include special bottlings from small, independent *almacenistas*, as an homage to both the bodega's past and the many small stockholders making superior wines. Lustau's Almacenista range was once more robust than it is today; the flailing economy and the continued extinction of small producers have brought the number to five producers, which

Lustau pulls from to bottle two wines for the *almacenista* range per year. To this day, Lustau's *almacenista* bottlings remain some of the finest in the Sherry Triangle.

GONZÁLEZ OBREGÓN (EL PUERTO DE SANTA MARÍA): Bodegas Obregón, a tiny bodega consisting of one small room, an alcove, and a *despacho* in front—where customers can taste the wines by the glass or fill their jugs or bottles to take away—is filled with bullfighting ephemera and religious icons. A hangout for locals, this bodega-cum-watering hole is run by José Luis González Obregón and his two sons. For Lustau, Obregón bottles a pungent, lemon-tinged five-year-old fino ($–$$, 500ml), sourced from a solera of just 143 barrels, as well as a saline, slightly funky amontillado ($$, 500ml)

Amontillado Botaina ($$, 750ml), the other standout, averages around fifteen years of age at bottling and shows a brisk iodine-like quality that sets it apart from Lustau's heftier takes on the style.

HOUSE STYLE: Like González Byass, the Lustau range is vast and varied, but tends toward a plusher, more forward style across much of the range.

TOP FIVE WINES: Fino La Ina ($, 750ml), Puerto Fino En Rama ($$, 500ml), Almacenista Manzanilla Pasada de Sanlúcar, Manuel Cuevas Jurado ($$, 500ml), Almacenista Amontillado de Sanlúcar, Manuel Cuevas Jurado ($$, 500ml), Almacenista Fino, Bodegas Obregón ($–$$, 500ml).

ESTABLISHED: 1896

averaging around fifteen years from a solera of just ten barrels, and lastly, an **oloroso** ($$, 500ml) that is also around fifteen years of age at bottling.

JOSÉ DE LA CUESTA (EL PUERTO DE SANTA MARÍA): This small bodega, which was founded in 1849 and is now owned by Grupo Caballero (owners of Lustau), still operates as an *almacenista*, bottling a single five-year-old bright, tangy **fino** ($, 500ml) sourced from a small solera of just 183 barrels.

MANUEL CUEVAS JURADO (SANLÚ-CAR DE BARRAMEDA): Bodegas Manuel Cuevas Jurado consistently bottles some of the finest wines in the entire Lustau collection of sherries. The bodega, which has holdings spread between three bodegas in Sanlúcar run by Don Manuel's grandson, bottles two wines from the bodega, a chalky seven-year-old **manzanilla pasada** ($$, 500ml) and an elegant, iodine-tinged twelve-year-old

manzanilla-amontillado ($$, 500ml), now simply labeled "amontillado."

GARCÍA JARANA (JEREZ DE LA FRONTERA): Juan García Jarana produces sherry as a hobby. By day, he owns a motorcycle shop in Jerez (Harley Davidson, surprisingly, is a big thing in these parts) and moonlights as a producer of oloroso. He produces one wine for Lustau—the rich, but finely textured **Oloroso Pata de Gallina** ($$, 500ml), the name of which refers to the "hen's foot" chalk mark used to identify olorosos with particularly high levels of glycerol. This classic is bottled at around twenty years of age.

VIDES (JEREZ DE LA FRONTERA): Bodegas Vides, a tiny bodega founded in 1958 by a member of the Domecq family, produces just one wine for Lustau: a musky, umami-rich **palo cortado** ($$–$$$, 500ml) that averages around fifteen to twenty years of age at bottling.

VALDESPINO

The Valdespino family's winegrowing activities in the Sherry Triangle date back to 1264, and the production of wine to at least 1430, but the story of Valdespino as we know it today begins in earnest in 1875 with the registration of the bodega under the family name.

By the late 1880s, the bodega was already considered among the most revered houses, known particularly for Inocente—which was then, as it is now, sourced exclusively from one of the Sherry Triangle's greatest vineyards, Macharnudo Alta. Today Inocente is labeled fino, but in the late nineteenth century and on through the first half of the twentieth, it was branded not by style but by the prestige of the vineyard, often being labeled simply Inocente Macharnudo.

While the quality of Valdespino's wines remained well regarded throughout the twentieth century, the bodega fell on hard times toward the latter part of the century. By 1999, when local entrepreneur and sherry lover José Estévez purchased the bodega, its facilities were in extreme disrepair. Realizing that most of Valdespino's old bodegas (some of them among the oldest in Jerez) were beyond salvaging, he moved the holdings to a new, modern facility on the outskirts of town. Of course, because of the unique importance of each bodega to the character of the finished wine, the move was met with skepticism. Yet ten years after the move was completed, the wines remain not only some of the best values in the region, but also among the finest examples of their type.

This is largely thanks to Eduardo Ojeda, who now serves as technical director for Grupo Estévez—which also includes Hijos de Rainera Pérez Marín (La Guita), among others—and one of the partners in Equipo Navazos (see page 123). He was hired right around the purchase of Valdespino and has been instrumental in furthering the traditions unique to the bodega, both in the cellar and in the vineyards. In fact, Grupo Estévez, as of 2012, is now the largest single landowner in the Jerez, giving Ojeda access to some of the finest grapes in the region. As a result, Valdespino's long-held dedication to the vineyard and the belief in its impact on wine quality and character remains remarkably intact.

NOTABLE WINES: Valdespino's most visible wines, Fino Inocente ($, 375ml; $–$$, 750ml) and Amontillado Tío Diego ($–$$, 750ml), are two of very few of single-vineyard wines (both are sourced from Macharnudo Alta) still being produced in the Sherry Triangle. The wines are also the only two in Jerez still fermented in cask. Once through the *sobretablas* stage, wherein the wines rest and are classified, Inocente is introduced into its own solera of ten *criaderas*, where it spends a remarkable ten years under flor, and Tío Diego goes into a separate solera of the same size, where it spends around twelve years under flor and five to six aging purely oxidatively, bringing its age to around seventeen to eighteen years at bottling. Both of these wines are among the finest expressions of their type and, at the time of writing, still among the most undervalued in the market.

Valdespino also bottles a small amount of their terrific Manzanilla Deliciosa ($, 375ml; $, 750ml), which is sourced from the La Guita cellars and averages around five years of age at bottling, as is Manzanilla Deliciosa En Rama ($), which is released in small quantities every spring.

The bodega bottles two fantastic VOS olorosos: Don Gonzalo ($$, 375ml; $$$, 750ml), which averages around twenty years of age at bottling and is rich and forward, but tense and lean on the palate; Solera 1842 ($$, 375ml; $$$, 750ml), on the other hand, receives a small dose of PX and is rich and slightly sweet but well integrated.

At the top of the Valdespino line are the VORS wines, which includes Amontillado Coliseo ($$$$), a stunning wine aged for the first twenty years of its life as a manzanilla before being transferred to Jerez and aging another forty years before bottling. The Oloroso Solera de Su Majestad ($$$$), which originates from the oldest solera system in the bodega and, at over thirty years old at bottling, is remarkably vibrant for an oloroso of its age. However, the pinnacle of the bodega's offerings is the Palo Cortado Cardenal ($$$$), which is sourced from a solera system containing just six barrels and bottled at over sixty years of age. It's a wine with a sinister sort of depth and intensity. It is fed by a younger solera of palo cortado, which is bottled in small quantities under the Palo Cortado Viejo C.P. ($$$, 750ml) label—the C.P. standing for Calle Ponce, the name of the street where the old bodega that housed this solera system was located. It's bottled at around twenty-five years of age.

The bodega also bottles two PXs, the younger El Candado ($, 375ml; $$, 750ml) and the VORS Niños ($$$$), but its finest sweet wine is the Moscatel Toneles ($$$$), a wine that is over eighty years old. The Toneles solera derives its name from the fact that it ages in *toneles*, or 1,000-liter barrels, rather than the usual 500 liters. The solera (oldest level) of this solera system contains just one *tonel*, which is kept under padlock in the bodega. No more than 250 liters of the wine is bottled per year.

HOUSE STYLE: The biological wines spend an unusually long period under flor, lending a strong biological imprint on everything from Fino Inocente to Amontillado Coliseo VORS. In a general sense, the house style is about as close as one can get to the Jerez archetype—bold, intense wines that still manage incredible subtlety.

TOP WINES: I found it impossible to limit myself to just five top wines for this bodega, since the range is not only vast but also of a consistently high quality. Fino Inocente ($), Manzanilla Deliciosa En Rama ($), Amontillado Tío Diego ($$), Amontillado Coliseo VORS ($$$$), Palo Cortado Viejo C.P. ($$$), Palo Cortado Cardenal VORS ($$$$), Oloroso Solera de Su Majestad VORS ($$$$), Moscatel Toneles ($$$$).

ESTABLISHED: 1875

BODEGAS TRADICIÓN

Bodegas Tradición was founded in 1998 by the billionaire construction entrepreneur Joaquín Rivero Valcarce, whose family ties to winegrowing and production in Jerez date back to the seventeenth century. His quest was simple: help sherry earn back its rightful place among the great wines of the world. He purchased a dilapidated bodega, restored it, and worked with a number of sherry experts to help source stocks of old, high-quality wines. Today the bodega focuses almost exclusively on VOS and VORS wines as well as small quantities of *añada* sherries—a rarity considering that the old wines at most bodegas constitute a barely mentionable percentage of their stock. Up until the release of their new Tradición Fino bottling in 2013, Bodegas Tradición had not released a wine younger than twenty years old to the U.S. market, making it the only boutique bodega of its kind.

Today the acquisition of old stocks and the maintenance of the wines is overseen by the *capataz* José María Quirós, while director Lorenzo García-Iglesias is the unofficial face of the company. His savvy has no doubt contributed to the success of this groundbreaking bodega.

NOTABLE WINES: While some of the vintage-dated releases, particularly the Oloroso 1970 ($$$$, 750ml), are among the bodega's more memorable wines, their efforts reach their height with the Amontillado VORS ($$$$, 750ml), released at over forty years of age. The bodega has a deft touch with oloroso as well. The Oloroso VORS ($$$$, 750ml) bottling is bold and smoky, but maintains plenty of finesse, as does the Palo Cortado VORS ($$$$, 750ml), which is nearly as full-bodied, but is countered by a notable pungency and intense saltiness. The bodega's Pedro Ximénez VOS ($$$$, 750ml), which is among its youngest offerings at just over twenty years of age, is spicy and well balanced. And the Tradición Fino ($$$$, 750ml), first released in 2013, and bottled *en rama* at a high average age of around twelve years, is savory and floral, showing a full monty of flavors thanks to its minimal filtration.

HOUSE STYLE: The bodega's offerings are focused on old, high-quality wines, either from very old soleras or vintage-dated (which is now a rarity in the Sherry Triangle). Because of the high average age of most of the bodega's wines, the house style can be summed up in one word: intense. This now extends to the bodega's expressive, mature fino.

TOP FIVE WINES: Tradición Fino ($$$$, 750ml), Amontillado VORS ($$$$, 750ml), Oloroso VORS ($$$$, 750ml), Oloroso 1975 ($$$$, 750ml), Oloroso 1970 ($$$$, 750ml).

ESTABLISHED: 1998

BODEGAS ALMOCADÉN

Bodegas Almocadén is one of the few bodegas in Jerez that is not only a sherry producer, but also a grape grower whose entire production originates from their own vineyard holdings. The family's presence in the wine business dates back to the nineteenth century, but the bodega was not established until 1915, when Don José González Granados purchased its first winemaking facilities.

The bodega is now run by the two grandsons of the founder, rugged men who seem to have absorbed the sun into their DNA. One of the brothers, Juan González Salguero, who chain-smokes with abandon, has skin that looks like a cross between kielbasa casing and rawhide. He's a third-generation farmer who's clearly no stranger to the wicked strength of Jerez's summer sun.

The bodega is popular among locals, and as noon rolls around on any given Saturday the bodega's *despacho* fills up with a never-ending stream of locals filling their jugs or liter plastic bottles, gossiping and snacking on the bodega's homemade *morcilla* (a recipe from the current owners' grandfather), which González Salguero likes to serve, in another gesture of formidability, with a hefty schmear of paprika-flavored lard called *manteca colorá*.

NOTABLE WINES: The sort of rusticity and simplicity of the Almocadén experience also defines the style of the wines. From the bodega's entry-level range, the Fino Paquiro ($, 750ml), named for a nineteenth-century bullfighter from Chiclana, is a simple, quaffable wine, as is the Manzanilla La Caletera ($, 750ml), which is purchased in Sanlúcar and bottled under the Almocadén label.

The mid-level range is labeled Caletero and contains an amontillado ($$, 750ml), an oloroso ($$, 750ml), and pedro ximénez ($$, 750ml), each with an average age of around twenty years at bottling, as well as a cream ($, 750ml), which is a blend of the Pedro Ximénez Caletero and Oloroso Caletero. Of the line, the amontillado is perhaps the most successful, showing a distinctive funk and a steeliness that keeps the wine lively.

The Almocadén line is the bodega's top tier, representing the same range of styles, but aged forty years at bottling. Here, too, the amontillado ($$$, 750ml) is the most successful of the lineup, while the pedro ximénez ($$$, 750ml) shows a remarkable amount of intensity, buttressed by aromas of smoke, jalapeño, and raisins. For fans of PX this is about as big as they get.

HOUSE STYLE: Rustic and humble.

TOP WINES: Amontillado Almocadén ($$$), Pedro Ximénez Almocadén ($$$).

ESTABLISHED: 1915

BODEGAS SÁNCHEZ ROMATE

Outside of Jerez, Sánchez Romate is best known for its flagship Cardenal Mendoza brandy, but its range of sherries—from Fino Marisemeño and Fino Perdido En Rama through its approximately twenty-year-old Amontillado NPU to the Old & Plus range of VORS sherries—represent some of the region's finest wines.

The bodega was founded in 1781 by Don Juan Sánchez de la Torre, a well-respected businessman and patron of the arts. It remained in the Sánchez de la Torre family until 1954, when it was purchased by five friends, all members of the same *tertulia*—the Spanish name for a club based around the sharing of music, wine, and ideas. The bodega is still owned by the families of those five men.

Most of the aging for the Romate wines is still carried out in the old bodega, built by Romate's founder in 1820, and is overseen by *capataz* José Luis Garcia Infante. Though many of the vineyards have been sold over the last ten years, the bodega still owns just over 100 acres of vines located in the *pago* of Balbaína, which supplies 95 percent of the fruit for the bodega's wines.

NOTABLE WINES: Sánchez Romate produces a total of sixteen sherries, divided into three ranges: the Romate line, the Special Reserves line, and Old & Plus line. The Romate line consists of the bodega's five entry-level wines: a manzanilla ($, 750ml) sourced from several suppliers in Sanlúcar de Barrameda, as well as a young fino ($, 750ml), an amontillado ($, 750ml), an oloroso ($, 750ml), and a pedro ximénez ($, 750ml)—all simple wines meant for everyday consumption.

The Special Reserves range is comprised of wines from separate soleras and higher average age. Fino Marismeño ($$, 750ml), sourced entirely from the bodega's Balbaína vineyards, undergoes a less aggressive filtration process and is bottled at around seven to eight years of age. As of 2011, Romate has also been bottling their limited-production eight-year-old Fino Perdido En Rama ($$, 750ml; *perdido* means "lost," and refers to the style of older, unfiltered fino, which fell out of favor beginning in the 1970s) sourced from three small soleras, totaling fifteen barrels. Originally bottled exclusively for The Wine Society in the United Kingdom, the wine will also be released to export markets beginning in 2014. Both are remarkable, full-bodied, complex finos that rank among the best in their class. The Amontillado NPU (*non plus ultra*; $$, 750ml), which averages around twenty years of age at bottling, is fed by the Marismeño solera and is one of the great values in amontillado, mastering the tension between oxidation and the steeliness of biological aging. Within the Reserva range, the

Palo Cortado Regente ($$, 750ml) is another standout. It's the only palo cortado bottled by the bodega and hails from just thirty *botas*, averaging around fifteen years of age at bottling. Of the sweet wines in this range, for my money the Pedro Ximénez Cardenal Cisneros ($$, 750ml), bottled at an average age of twenty years, has a bit more verve and complexity than the bass-thumping Pedro Ximénez Duquesa ($$, 750ml).

While the Special Reserves range is comprised of some of the region's best values, the most stunning wines in the Romate lineup are the VORS wines in the Old & Plus range ($$$$, 500ml). Of the three wines in this range—an oloroso, an amontillado, and a pedro ximénez—the amontillado and oloroso are among the finest old wines available on the market, with the amontillado having the edge in my book.

HOUSE STYLE: Defined by a clear dedication to classicism with a bit of modern polish.

TOP FIVE WINES: Fino Marismeño ($$, 750ml), Fino Perdido En Rama ($$, 750ml), Amontillado NPU ($$, 750ml), Palo Cortado Regente ($$, 750ml), Amontillado Old & Plus ($$$$, 500ml).

ESTABLISHED: 1781

BODEGAS DIOS BACO

While the soleras that the bodega was founded on can claim a history that dates back to 1765, Bodegas Dios Baco's history begins in 1992 with the Morilla family's (famed producers of sherry vinegar) purchase of one of the twelve bodegas once owned by the historic firm of Palomino & Vergara. With this purchase the Morillas also acquired several old soleras that have been expanded to form what is now Dios Baco.

The bodega's current production is managed by *capataz* José Paez Morilla, while the commercial side of the business is run by his daughter, Alejandra. The bodega produces a relatively small amount of wine—the vast majority of which is sold outside Spain's borders. As such, the bodega is a bit of ghost within the town of Jerez, but is worth seeking out, particularly for their Baco Imperial line.

NOTABLE WINES: The Dios Baco wines can be separated into three ranges: the classic range, which includes the bodega's flagship Fino Bulería ($$, 750ml), a full-bodied, umami-driven fino aged around five years at bottling; a line of sweetened blended sherries labeled "Baco de Elite"; and the bodega's older wines, labeled Baco Imperial.

In addition to the Fino Bulería, the classic range also includes the manzanilla Riá Pitá ($, 500ml), which, in keeping with the style of the fino is also flor-forward and full-bodied in the context of manzanilla. The bodega bottles several sweetened wines under their Baco de Elite range, as well as the dry Amontillado Dios Baco ($, 750ml), which is a solid value for the style. The same is true of Oloroso Dios Baco ($, 750ml), but, unfortunately, the less refined Oloroso Baco de Elite ($$, 750ml) is more widely available in the market. The range is rounded out with the fairly simple, raisiny Pedro Ximénez Oxford 1970 ($, 500ml), and the Moscatel Pasa Esnobista ($$, 500ml), which is bottled at around twelve to fifteen years old.

The bodega's finest offerings can be found within the Baco Imperial range ($$$$, 750ml) which includes an amontillado and pedro ximénez, both labeled VOS, and an oloroso and palo cortado, both labeled VORS.

HOUSE STYLE: Rustic, full-bodied wines.

TOP WINES: Fino Bulería ($$, 750ml), Baco Imperial Palo Cortado ($$$$, 750ml).

ESTABLISHED: 1848/1992

BODEGAS WILLIAMS & HUMBERT

There isn't a trace of Spain in the name, yet there are few bodegas that are, historically, more synonymous with sherry. The bodega was founded in 1877 by Alexander Williams—a sherry lover who'd left England to take a job working in the offices of the now-defunct bodega Wisdom & Warter—and Arthur Humbert, a specialist in international relations. The impetus for their union was born out of a steamy love affair between Williams and Amy Humbert, Arthur's sister (imagine *Out of Africa,* but in Spain and without all the tragedy). He earned a modest salary working at the bodega and after his attempt at entering into partnership with the Warter half of Wisdom & Warter, he set out to establish a bodega of his own with the help of Humbert's father, and with Amy's brother as his partner. The result was Williams & Humbert.

The firm grew steadily during the latter half of the nineteenth century, but hit its stride in the beginning of the twentieth century with the introduction of Dry Sack, a blend of oloroso, amontillado, and pedro ximénez that would go on to become one of the most iconic sweetened sherries ever produced. It remains the house's signature wine to this day.

MY ESSENTIAL SHERRIES

BELOW I'VE LISTED SOME OF MY FAVORITE sherries in each category. While there is at least one (but in almost every case, several) Equipo Navazos La Bota wines that *belong* on this list, I chose not to include them: the supply and availability of each release is too limited.

Fino
- El Maestro Sierra Fino ($)
- Valdespino Fino Inocente ($)
- Gutiérrez Colosía Fino Amerigo ($)
- Fernando de Castilla Fino En Rama ($$)
- Emilio Hidalgo Fino Especial La Panesa ($$$, 750ml)
- González Byass Tres Palmas ($$$$, 500ml)

Manzanilla
- La Guita Manzanilla ($)
- Barbadillo Manzanilla Solear En Rama ($)
- Hidalgo–La Gitana Manzanilla Pasada Pastrana ($$, 750ml)
- Manuel Cuevas Jurado Manzanilla Pasada de Sanlúcar ($$, 500ml)
- Equipo Navazos Manzanilla 'I Think' En Rama ($)

Amontillado
- Valdespino Amontillado Tío Diego ($)
- Sánchez Romate Amontillado NPU ($$, 750ml)
- La Cigarrera Amontillado VOS ($$$$, 500ml)
- Hidalgo–La Gitana Amontillado Napoleon VORS ($$$$, 500ml)
- El Maestro Sierra Amontillado 1830 VORS ($$$$)

Palo Cortado
- Delgado Zuleta Monteagudo Palo Cortado ($$, 750ml)
- Fernando de Castilla Palo Cortado Antique ($$$$, 500ml)
- Emilio Hidalgo Palo Cortado Especial Marqués de Rodil ($$$$, 750ml)
- Gutiérrez Colosía Solera Familiar Palo Cortado ($$$$, 500ml)
- Valdespino Palo Cortado Cardenal VORS ($$$$)

Oloroso
- Gutiérrez Colosía Oloroso Sangre y Trabajadero ($$)
- Gracia Hermanos Oloroso Tauromaquia ($, 750ml)
- Emilio Hidalgo Oloroso Gobernador ($$, 750ml)
- Barbadillo Oloroso Seco Cuco ($$$, 750ml)
- Tradición Oloroso VORS ($$$$, 750ml)

Pedro Ximénez
- Valdespino Pedro Ximénez El Candado ($)
- Pérez Barquero Pedro Ximénez La Cañada ($$$$, 750ml)
- Toro Albalá Pedro Ximénez Don PX Gran Reserva 1983 ($$)
- Alvear Pedro Ximénez Solera 1830 ($$$$, 500ml)

Moscatel
- Delgado Zuleta 'Zuleta' Moscatel ($, 750ml)
- César Florido Moscatel Pasas ($)
- Valdespino Moscatel Toneles ($$$$)

The bodega remained within the Williams & Humbert family until 1972, when it was purchased by Rumasa—a large company that had acquired several bodegas before being seized by the Spanish government in 1983. Its fall, the result of a laundry list of wrongdoings, severely damaged not only the bodegas under Rumasa's control but also the entire sherry industry.

Today the bodega is under the majority ownership of the Medina family, who oversee around 750 acres of vineyard land spread between two vineyards, Las Conchas in Balbaína, which includes a plot of some of the oldest vines in the Sherry Triangle, and Dos Mercedes in Carrascal.

While the majority of the bodega's production is focused on Dry Sack—particularly in the export markets—the house also produces some well-made and underexposed dry sherries.

NOTABLE WINES: Williams & Humbert produce two finos, the Dry Sack Fino ($, 375ml; $, 750ml), which was originally bottled under the Pando label and was the first-ever wine shipped by the bodega in 1878. It's the light but stylish intro, at five to six years of average age, to the Fino Collection ($, 750ml), an eight-year-old, golden, floral fino that is just starting to show the mature, mushroomy flavors associated with older fino. The bodega also bottles the roughly six-year-old almond-tinged Manzanilla Alegría ($, 375ml; $, 750ml) and the Manzanilla Collection ($, 750ml), which is roughly the same age as the fino. The twelve-year-old Amontillado Cóllection ($, 750ml), is light on its feet, but lacking in complexity to the point of feeling a tad diluted. The Oloroso Collection ($, 750ml) also suffers the same fate, lacking both complexity and concentration. The Jalifa Amontillado VORS ($$$$, 750ml), however, lacks nothing in intensity, showing all of the burnished pungency and high-toned citrus peel notes that are often hallmarks of old amontillado. The bodega's other top dry bottling is the Palo Cortado Dos Cortados VOS ($$$, 750ml) a robust but balanced take on the style.

HOUSE STYLE: Beyond the predictably plush sweetened wines, the dry wines are varied, lacking in character and balance within the Collection line, but showing refinement and concentration in the VOS and VORS wines.

TOP WINES: Fino Collection ($, 750ml), Amontillado Jalifa VORS ($$$$, 750ml).

ESTABLISHED: 1877

BODEGAS SANDEMAN

This historic house was founded in 1790 by George Sandeman, a Scotsman who grew up in Perth, Australia. He first established a business as a wine agent in London and went on to root himself and his business in both Portugal and Jerez simultaneously. The bodega remained under the sole direction of the Sandeman family until 1980, when it was purchased by Seagram and then eventually sold in 2002 to Sogrape, Portugal's largest wine company.

Despite the fact that the bodega is now almost exclusively focused on sweetened, blended sherries, it remains one of the most recognizable (who could forget the iconic caped, Zorro-esque Sandeman mascot?) in the Sherry Triangle as well as in Portugal. And while for years the company has been far more synonymous with port, it still produces a few excellent sherries, most notable among them the limited and thus aptly named Rare Fino. Unfortunately, the bodega's dry wines can be difficult to find in export markets, where inexpensive cream and medium sherries—which make up the majority of their total sherry production—tend to dominate the shelves.

NOTABLE WINES: The house produces three main dry wines. The mid-level (the bodega bottles an entry-level fino distributed within Europe) Don Fino ($, 750ml) is a rich fino aged around five years at bottling that sees a second fortification to 17 percent (for bottles destined to be released in Spain, a second fortification is not conducted), making it one of only a few finos still made in this style. While the wine feels slightly disjointed due to its alcohol level, it still retains a classic fino profile. Better, though, is the limited-release Rare Fino ($$, 500ml), a roughly seven-year-old wine bottled from selected casks within the Don Fino solera system once per year and bottled with only minimal filtration. Bottles destined for the United States also see a second fortification.

Beyond fino, the bodega bottles only one more dry wine, the Royal Esmeralda Amontillado VOS ($$, 500ml). Bottled at more than twenty years of age, it is round and caramelly but still maintains a salinity and pungency that is true to the style. Also within this range is the Royal Corregador Rich Oloroso ($$, 500ml), a wine that is sweetened with PX but remains balanced and elegant. Also within the VOS range is the classic Royal Ambrosante PX ($$, 500ml), which is rich and expressive.

Beyond the finos and the range of VOS wines, the house focuses exclusively on sweetened sherries.

HOUSE STYLE: Rich and bold wines, with a near total preference for sweetened wines.

TOP WINES: Rare Fino ($$, 500ml), Royal Esmeralda Amontillado VOS ($$, 500ml).

ESTABLISHED: 1790

EQUIPO NAVAZOS: THE PRIVATE CLUB THAT HELPED SPARK A RENAISSANCE

WHEN EQUIPO NAVAZOS BEGAN IN 2005 as a private club of collectors and friends, Eduardo Ojeda and Jesús Barquín certainly couldn't have imagined that it would turn into one of the driving forces behind the modern sherry renaissance.

It started with a single barrel of amontillado that, like so many other exceptional sherries, hadn't been touched for decades. At the time, there was very little demand for older, high-end sherry, but Ojeda and Barquín were determined to bottle the wine. They pooled funds from the small wine club they'd assembled and purchased one cask from Bodegas M. Sánchez Ayala in Sanlúcar of what became their first private release, La Bota de Amontillado, or "The Cask of Amontillado," a reference to the Edgar Allan Poe short story of the same name.

At the urging of club members, Ojeda (by day the technical director of Grupo Estévez, overseeing production for Valdespino and Hijos de Rainera Pérez Marín) and Barquín (a longtime sherry lover and a professor of criminology at the University of Granada) continued to seek out top wines from a handful of bodegas in the Sherry Triangle. The hits kept coming. Eventually, demand from outside

the group began to grow and by their sixth bottling they'd gone commercial, releasing tiny quantities of limited-edition sherries that, to them, represented the purest—and most unique—expressions of everything from fino to old palo cortado.

At the time of writing, Ojeda and Barquín have released forty-six "La Bota" bottlings sourced from more than ten different producers and have collaborated on a number of alternative projects, from a white table wine based on Palomino Fino in conjunction with Douro wine producer Dirk Niepoort to a sparkling wine made with the cava producer Sergi Colet that is aged under flor and dosaged with sherry instead of the typical mixture of wine and cane sugar. Their interests also extend to spirits: since 2012, they've been collaborating with artisan Cognac producer and importer Nicolas Palazzi on a number of exceptional bottlings of Brandy de Jerez, as well as Caribbean rum aged in the Sherry Triangle.

The idiosyncratic nature of their wines and the unlikeliness of the project has not only helped turn attention back to the Sherry Triangle, but it's also proven that one can respect tradition and history— even be driven by it—and still innovate.

CONTINUED

When it comes to selecting and blending sherry, the skill of Barquín and Ojeda is undeniable, but the success and rapid reach of Equipo Navazos is not the story of a maverick wine producer making groundbreaking wines in a sea of mediocrity. It's the story of a group of sherry lovers who've helped reveal the greatness and diversity of wines that have always existed here, but had been left to languish due to lack of perceived marketability for sherries that fell outside the more widely accepted modern expressions of each style.

Of course, things have changed drastically since the project began in 2005; a new fino or manzanilla *en rama* seems to hit the market every other week and producers are increasingly interested in capitalizing on a market that is more adventurous than it has been in more than a century. But something like La Bota de Manzanilla Pasada 20—bottled, like all of the Equipo Navazos wines, nearly unfiltered or not filtered at all—when I first tasted it, was so foreign stylistically that it was both enlightening and shocking in equal measure. I'd never tasted a manzanilla with that depth of flavor and intensity and still, despite the growing number of new, interesting sherries in the market, the Equipo Navazos wines remain consistently singular, revealing new heights for each style.

What makes them so different? I am often asked this question and further prodded to define the "style" of the wines. But trying to pin a style on Equipo Navazos is difficult. Unlike the traditional bodegas of the Sherry Triangle, they do not have a house style to protect—which allows them to release a dizzyingly variable line of wines. In fact, their house style is predicated on *not* being beholden to one style. They're looking for the wines in a bodega that are, as Ojeda calls them, "the funny ones," or the casks that stand out as remarkably unique or divergent in the context of a solera system.

In a traditional bodega, these divergent casks are assimilated into a blend that's meant, like a Champagne house's nonvintage cuvée, to remain consistent from year to year. The adverse effect of such an approach is that some of the singularity of certain casks is never truly reflected in bottle.

What Equipo Navazos aims to do is preserve the character traits that make certain casks stand out. "If the wine is extreme in the cask, it will be extreme in the bottle," says Barquín. "We don't want to compromise."

Thus, the one characteristic that defines all of the wines is intensity of expression. Part of this is seeking particularly outgoing casks, part of it is the minimal filtration of the wines, and part of it is

the age of the wines. Even the biological wines tend to be bottled at a higher average age than the majority of finos and manzanillas that are widely distributed. Of course, once one is familiar with the Equipo Navazos wines, a pattern emerges in the preferences of Ojeda and Barquín, but trying to bundle their offerings misses the point. The quest to capture the varied and changeable nature of the solera system is precisely what's driving Ojeda and Barquín forward.

Beyond traditional sherry, their most fascinating effort is Florpower, an unfortified 100 percent Palomino Fino sourced primarily from the *pago* of Miraflores

near Sanlúcar, bottled at 11.5 percent alcohol and aged for a total of thirty-two months under flor—eight of those in cask, and twenty-four in stainless steel tanks. The release is part of an ongoing research project meant to prove the importance of vineyard site to the character of sherry and reproduce the "natural," unfortified, and unfiltered sherries that once captivated England in the late nineteenth century. While the impact of flor is evident in the wine's aromas, it speaks less to biological aging and more to the underappreciated expression of *terroir*, in the traditional sense, in the wines of this region.

Sanlúcar de Barrameda

"San Lucar de Barrameda is a small but pretty town with near 5000 inhabitants situated on the left bank of the Guadalquivir. It is famous for smuggling and frauds of every kind. Its foreign commerce produces a certain degree of luxury in furniture, dress, and the pleasures of the table, and there is a white wine called Vino de Manzanilla, so called from a small town seven leagues from Seville, which is a good deal like Burgundy."

—Frederick Augustus Fischer, *Travels in Spain in 1797 and 1798* (published 1802)

Here in Sanlúcar, where the Guadalquivir River flows down from Sevilla to meet the Atlantic, a gloriously confused mix of flora litters the edge of the water—bamboo-like reeds tangle with pine brush, and palm trees stand tall in a prideful reminder of Andalusia's latitude. While the city's fortunate location on the sea—and its centuries-long reputation as a great place to take it easy—has produced pockets of more modern development, it's also not difficult to imagine the town as it was over a hundred years ago.

The Barrio Alto—the oldest part of the city, perched atop a bluff overlooking the sea—still looks much like it did in the nineteenth century (albeit a bit more timeworn). And the Barrio Bajo is still dotted with palaces built during boom times, now in various stages of disrepair.

To Sanlúcar's nineteenth-century aristocracy, today's city would've likely been their imagination of end times. Yet what makes this city great has nothing to do with a polished appearance or economic prosperity. Sanlúcar is built on something far stronger: state of mind. And if the world were ending, or had ended and I managed to survive, I'd want to be in a bar on the Bajo de Guía.

Here along the stretch of boardwalk overlooking the mouth of the Guadalquivir, fishermen travel in small boats to and from the Atlantic, offering the view for a strip of seafood restaurants and bars packed with locals feasting on the bounty they've supplied. Sitting at any one of them it's not hard to wish that life was one long Spanish Saturday punctuated by plates of *langostinos* and an endless parade of manzanilla—from the half bottle, of course. In a testament to the lifestyle in Sanlúcar, manzanilla is rarely ordered by the glass here. If you don't have time for at least a half bottle, you don't have time for lunch.

Identifying as Sanluqueño, whether or not one even lives there, refers partly to this particular talent for relaxation. But it's also something deeper, something that has to do with the town's subtly rebellious bent—a revolutionary spirit stifled by economic despair, but not stomped out. While there have always been bodegas here that matched Jerez's in grandeur and scale—

Hidalgo–La Gitana and Barbadillo notable among them—Sanlúcar has historically been a cottage industry in comparison, a city whose wine business was always run by many rather than a noble few.

At its height, it was home to hundreds of growers and more than eighty independent bodegas or *almacenistas*, but regulations enacted in the 1970s—which forbade producers' owning fewer than 2,500 barrels (or 12,500 hectoliters of wine) to bottle and ship their own wines—either turned many of Sanlúcar's small bodegas into *almacenistas* dependent on larger producers or put them out of business. After the restriction was lifted in 1996, the industry never fully recovered. And while the landscape of the wine industry has changed here, the cultural identity that Sanlúcar's cottage industry created has not. And today, a general lightness of being still persists here despite the city's many challenges. You feel it almost immediately, in a greater propensity to smile, to tell a joke to a stranger, to order just one more bottle of manzanilla.

Maybe it's the proximity to the sea or the embarrassment of riches plucked from it. Whatever it is, it's produced a powerful sense of joy, and today Sanlúcar remains—as Rupert Croft-Cooke described it in his 1956 *Sherry*—"one of the most naturally happy places in the world."

BODEGA HIJOS DE RAINERA PÉREZ MARÍN (LA GUITA)

Bodega Hijos de Rainera Pérez Marín—which is more commonly known for the name of the only wine it produces, La Guita—was founded in 1852 by Don Domingo Pérez Marín. The name La Guita refers not only to a nineteenth-century slang word for "cash" (stories about Don Domingo suggest he was a bit of a hustler) but also to the Spanish word for "string"—hence the tiny piece of raffia affixed to each bottle.

La Guita is Spain's number one selling manzanilla. In wine, mass popularity is often synonymous with low quality (in America, Sutter Home is still one of our most popular brands, after all), but La Guita has been able to avoid the sort of banality long associated with large-scale wine production.

Today the La Guita solera system is split into two cellars: one old and one new. The old cellar, originally built in 1526, is called Misericordia and is situated at one of the highest points in Sanlúcar's Barrio Alto. Between 1867 and 1868 the building, originally a hospital, was transformed into a bodega and today houses around 2,000 of the more than 14,000 barrels (which, filled to 500-liter capacity, would translate to more than nine million bottles of wine) that make up the solera system.

The new cellar, Bodega Pago Sanlúcar Viejo, which is located outside the city center, was purchased in 1993 and renovated to become a bi-level bodega—complete with temperature control, which is still a rarity in the Sherry Triangle—in the early 2000s. It houses around 12,000 barrels organized into five *criaderas* and one *solera*.

Before the 1980s, La Guita was bottled with a higher average age than it is now, and it originated from a single vineyard. As demand for younger "manzanilla fina" grew throughout the last several decades, La Guita was bottled at an increasingly younger age. And as demand grew, so too did the need for more grapes and more wine. Eventually, La Guita outgrew its single vineyard, but it is still produced entirely from grapes grown within the famed *pago* of Miraflores.

Toward the latter part of the twentieth century, the bodega changed ownership several times before being purchased by Grupo Estévez (also the owner of Valdespino) in 2007. Since then, the group's technical director, Eduardo Ojeda, has significantly improved the quality of production, restoring La Guita's reputation as one of the best values in the region and a classic example of just how complex—and reflective of a place—manzanilla can be.

NOTABLE WINES: In the spring of 2013, over a glass of amontillado at Bar La Moderna, a favorite of Ojeda's in Jerez, I asked him what he loved about La Guita ($, 375ml; $, 750ml) and what he thought made it distinctive. He used to drink more fino from Valdespino than anything else, but in recent years La Guita has become something of a revelation for him. "[Valdespino] Inocente [fino] is evident, like a tall man with strong character," he said. "But La Guita is about subtlety; La Guita is soil." While the original 370 acres of vineyards that were owned by the bodega were sold during a change of hands, the company—shortly after—bought the Miraflores Growers' Co-op, giving them exclusive access to hundreds of growers within the Miraflores *pago*, as well as the ability to continue to make La Guita as a single-*pago* wine. In 2013, Ojeda discovered a portion of the original La Guita vineyard still in production and has entered into a contract with the owner to purchase fruit for La Guita from these vines, which at seventy to eighty years old are some of the oldest in the region.

HOUSE STYLE: Approachable, but more complex and defined than many of its counterparts.

TOP WINE: There is only one wine: La Guita ($).

ESTABLISHED: 1852

BODEGAS BARBADILLO

Barbadillo was established in 1821 by Benigno Barbadillo, who'd recently transplanted to Spain after spending the previous twenty years in Mexico running an import-export business. When he returned, fortune in tow, he entered the wine trade, purchasing the Bodega del Toro cellar in the Barrio Alto in 1824, which is still owned by the bodega today. He died ten years later and his widow went on to marry Pedro Rodríguez, which led to a brief period wherein the bodega was known as Bodegas Pedro Rodríguez e Hijo, as recorded in Henry Vizetelly's *Facts About Sherry*, published in 1875.

The current name of the company, Bodegas Antonio Barbadillo, is an homage to Benigno's grandson, who was born in 1863 and led the company through a period of great expansion until his death, in 1921.

Today, Barbadillo is run by the sixth generation of the family and has grown to become one of the largest producers in the Sherry Triangle, with seventeen bodegas and over 1,200 acres of vineyards spread between two main growing areas—Gibalbín and Santa Lucía—in addition to around thirty different growers they purchase fruit from all over the region.

The cellar is currently under the guidance of Montse Molino. Since signing on with Barbadillo sixteen years ago, she's spearheaded a number of alternative projects—including a sparkling wine made from Chardonnay and Palomino Fino grown in *albariza* soil—and has further established the more robust style of the house's flagship wine, Manzanilla Solear.

NOTABLE WINES: While the meat of the Barbadillo business comes from their table wines—including Spain's number one selling white wine, Castillo de San Diego—their sherries still represent an important part of their business, at least philosophically. Manzanilla Solear ($) remains one of the most popular mazanillas locally. It's sourced from a solera system of around 12,000 barrels, housed in numerous bodegas, including the house's spectacular La Arboledilla cellar, and is bottled at around six and a half years of age. The top of the range for manzanilla is Barbadillo's seasonal Manzanilla Solear En Rama ($), bottled from a relatively small solera system of just 550 *botas* of manzanilla refreshed with only the finest *botas* of Solear. It's bottled four times per year—which is meant to illustrate the fluctuation in flor growth with the seasons and its impact on the character of the wine—at an average age of around eight years at bottling. It's consistently, with each season's release, one of the best manzanillas on the market.

Beyond manzanilla, Barbadillo's classic line includes Amontillado Principe ($$$, 750ml), a briny, intense amontillado bottled at around fifteen years of age from a solera fed by the Manzanilla En Rama solera system. While it has all of the hallmarks of Sanlúcar—the fine texture and salinity—it also has a higher than average alcohol level (19.5 percent), giving the wine a tension between robust and lean that is characteristic of the house style. Oloroso Seco Cuco ($$$, 750ml), bottled at the same age, is a forward, expressive wine with that Sanlúcar texture still lurking underneath. The Palo Cortado Obispo Gascón ($$$, 750ml), bottled at close to twenty years of age, is one of the finest values in palo cortado, but it's not for the faint of heart. It, too, is bottled at a high average level of alcohol (21.5 percent). These three wines in all of their intensity are the whiskey lover's gateway to sherry.

Each of the three wines from this classic line feeds soleras of the house's VORS line, save for the Obispo Gascón, which is bottled from the house's single palo cortado solera system, each of the three drawn from different *criaderas*. Of the VORS line, the amontillado ($$$$, 750ml) and the palo cortado ($$$$, 750ml), both bottled at around forty years of age, wear well the particular pungency that results from long aging in wood.

The pinnacle of the house's offerings is the Reliquia line ($$$$, 750ml), which consists of four wines—amontillado, oloroso, palo cortado, and pedro ximénez—that are among the most expensive and sought-after wines in the Sherry Triangle. Only forty bottles of each style are released each year.

HOUSE STYLE: Bold and forward, particularly for Sanlúcar.

TOP FIVE WINES: Manzanilla En Rama Solear seasonal series ($), Amontillado Principe ($$$, 750ml), Amontillado VORS ($$$$, 750ml), Palo Cortado VORS ($$$$, 750ml), Reliquia line ($$$$, 750ml).

ESTABLISHED: 1821

BODEGAS LA CIGARRERA

A small operation consisting of just five hundred barrels, La Cigarrera was founded in 1758 by José Colóm Darbó. The bodega changed hands within the family several times before Manuel Hidalgo Colóm, a descendant of Colóm Darbó, took over in the late 1800s, purchasing the current bodegas and launching La Cigarrera's namesake manzanilla—the label and name an homage to the ladies, called "cigarreras," who used to sell rolled cigarettes on the streets of Sanlúcar.

Today, in order to reach the tiny bodega complex you have to follow a narrow street that runs along the border of the Barrio Alto and the Barrio Bajo until you see the sign perched at the top of an arch that reads, in English, "Typical Tavern." Without it, it'd be impossible to guess that, behind the doors of this former convent, is a trio of bodegas—organized around a central patio—that rank among the oldest in Sanlúcar.

By the time the current owners, brothers Ignacio and Pedro Hidalgo García de Velasco—great-grandsons of Hidalgo-Colóm and ninth-generation descendants of Colóm Darbó—took over in 1997, La Cigarrera was operating as an *almacenista*. But export regulations on small producers had recently been lifted, and the brothers once again began bottling Manzanilla La Cigarrera, eventually building production of the wine to a still tiny 11,000 cases of half bottles per year. While their flagship manzanilla makes up around 90 percent of their total production, they also bottle small quantities of manzanilla pasada, amontillado, and oloroso for the U.S. market.

NOTABLE WINES: The majority of La Cigarrera's production is comprised of their manzanilla ($), sourced almost entirely from grapes grown in vineyards around Sanlúcar, a wine that averages just under five years of age at bottling and is marked by an ashy, herbal quality that has become a calling card of the house. The bodega recently began releasing very small amounts of their manzanilla pasada ($$$), bottled from just three barrels that, as Ignacio says, contain nearly the same wine that they did twenty-two years ago, as the family stopped drawing wine from the barrels when he passed away in 1990. Previously, the barrels were only drawn off for special family occasions and were refreshed only minimally each year. It's a wine with tremendous depth, but more striking is the freshness and steeliness the wine still possesses at this age.

In addition to manzanilla, the bodega bottles an amontillado, an oloroso, a moscatel, and a pedro ximénez from the standard line, but they are not exported to the United States. Of the older wines, the bodega has also recently bottled an Amontillado VOS ($$$$) from a single barrel of three that make up a small solera started for the brothers' grandmother. It's an intensely saline, iodine-tinged wine that shows not only the strength of the house style but also the remarkable influence of Sanlúcar's climate in maintaining freshness and tension in wines of considerable age.

HOUSE STYLE: Classic, über-lean wines with a strong saline steeliness to the manzanilla that speaks to the prime location of the cellar, wedged in between the Barrio Bajo and the Barrio Alto.

TOP WINES: Manzanilla ($), Manzanilla Pasada ($$$), Amontillado VOS ($$$$).

ESTABLISHED: 1758

BODEGAS HIDALGO–LA GITANA

Throughout the many changes to the landscape of Sanlúcar's wine industry and its economic ups and downs, Hidalgo–La Gitana has remained a name synonymous with prosperity and top-quality wine production.

The bodega was established by the Hidalgo family in 1792 with the purchase of a piece of land in the Barrio Bajo, where the current bodega stands to this day. The bodega, then called Eduardo Hidalgo y Cía (and, later, Viuda de Eduardo Hidalgo), rose to fame in the mid-1800s, and by 1875, when Henry Vizetelly's *Facts About Sherry* was published, it was already considered the premier producer of manzanilla.

During the latter part of the nineteenth century the bodega would go through several name changes before settling on Bodegas Hidalgo–La Gitana, which translates to "the gypsy." As the story goes, in the early nineteenth century, Hidalgo's wines became popular at a certain bar in Málaga frequented by fishermen and owned by a beautiful gypsy woman. Locally, the wine simply became known as *vino de la gitana* or "the gypsy lady's wine." The name stuck, and when Hidalgo began bottling the wines in the early part of the twentieth century, the label—which was commissioned in 1901 and reworked in 1920—bore the image of "la gitana," in commemoration of the woman who helped popularize the wine.

The bodega is now under the watch of Javier Hidalgo, the seventh generation of the Hidalgo family to care for it. Hidalgo is famously brusque, but underneath the unflappable exterior is a man with an intense passion, not only for sherry—it is, as he says, "in my genetic information"—but also for birds and horses (he is an ornithologist and an amateur jockey). Under his leadership the bodega has continued to prosper and evolve, and while Manzanilla La Gitana remains the bodega's most well-known wine, it is merely the starting point for what is a fantastic line of sherries from top to bottom.

NOTABLE WINES: Like most enduring manzanilla brands, Manzanilla La Gitana ($, 500ml)—often referred to as "Tío Pepe's girlfriend" because of its light style and similar prominence in the region—evolved from a manzanilla pasada into a much younger, lighter style. It is now considered one of the archetypes of modern manzanilla. The bodega's Manzanilla Pasada Pastrana ($$, 750ml) remains a reminder of the old style, bottled at around eight to nine years of average age and sourced from a single vineyard of the same name. It's one of the finest wines to bear the name manzanilla. As of 2011, Hidalgo began releasing a small amount of Manzanilla La Gitana En Rama ($$, 750ml), bottled twice per year in spring and autumn. It's a wine with the same skeleton as La Gitana but with a bit more meat and a heavy aromatic dose of chamomile.

While Hidalgo–La Gitana bottles a simple Clasica range of young sherries, they do not have a major presence in the export markets. Of the consistently value-driven Premium range—which includes Amontillado Napoleon ($, 500ml), Oloroso Faraón ($, 500ml), Cream Alameda ($, 500ml), and Pedro Ximénez Triana ($, 500ml), each bottled with at least twelve years of average age—the elegant, iodine-laced Napoleon and the nutty, orange blossom–tinged Faraón are standouts. So is the Cream Alameda, a balanced take on the style that ranks alongside Emilio Hidalgo's Cream Morenita as one of the best examples of its type.

Outside of Hidalgo–La Gitana's core trio of manzanilla bottlings, the house reaches its zenith with the its age-designated sherries. The youngest of the bunch, the Palo Cortado Wellington VOS ($$$, 500ml) is a bright, tangy palo cortado aged around twenty years at bottling. Its senior, the Palo Cortado Wellington VORS ($$$$, 500ml), is, along with the Amontillado Napoleon VORS ($$$$, 500ml), the finest wine that the bodega produces, the former bottled at around fifty years of age and the latter at around forty. Both are great examples of the persistence of the house style, which combines elegance with approachability. The Oloroso Faraón VORS ($$$$, 500ml) is no slouch either, staking its claim as the most aromatic of the bunch with an intense aroma of smoke, roasted nuts, and candied orange peel. The youngest of the VORS group is the fruity Pedro Ximénez Triana VORS ($$$$, 500ml), which averages around thirty-five years (a tween in PX years) at bottling.

HOUSE STYLE: Classic Sanlúcar. Finely textured and intensely saline, with remarkable approachability across the entire range.

TOP FIVE WINES: Manzanilla La Gitana En Rama ($$, 750ml), Manzanilla Pasada Pastrana ($$, 750ml), Amontillado Napoleon ($, 500ml), Amontillado Napoleon VORS ($$$$, 500ml), Palo Cortado Wellington VOS and VORS ($$$–$$$$, 500ml).

ESTABLISHED: 1792

BODEGAS HEREDEROS DE ARGÜESO

Argüeso was founded in 1822 by León de Argüeso y Argüeso, who came to Sanlúcar from Burgos in 1820. He established himself as a grocer, quickly prospered, and just two years after he arrived, bought several old soleras and the cellar of San José on Calle Santo Domingo, now part of a complex of bodegas in the Barrio Bajo belonging to Argüeso. These original soleras are still in production and are estimated to be between 225 and 250 years old.

At the time of his death, León de Argüeso had never married and had no children. He left the bodega to his niece and nephew, hence the winery's seal, which reads "Los 2 Herederos de Don León de Argüeso" (the Two Heirs of Mr. León de Argüeso) with the initials "J & F" for their names, Juan and Francisca.

Today, Argüeso's holdings include several bodegas around a complex that covers around 280,000 square feet and produces around 1.5 million bottles of sherry per year under the guidance of longtime *capataz* Mariano Galan. Although much of the architecture of the bodegas was added during the nineteenth century, two buildings, the *sacristía* and the *refectorio*, both of which house wine, contain original coffered ceilings from the old, sixteenth-century convent of Santo Domingo. They're among the more dramatic and silencing spaces to be found in all of the Sherry Triangle.

NOTABLE WINES: While Argüeso is well regarded for the quality of its wines, the bodega has never enjoyed the international acclaim of its contemporaries of a similar size and quality level. But as the wines continue to gain more visibility in the export markets, this is likely to change. From top to bottom, the house's manzanilla offerings are a tremendous value. While the bodega does produce a manzanilla fina, it's largely for local consumption. The starting point for the bodega's manzanillas is the Las Medallas ($, 375ml; $, 750ml), a bright, citrusy wine bottled at around four years of age. The bodega's flagship, Manzanilla San León ($, 375ml; $, 750ml), is a big step up in terms of both age and complexity. Bottled at around six to eight years of age, it's just starting to show notes of earthy umami character, giving the wine another layer of complexity on top of the eminently likable citrusy quality of the house's manzanillas. The finest of the bunch is the Manzanilla San León Reserva de Familia ($, 375ml; $$, 750ml), which averages around ten years of age at bottling and is sourced from a solera of just forty-four *botas*, from which only two *sacas* are performed each year, totaling just 2,000 liters released annually.

Beyond manzanilla, the house bottles a fifteen-year-old amontillado ($$, 750ml), which shows the citric pungency and leanness that is characteristic of all three manzanilla bottlings. The bodega's oloroso ($, 750ml) is less compelling, showing marked leanness, but lacking complexity. Better is the pedro ximénez ($, 375ml; $$, 750ml), which, at five years of age, is fruity and light on its feet despite its sweetness.

The bodega's finest wine is its single VORS bottling, a seventy-year-old Amontillado Viejo ($$$$, 750ml)—a stunningly saline and complex wine that is one of the finest old amontillados in Sanlúcar.

HOUSE STYLE: Pungent, flor-forward wines with a tinge of rusticity that makes them easily recognizable.

TOP WINES: Manzanilla San León ($), Manzanilla San León Reserva de Familia ($$), Amontillado Viejo VORS ($$$$).

ESTABLISHED: 1822

BODEGAS DELGADO ZULETA

Founded in 1744 by Don Francisco Gil de Ledesma y Sotomayor, Bodegas Delgado Zuleta's primary goal was to supply wine to the ever-thirsty and increasingly prosperous American colonies.

It wasn't until the late nineteenth and early twentieth centuries that the bodega and its flagship Manzanilla La Goya established itself as "la manzanilla de Sanlúcar," or, as the bodega translates it, "the wine of the people of Sanlúcar." La Goya—which is named for Aurora Jauffré, a famous flamenco dancer of the time who used La Goya as her stage name—became King Alfonso XIII's drink of choice when he declared Sanlúcar de Barrameda his main vacation spot in the early twentieth century.

Stroll through the town's main square, Plaza Calbido, and it's hard not to notice the La Goya advertisement in mural form emblazoned on the side of Hotel Barrameda, lit up like a cabaret singer in the late afternoon sun. It has loomed over the plaza for more than twenty years. Take a right and you'll find the best *papas aliñas* (see page 243) you'll eat in your life. They're served at Barbiana, the namesake bar of Zuleta's other beloved manzanilla, where they serve the sherry directly from cask.

While this strong local presence has persevered since King Alfonso days, of the 800,000 bottles of sherry Zuleta produces each year, most of it—upward of 85 to 88 percent—never makes it beyond Spain's borders.

NOTABLE WINES: While the Zuleta wines are not well known in the United States, the bodega has plans to increase distribution in the near future, which will hopefully provide greater exposure for what is a fantastic line of wines. Both flagship manzanillas, La Goya ($, 375ml; $, 750ml), a wonderfully approachable manzanilla, and Barbiana ($, 375ml; $, 750ml), a more full-bodied, umami-forward variation on the style, are fantastic values, both bottled at over six years of average age. In 2012 Zuleta began bottling Goya Manzanilla XL En Rama ($$, 500ml) an exceptional old manzanilla sourced from a selection of barrels in the La Goya solera as well as the *reposado* portion of that solera, so called because it's been left apart for longer aging. The wine averages over ten years of age at bottling and is released in very small quantities.

Beyond manzanilla, the Amontillado Goyesco (released to the United States, as of 2014, as Amontillado Delgado; $$, 750ml) is one of the rare wines that offers a true snapshot of the transition between manzanilla and amontillado. It is technically a manzanilla-amontillado, averaging around eight years of age and showing a strong flor character. Pungent, tense, and elegant, this is one of the finest wines in the Zuleta line.

The house also maintains a line of premium sherries—an amontillado, a palo cortado, a pedro ximénez, and a cream—within their Monteagudo line. Of them, the palo cortado ($$, 750ml), bottled at fifteen years of age, is true to style and a terrific value. The bodega also bottles a fantastic moscatel ($, 750ml), which is a combination of both rasinated grapes and those fermented to dryness, adding freshness and acidity to keep the sweetness in check.

Within the premium range is one of the Sherry Triangle's most distinctive wines, Amontillado Muy Viejo Quo Vadis? ($$$$, 750ml), an over forty-year-old wine that originated with La-Cave, a now-defunct bodega that Zuleta merged with in 1978, taking over several brands, including this wine and Barbiana. One of the strangest experiments to be commercialized, Quo Vadis? was sourced entirely from young vines and fermented in new oak casks, a rarity considering new wood is never used in the production of sherry (wood tannins are the enemy of flor). Without a buyer for a wine that was undoubtedly peculiar to begin with, the barrels were set aside and the wine eventually matured into an amontillado. It's one of the most idiosyncratic wines in the region—elegant and delicately perfumed on the nose, but unusually tannic.

The bodega also bottles another premium wine, the Amontillado Viejo ($$, 750ml), bottled at around twenty years of age, and a sweetened oloroso, Las Señoras ($, 750ml, bottled at around ten to twelve years of age.

HOUSE STYLE: Full-bodied, expressive wines that couple intensity of flavor with elegance across the range.

TOP FIVE WINES: Manzanilla Barbiana ($), Goya Manzanilla XL En Rama ($$, 500ml), Amontillado Goyesco (Amontillado Delgado; $$, 750ml), Palo Cortado Monteagudo ($$), Moscatel 'Zuleta' ($).

ESTABLISHED: 1744

SACRISTÍA AB (SELECCIÓN DE ANTONIO BARBADILLO MATEOS)

In 2010, Antonio Barbadillo Mateos, a sixth-generation descendant of the founder of Bodegas Antonio Barbadillo, left his post with the family business—where he'd worked on the commercial side for seventeen years—to establish Sacristía AB.

He founded the company on one wine, an eight-year-old manzanilla sourced and blended from several bodegas and bottled *en rama*. While most sherries labeled *en rama* still undergo a light filtration, Manzanilla Sacristía AB sees no filtration at all; it's bottled directly from cask. Barbadillo bottles around twenty-four hundred 375-milliliter bottles twice annually, in autumn and late spring, labeling these two *sacas* by the year and either Primera Saca (conducted in May or June) or Segunda Saca (conducted in October or November).

While mature manzanilla is Barbadillo's passion, he also began bottling an amontillado de Sanlúcar, which has been available in the U.S. since the spring of 2014.

NOTABLE WINES: Because of the complete lack of filtration in Manzanilla Sacristía AB ($$–$$$), this is a wine that tends to perform best closer to bottling, though the wines can improve over the coarse of a year if correctly stored. Across releases, the manzanilla is intensely savory, showing flavors of mushroom and bouillon, but also has a strong chamomile character that is remarkably pronounced even after the wine has developed in bottle.

HOUSE STYLE: Expressive and mature manzanilla that closely mirrors the experience of tasting from barrel.

TOP WINE: Manzanilla Sacristía AB ($$–$$$). (At the time of writing the amontillado was not yet available in the market.)

ESTABLISHED: 2010

CHIPIONA AND BODEGAS CÉSAR FLORIDO

TUCKED AWAY ON THE COAST, JUST OVER five miles from Sanlúcar along the road that wraps around Rota on the way to El Puerto de Santa María, is the small village of Chipiona. Famous for its lighthouse (the tallest in Spain, built in 1867), Chipiona has historically been associated with Moscatel, which thrives in the sandy *arenas* soils surrounding the town. While Moscatel has always been the least planted of the main sherry grapes, today it makes up about 2 percent of total vineyard plantings in the region, and continues to decline. As such, the town, which was once home to dozens of bodegas as late as the 1940s, is now home to only two producers still operating independently of the town's agricultural cooperative, and only one that exports beyond Spain's border: Bodegas César Florido.

If selling sherry in a down economy to an audience trained to think of it as a warm, sweet substance is a thankless job, hedging on moscatel is practically masochistic.

But César Florido (also known as "Mr. Moscatel"), the fifth generation tending to Bodegas César Florido, doesn't mind playing the outsider.

A longtime *almacenista*, Florido began bottling his wines for export in 1988. Not only does he produce three fantastic moscatels that have earned him his Mr. Moscatel moniker, he also produces three dry wines—a fino, an oloroso, and an old palo cortado. Though they fall outside of the official "zona de crianza" for these styles and cannot wear the official "Jerez-Xérès-Sherry" back label, they're some of the most singular Palomino Fino–based wines in the region.

Florido owns three bodegas in the town of Chipiona—one of which is just over a hundred feet from the sea—and buys grapes directly from growers, pressing and fermenting the wines himself in his own facilities with native yeasts. Though Florido is technically no longer an *almacenista*, the scale and mentality of the bodega is firmly rooted in the independent spirit, both past and present, that has defined the *almacenistas* of the Sherry Triangle.

NOTABLE WINES: César Florido produces seven wines. The three-year-old **Fino César** ($) is one of the most interesting finos produced in the region, literally tasting like the sea, with distinct oyster shell and herbal aromatics and intense salinity. The grapes for this wine are all sourced from the *pago* of Balbaína, in Jerez. The **Oloroso Seco Cruz del Mar** ($) is a steal at twelve years old, maintaining the freshness and lean structure that defines all of the wines. The finest of the dry wines is the nearly forty-year-old, intense and briny **Palo Cortado Peña del Aguila** ($$$$), a wine formerly reserved only for the family and special occasions. Only 384 (375ml) bottles were released in 2013.

On the moscatel front, the bodega produces three wines, the young **Moscatel Dorado** ($), produced from grapes that are not dried, but instead fermented to 1 to 2 percent alcohol to retain sweetness. The wine is then fortified to 18 percent before aging in the solera system. The **Moscatel Especial** ($) is made in a similar fashion, but *arope* (unfermented grape must that has been cooked down into a sort of molasses) is added, making this darker, more caramelly wine the brawnier counterpart to the Dorado. The flagship **Moscatel Pasas** ($) is made from grapes hand-selected on the vine and dried for two to three weeks in the sun, then fermented, fortified, and aged in the solera for between three and five years.

HOUSE STYLE: Intensely saline and steely with a razor-sharp focus that defines the texture of the wines, from the fino to the three moscatels.

TOP WINES: **Fino César** ($), **Oloroso Seco Cruz del Mar** ($), **Palo Cortado Peña del Aguila** ($$$$), **Moscatel Pasas** ($).

ESTABLISHED: 1887

El Puerto de Santa María

El Puerto de Santa María is admittedly a long way from Laguna Beach, California. But there is something about the town that reminds me of where I grew up. In the 1960s and 1970s, Laguna was one of the capitals of weird California coastline, dotted with art galleries, hippie health food stores, and gay bars. But the real estate boom of the 1980s and early 1990s turned it into a resort town, typified by golf clubs, gated communities, McMansion tract housing, and oceanfront property that seemed to exist only as a game of Monopoly for the rich. And so, I can't help but identify with those who lament comparable changes to El Puerto. Pretty places rarely develop the way we think they ought to (which is, generally, not at all).

For almost the entirety of its existence, fishing and wine have been El Puerto's most important industries. But the town's long shift toward beach getaway has changed the landscape of the town dramatically. There are only five remaining bodegas or *almacenistas*—Grant, Gutiérrez Colosía, Obregón, Osborne, and Caballero—down from more than thirty just three decades ago. Many of the old bodegas have been abandoned or converted, mostly due to rising real estate values and the increasingly absent economic incentive to stay in the wine industry. Of the three sherry towns, El Puerto's wine industry has suffered the most.

It's a hard pill to swallow for sherry lovers, as El Puerto was once the capital for fino, its creamy, elegant wines—the result of the town's fortunate location, wedged in between the Guadalete River and the sea—historically among the most sought after in the region. But in exchange for the loss, El Puerto has managed to maintain a feeling of prosperity that the other, more timeworn sherry towns have not.

Driving through the city in the backseat of Carmen Pou Riutort's car for the first time—the Technicolor stucco buildings lining the edge of Playa Del Puerto, pine brush creeping over the edge of sandy bluffs as if curious about the shore—it's not hard to get why most of the Sherry Triangle's wine industry lives (or wants to live) here, even if their bodegas or employers are located in other towns. There are condos, mansions—many of them summer homes of wealthy Spaniards from Sevilla and Madrid—marinas, seaside golf clubs, and Michelin-starred seafood restaurants. But there are still glimpses of the old El Puerto, enough that you become familiar with the town's particular way of juxtaposing old and new.

In the center of the town, bullfighting ephemera tangles with all manners of Catholic devotional items and classic Andalusian mosaic tilework. The whitewashed buildings nearly squeeze out the streets below, their Juliet balconies draped in drying laundry. The center of the city is less populated and not as well maintained, signaling the steady diaspora of El Puerto's residents to the beaches and communities surrounding them. Within the context of greater Western Europe—which is largely typified by towns built around a central square—El Puerto's sprawl makes it feel a bit like the Sherry Triangle's own little Los Angeles. And sometimes you just can't help but want to be where the sun almost always shines.

BODEGAS GUTIÉRREZ COLOSÍA

Producing sherry may not be a great business, as Carmen Pou Riutort—or "Señora de Gutiérrez Colosía" as she is often called—is quick to acknowledge, but it is "a nice way of living."

"We work in the bodega every day, smelling the wine and meeting visitors; our holidays are when we go to different countries for tastings; our distributors and clients are our friends." Their joy in what they do and their dedication to upholding the legacy of El Puerto is evident in the wines. There is an openness to innovation, but always with the intention of better exposing people to true sherry. As such, their wines remain some of the best values in the region, not only for their ability to express the character of El Puerto de Santa María, but also for their dedication to keeping each style true to form.

Juan Carlos Gutiérrez is the third generation of the Gutiérrez family to look after the wines since his great-grandfather purchased the bodega in the early 1900s. (It was originally founded in 1838 under a different name.) After his father's untimely death in 1966, Juan Carlos, then only twenty years old, took over a large part of the responsibility for the bodega. Three years later, he purchased the ruins of the Count of Cumbre Hermosa's palace—the home of one of the many rich merchants who populated El Puerto throughout its history—and expanded the bodega's production.

For the better part of the last century the bodega operated as an *almacenista*, selling to larger bodegas like Osborne until the regulations on bodega size and exportation were loosened in 1996. Since then, the bodega has won a loyal following among sherry lovers, as well as some of Europe's top sommeliers—not least among them Josep Roca of El Celler de Can Roca, Nicolas Boise of Mugaritz, and Juli Soler, formerly of El Bulli.

The bodega is the last with cellars along the banks of the Guadalete River where it swells out into the Bay of Cádiz. The rest of the bodegas that once lined this prime stretch of winemaking real estate have been either converted or abandoned. Gutiérrez Colosía's proximity to the river and the sea has a notable moderating effect, keeping temperatures more consistent and the humidity higher, resulting in the creamy, saline character that has come to define the bodega's wines.

NOTABLE WINES: In order to test the vigor of the flor in El Puerto, Juan Carlos began making Fino Amerigo (which is labeled Fino En Rama outside of the U.S.; $), a wine fortified to 16 percent (above the level considered ideal for flor growth) before entering the solera. It's bottled at about six years old, very minimally clarified to remove solids, and is one of the great values in fino on the market. The bodega's Fino Elcano ($) is bottled at an average four years of age and is a terrific entry point for understanding the El Puerto style of fino.

Beyond their flagship Fino Elcano, the bodega is perhaps most well known for its Oloroso Sangre y Trabajadero ($–$$), bottled at around twelve years of age. The wine originated from a solera formerly owned by the now-defunct bodega Cuvillo y Cía and was purchased by Gutiérrez Colosía in 1982. The wine was originally made by a cooper located on Calle Sangre or "Blood Street," in Jerez, so named because it was the street where all of the butchers resided. The oloroso from this solera became quite famous among Jerezanos and was purchased by Cuvillo, who—in homage to its original creator—named it "Blood and Work." Today the style has shifted from its origin as a sweeter wine under the Cuvillo label to a dry oloroso that embodies the lean, vibrant style synonymous with El Puerto.

The finest wines in the bodega are part of a collection of four wines—an amontillado, a palo cortado, an oloroso, and a pedro ximénez—labeled Solera Familiar, averaging between thirty-five and over fifty years of age. The oloroso ($$$$, 500ml) is the youngest of the bunch, but it too shows the deft hand of Juan Carlos when it comes to the style: it's at once intense, smoky, and laced with iodine, but retains a unique delicacy. The amontillado ($$$$, 500ml) at upwards of fifty years old is pretty and saline, showing the strength of El Puerto's maritime influence. The palo cortado ($$$$, 500ml) is slightly older than the amontillado and is a classic take on the style, showing both intensity and elegance in equal measure. The pedro ximénez ($$$$, 500ml) is the oldest wine in the house, pulled from a solera system of just four barrels, and averaging around eighty years old at bottling.

HOUSE STYLE: Classic, flor-forward, creamy, and saline El Puerto–style wines. Elegance rules from top to bottom.

TOP FIVE WINES: Fino Elcano ($), Fino Amerigo ($), Oloroso Sangre y Trabajadero ($), Solera Amontillado Solera Familiar ($$$$, 500ml), Oloroso Solera Familiar ($$$$, 500ml).

ESTABLISHED: 1838

BODEGAS GRANT

One of only three completely family-owned bodegas—Gutiérrez Colosía and Bodegas Obregón, an *almacenista*, being the other two—left in El Puerto de Santa María, the fourth and fifth generation of Grants—Edmundo and his son, Edmundo—currently care for this petite bodega.

In Edmundo senior's face there are still strong traces of his Scottish heritage (small nose, high cheekbones) and with the name Grant engrained in one's mind, it's almost startling to hear him speak Spanish. Yet the Grants are as *Andaluz* as they come, always khakied with a perfectly pressed button-down or understated yet elegant scarf—traditionally mannered and affable in equal measure.

The bodega was founded in 1841 and spent the majority of its existence as an *almacenista*, selling stocks of sherry to larger producers. It wasn't until 2011 that they began bottling their own wines. When their American importer, André Tamers, first stumbled upon the Grants the bodega was near extinction, kept alive by the jewelbox restaurant they run in a patio off the cellar. While their business has grown with exports to the United States, they are still a very small bodega, bottling just twelve thousand 750-milliliter and one thousand 375-milliliter bottles per year, and most of their production is still consumed locally and sold out of the bodega.

NOTABLE WINES: There is a leanness across the very small range of Grant bottlings that—though wrapped in a style more rustic than their other El Puerto counterparts—embodies the town's style.

The La Garrocha line, whose name and label pay homage to the traditional Andalusian dance on horseback of the same name, includes an herbal, lemony fino ($), a funky, seaweed-and-salt-laced amontillado ($), and a bitter orange–tinged oloroso ($)—all of them showing a briskness that speaks to the location of the bodega, which is just a few blocks from the River Guadalete.

At the top of the bodega's offerings is the Oloroso Viejo ($$$$) and the Amontillado Viejo ($$$$), both averaging around thirty-five to fifty years of age. The bodega also keeps a small *bota* of palo cortado, consisting of just 75 liters for consumption by esteemed guests and family members.

HOUSE STYLE: Rustic, and unique within El Puerto, but still representative of the town's elegant, flor-forward style.

TOP WINE: Fino La Garrocha ($).

ESTABLISHED: 1841

BODEGAS OSBORNE

The history of the bodega begins with the arrival of Thomas Osborne Mann in Cádiz in 1772, where he took a job with the now-defunct Lonergan & White. By 1804 Osborne began shipping his own sherries with the help of James Duff, already a veteran of the wine industry and one-half of what would become Duff Gordon. He allowed Osborne to store his wines in his facilities, developing a relationship with him that would eventually lead to a partnership in 1833. By 1836, after the death of Duff and the managing partner of the bodega—whose daughter Osborne ended up marrying—he took over management and majority ownership of Duff Gordon.

He was succeeded by his son, Thomas Osborne Böhl de Faber, who erected the famous bullring in the center of El Puerto de Santa María. In 1872, the Osborne family bought out the remaining Duff Gordon interests, and in 1890 they began marketing sherries under the Osborne name alongside the already established Duff Gordon brands. While the Osborne wines were initially only sold in Spain, eventually, the Duff Gordon name was dissolved and the former brands began being bottled under the Osborne name.

The bodega grew in prominence under Ignacio Osborne Vázquez, who, between 1935 and 1972, all but corned the market for Spanish brandy with the now-legendary Veterano brand. The sherries also established themselves both on the high end and in the local fino market, further cementing the Osborne name within the Spanish psyche.

Today the company has grown to become a multi-business empire with interests in everything from *jamón* to liqueurs to energy drinks. In recent years, sherry has become an increasingly small portion of the business, but the quality of the wines remains high. And thanks to a recent acquisition of import rights to some of the bodega's prized older wines—some of them from soleras started in the eighteenth century—the bodega is reestablishing itself abroad as a producer of fine sherry.

NOTABLE WINES: Osborne bottles two flagship finos, Fino Quinta ($, 750ml), which is aged just over four years at bottling and is simple but well crafted, and Fino Coquinero ($, 750ml), which was, up until the term was banned, bottled as a fino-amontillado. It ages for four to five years under flor, undergoes a second fortification to 17 percent, and then ages for two years oxidatively. It's a bold, savory fino that shows the character of flor and the early signs of oxidation.

While Osborne makes a number of other sherries within its Premium Sherry range, the bodega's most notable bottlings beyond the finos belong to

its old wines, which are comprised of their own ancient soleras as well as four VORS soleras purchased from Bodegas Pedro Domecq following its demise. From the latter line is the Amontillado 51-1a VORS ($$$$, 500ml), a smoky, concentrated wine sourced from a solera started in 1830. The Palo Cortado Capuchino VORS ($$$$, 500ml) is even more intense and rich, sourced from a solera system of just twenty-five barrels started in 1790. The Oloroso Sibarita VORS ($$$$, 500ml), sourced from a solera started in 1792, is perhaps the finest wine in the lineup; the small addition of sweet Pedro Ximénez (2 percent) at the beginning of its life adds just enough cushion to balance the intensity that wood aging has imparted. This line is rounded out with the Pedro Ximénez Venerable VORS ($$$$, 500ml).

Osborne's own collection of soleras is responsible for five excellent old wines that are released in very limited quantities: Amontillado Solera AOS (Antonio Osborne Solera; $$$$, 500ml), Palo Cortado Solera PΔP (the delta symbol is meant to represent the Sherry Triangle; $$$$, 500ml), Oloroso Solera BC 200 ($$$$, 500ml), Oloroso Solera India ($$$$, 500ml), and finally the sweet Pedro Ximénez Viejo ($$$$, 500ml). Like Sibarita, in this range the palo cortado and both olorosos are blended with varying percentages of Pedro Ximénez, which is added at the very beginning of each wine's life. Each of the wines proves that with wines of exceptional age, the addition of small amounts of PX not only integrates with age, but can create complexity and balance.

HOUSE STYLE: Full-bodied, generous wines that still exhibit the freshness and vivacity long associated with El Puerto wines.

TOP FIVE WINES: Fino Coquinero ($, 750ml), Amontillado Solera AOS ($$$$, 500ml), Oloroso Sibarita VORS ($$$$, 500ml), Palo Cortado Capuchino VORS ($$$$, 500ml), Palo Cortado Solera PΔP ($$$$, 500ml).

ESTABLISHED: 1772

Montilla-Moriles

The wines of Montilla-Moriles—an Andalusian region roughly one hundred miles and one very convoluted train-to-bus journey from Jerez—are not sherry, in that they are not produced in the DO of Jerez-Xérès-Sherry, yet avoiding their connection is impossible. Simply referred to as "montilla," the wines are grown primarily in *albariza* soil (which is called *albero* locally) within two main subzones, called Moriles Alto and Sierra de Montilla.

In comparison to the Sherry Triangle, the climate here is drier, the altitude higher, and the diurnal shifts more drastic. But the major difference between sherry and montilla comes down to grape variety. Here the dominant grape for both sweet *and* dry wines is Pedro Ximénez, not Palomino Fino. As a result of the higher ripening potential of Pedro Ximénez, and the warmer growing season here, the grape can reach the 15 percent alcohol mark—the level optimal for biological aging—on the vine. Thus the wines destined to become fino are rarely fortified; most amontillados, and even some olorosos, are bottled unfortified as well.

While the wines from Montilla-Moriles are easily confused with the wines of the Sherry Triangle, they're often fruitier across all styles, and the biological wines, in particular, tend to be richer, with less cut than those produced in Jerez, Sanlúcar, and El Puerto. This is often attributed to the thinner layer of flor here, which is much more difficult to maintain without the humidity and moderating effect produced by the Sherry Triangle's proximity to the Atlantic Ocean.

With experience, the differences between the wines of this region and the wines of the Sherry Triangle become more obvious, yet Montilla-Moriles has struggled for centuries to carve an identity that is separate from sherry.

Part of this is the lack of visibility of the wines. With only three bodegas with a notable presence in the export markets, it's counterproductive to try and draw a separation between montilla and sherry. Yet these three bodegas, whose wines are gaining an ever larger presence abroad, are helping establish Montilla-Moriles as a region that deserves recognition for both the high quality of its wines and their singularity.

BODEGAS ALVEAR

If there's any one producer intimately acquainted with the unique predicament Montilla faces producing sherry-like wine in a region that is not the Sherry Triangle, it's the Alvear family. The bodega is not only Montilla's oldest producer, but it is also the oldest bodega in Andalusia still in production, with a winemaking history that dates back to the first half of the eighteenth century. Today the bodega remains exclusively family owned, the eighth generation now at the helm.

In the context of Montilla, Alvear is next of kin to the winemaking traditions and cultures of Jerez. The great-great-grandfather of Maria Alvear, the current export manager, married into an English family and established Alvear as a shipper to the United Kingdom in the middle of the nineteenth century, during a time when the region and its wines were little more than a supplier to Jerez. Since then, Alvear has maintained a healthy export business, establishing itself in the United States before many of the Sherry Triangle's most recognizable bodegas had a presence.

Of the handful of producers in Montilla-Moriles that currently export wine beyond Spain's borders, Alvear remains the most established and certainly one of the most progressive—experimenting with vintage-dated finos and bottling and labeling *en rama* as early as 1998, years before the trend found footing in the export markets. Alvear also remains a significant landowner, managing around 500 acres of vines.

NOTABLE WINES: While Alvear's bottlings of pedro ximénez remain the bodega's most prized offerings, they produce a number of compelling dry sherries. Their entry-level Alvear Fino ($, 750ml) is a simple but well-made introduction to fino made from pedro ximénez. Their Fino En Rama ($, 500ml) is bottled *añada*, or by vintage, rather than being blended via the solera system. Generally released five years after the harvest, it's truly the only one of its kind. The Amonillado Carlos VII ($$, 500ml), bottled at around fifteen years, shows a classic tension between caramelly oxidation and the tug of leanness, with floral aromatics to match. It's consistently the finest wine in the Alvear range of dry sherries. The Oloroso Asunción ($, 500ml) is rich, feeling a bit weighed down by residual sweetness.

Of the range of sweet pedro ximénez wines, the Pedro Ximénez Solera 1830 ($$$$, 500ml) represents the very top of the range. It's bottled at just over 11 percent alcohol and with its notes of tar and tobacco, it uniquely showcases how nuanced pedro ximénez can be. Right alongside it is the Solera 1920 ($$$$, 750ml), which shows a vibrancy not often associated with pedro ximénez and lots of peppery spice and pungency. The younger Solera 1927 ($$, 500ml) is Alvear's best value. Since 1998, the bodega has bottled vintage pedro ximénez, which is generally released three years after the harvest. Of these releases the 2002 ($, 500ml) is a standout.

HOUSE STYLE: True to Montilla, with the dry wines showing an expressive aromatic profile and a bit more weight and body, while the sweet wines maintain the finesse and definition that only pedro ximénez from Montilla can so easily achieve.

TOP FIVE WINES: Fino en Rama ($, 500ml), Amontillado Carlos VII ($$, 500ml), Pedro Ximénez Cosecha 2002 ($, 500ml), Pedro Ximénez Solera 1920 ($$, 500ml), Pedro Ximénez Solera 1830 ($$$$, 500ml).

ESTABLISHED: 1729

BODEGAS PÉREZ BARQUERO

While the history of Pérez Barquero dates back to 1905, the bodega began its modern renaissance in 1985, when it was purchased by the current owner, Rafael Córdoba García. The bodega has since increased in both prominence and quality, producing some of the best wines in the region.

Today Pérez Barquero owns about 500 acres of vineyard land in the two finest subzones in the region—Moriles Alto and Sierra de Montilla—which supply around 35 to 50 percent of the bodega's production. Showing both a dedication to tradition and an openness to innovation, the bodega has become a beacon for the region and is an increasing presence in the U.S. market. In addition to the wines bottled under the Pérez Barquero label, the company bottles wines under three other labels: Hermanos Gracia, Vinícola del Sur, and Tomás Garcia. While the latter labels are not exported outside of Spain, Gracia is becoming more and more visible in the United States via its more full-bodied fino and the fantastic Oloroso Tauromaquia, which ranks among the finest wines in the region.

NOTABLE WINES: The Pérez Barquero line consists of three finos: Solera 13 ($, 750ml), a young fino only released in Spain and Germany; Los Amigos ($, 750ml), a three- to four-year-old fino, fruity and lovable; and the top of the line, Fino Gran Barquero ($, 750ml), an eight- to ten-year-old herbal and saline fino that is one of the best values in the house. From Hermanos Gracia is the Fino Maria del Valle ($, 750ml), a full-bodied fino aged around eight to ten years. It does not have quite the complexity or finesse of Gran Barquero, but is a fine wine nonetheless.

Within the Gran Barquero range, the bodega's more than twenty-year-old amontillado ($$, 750ml) is a standout. Lean, finessed, and floral, it's another fantastic value. The Oloroso Gran Barquero ($, 500ml), aged around twenty-five years, is dosed with a touch of sweet pedro ximénez that adds an unnecessary weight to the wine. Better is the completely dry iodine-and-smoke-laced Oloroso Tauromaquia ($, 750ml), bottled under the Bodegas Gracia label without the addition of pedro ximénez. Lean and stylish, it's easily one of the best wines under the Grupo Pérez Barquero umbrella.

Among the excellent sweet pedro ximénez wines produced under both the Pérez Barquero and the Gracia labels, the Pérez Barquero La Cañada ($$$$, 750ml) is a standout. Bottled at around twenty-five years of age, it's thick, meaty, and smoky, but remarkably elegant on the palate, showing the sort of freshness that is characteristic of the best sweet wines of Montilla. The Gracia Dulce Viejo ($$, 750ml), which is fortified with oloroso instead of grape brandy, is also fantastic.

At the top of the Grupo Pérez Barquero range are the three wines—an amontillado, an oloroso, and a pedro ximénez—in the 1905 series ($$$$, 750ml), of which only one thousand bottles of each wine have been released to date. Each wine is bottled from small soleras set aside the year the bodega was founded, and all three are among the finest old examples of their type, not only in Montilla, but in all of Andalusia.

HOUSE STYLE: Classic montilla in expressiveness, but showing a particular brightness and refinement across the range. The Gracia wines show a bit more plushness than the Barquero wines as a whole, but still maintain the finesse characteristic of the entire group.

TOP FIVE WINES: Fino Gran Barquero ($, 750ml), Amontillado Gran Barquero ($, 750ml), Oloroso Tauromaquia ($, 750ml), Pérez Barquero Pedro Ximénez La Cañada ($$$$, 750ml), 1905 range ($$$$, 750ml).

ESTABLISHED: 1905

BODEGAS TORO ALBALÁ

Located in the tiny town of Aguilar de la Frontera, just south of Montilla, Toro Albalá's history dates back to 1844. However, the bodega as we know it today begins its modern genesis in 1922, when José María Toro Albalá moved the winery into an old power station in the center of Aguilar.

The bodega is still centered around this facility and is currently under the direction of *capataz* Antonio Sánchez Romero, the fifth-generation descendant of the bodega's 1844 founder, Antonio Sánchez, and the nephew of José María Toro Albalá.

The bodega owns half of their vineyard land and directly manages the other half, totaling just over 350 acres in the subzone of Moriles Alto. The wines, which have mostly flown under the radar in the United States for the last decade, are some of the finest and most unique wines—both sweet and dry—currently produced in Montilla-Moriles.

NOTABLE WINES: The bodega produces a number of excellent dry wines. The Fino Eléctrico ($, 500ml) aged around ten years old at bottling, is remarkably fresh, showing the fruitiness of pedro ximénez, but maintaining more cut than the average fino from Montilla, particularly at this age. The Marqués de Poley Amontillado Viejísimo ($$–$$$, 500ml), bottled at around thirty to thirty-five years of age, shows the tension between round, caramelly concentration and a structure that is remarkably delicate given its age and alcohol content (21 percent without fortification). The Marqués de Poley Oloroso ($, 500ml), aged around fifteen years at bottling, is one of the best values in the range. It, like the amontillado and the fino, is not fortified, reaching 14 percent alcohol at primary fermentation and eventually gaining three more degrees before bottling. Its touch of residual sweetness is matched by pungent freshness. The bodega also bottles a unique Marqués de Poley Pedro Ximénez Cream ($, 500ml)—the blend of pedro ximénez, oloroso, and fino—that's a saline, balanced take on the style.

While the dry wines can be exceptional, the bodega is at its best with sweet pedro ximénez wines. The Don PX ($), a vintage pedro ximénez aged only in stainless steel that the bodega first began bottling in 1997, is a fine value in its youth, but is really a wine that deserves cellaring. The spicy, fresh passionfruit-laced Don PX Gran Reserva ($$), which is typically labeled by the oldest wine in the blend (the excellent 1983 and 1985 being the two most recent releases), is consistently one of the best pedro ximénez wines in the region. In addition to these two core bottlings, the bodega releases small quantities of several older pedro ximénez wines bottled under a variety of different names, like the recent releases Don PX Gran Reserva Especial ($$$$, 750ml) and Don PX Convento 1946 ($$$$, 750ml).

HOUSE STYLE: Bold wines that are classic montilla with a bit more added cut and finesse.

TOP WINES: Fino Eléctrico ($, 500ml), Marqués de Poley Oloroso ($, 500ml), Don PX Gran Reserva ($$).

ESTABLISHED: 1844/1922

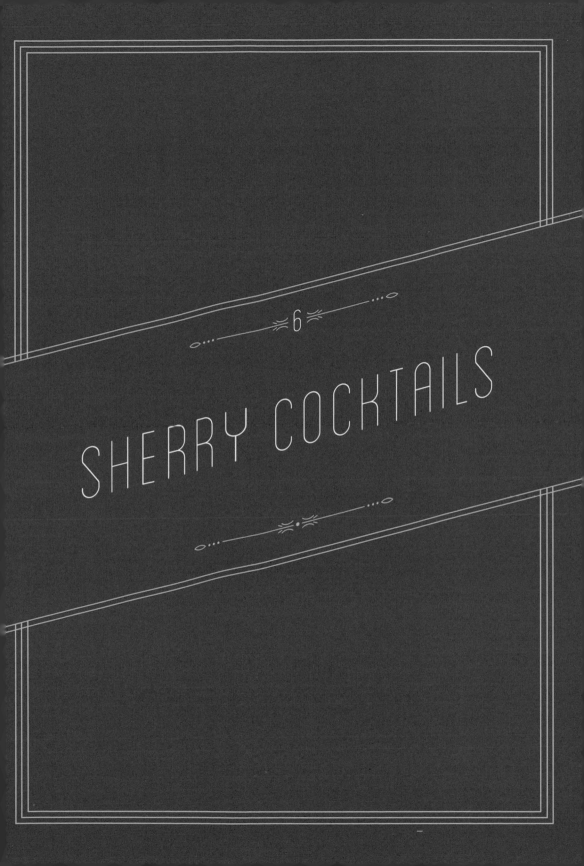

6

SHERRY COCKTAILS

Purists will likely balk at the notion, but like it or not, many of sherry's greatest American moments have been spent on crushed ice. That's not to say it has not been sipped on its own plenty. But the connoisseurship of sherry—and wine in general—was inherited from the English. The seemingly vulgar penchant for mixing wines and spirits, tossing them in a glass, and turning it into entertainment—that's ours. Some might call it adulteration; I'd call it the very spirit of reinvention and experimentation that has come to define America itself.

From sangarees to punches to flips and cobblers, during the eighteenth century and on through the cocktail's late-nineteenth-century Golden Age, sherry was an integral part of the barman's repertoire.

It began its transition from an ingredient in hot and cold punches of the late 1700s slowly, via two-ingredient cocktails like sherry and bitters, sherry and ice, and sherry and egg. These drinks, most from the dawn of the nineteenth century, populated the first American cocktail book—Jerry Thomas's now legendary *How to Mix Drinks*, originally released in 1862.

But by then another drink had captured America's fancy: the Sherry Cobbler. Thomas describes it as a simple mixture of sugar, sherry, and muddled citrus (orange, to be exact) over crushed ice, ornamented with "berries in season" and sipped through a straw—a novelty at the time. In fact, were it not for the Sherry Cobbler, which is credited with introducing the straw to popular consciousness, we might still be dumping ice down our chins to get to the bottom of a drink.

The Sherry Cobbler's popularity managed to transcend both age and gender, becoming the country's most ubiquitous cocktail, consumed by everyone from society ladies to newspapermen to—according to an 1882 article in the *Boston Daily Globe* titled "A Lecture to Young Men"—students "sowing their wild oats." Sadly, by the time I reached my oats I was sowing them with Jose Cuervo and Irish Car Bombs. If only the Cobbler was still in vogue then.

Before the Civil War, when the Mint Julep was in its Cretaceous period and a far more varied drink, it called for the addition of things like sherry, madeira, and port. And dare I say—and risk crucifixion south of the Mason-Dixon line—that the julep, in all its modern glory, still benefits from a dash or two of sherry.

The 1880s and 1890s were cocktail boom times and saw the creation of two of the most enduring sherry aperitif drinks—the Adonis and the Bamboo. The latter originated in the 1890s at Grand Hotel in Yokohoma, Japan, and by 1900, it was a regular fixture on American menus, finding enough fame that it was eventually sold in premixed bottles across the country. The Adonis is essentially a variation on the same composition (as many of the drinks of this time were), with Italian vermouth moonlighting for French.

By the first two decades of the twentieth century, sherry had evolved from being an ingredient in simple drinks that combined fortified wines and bitters to being either a base or a modifier in drinks that contained everything from crème de roses to cracked pepper.

It continued to be a major ingredient in cocktails until 1920, when Prohibition killed all motivation to smuggle in anything that wasn't overproof. Cocktails served in speakeasies were often strong, simple, and stirred. But across the Atlantic the English had already taken up where we'd left off. Harry Craddock had left the United States—apparently only after mixing the last legal cocktail in New York—and set up shop at the American Bar at London's Savoy Hotel. In Paris, another Harry (last name MacElhone) purchased Paris's New York Bar, appended his name, and turned it into a haven for American expatriates—Ernest Hemingway, Humphrey Bogart, and Rita Hayworth among them—as well as the source of some of the most interesting Prohibition-era cocktails. The two Harrys, among many others, helped usher in Europe's Golden Age of cocktailing.

Back in America, after Repeal sherry was left to reenter the market anew. But the fallout from Prohibition had helped brand the cocktail as an evil creation. Wine salesmen saw an opportunity to pounce, pitting sherry against cocktails in a battle for the American preprandial drink.

Despite the best efforts of the wine distributors to use the cocktail's perceived vulgarity as a springboard, it continued to flourish, of course. But Prohibition had planted something deep in the American psyche—a fear of alcohol as a health hazard and a symbol of the gauche underbelly of America—that continues to fester even today. The country's attempts at temperance certainly didn't die with Prohibition, and even though we saw the rise of the famed "three-Martini lunch" in the 1950s and 1960s, Americans began to drink less in the 1970s. And when they drank, they increasingly reached for a bottle of wine, and that bottle was rarely sherry.

The cocktails that survived during the rise of wine were famously grim drinks like Sex on the Beach, the Golden Cadillac, and the Midori Sour—cocktails one might find on the list of "do-nots" for diabetes patients, right alongside doughnuts. When it came to the cocktail, American ingenuity had apparently hit a roadblock and gone headfirst into a gulch, leaving a trail of blue curaçao and canned cranberry juice in its wake.

We survived. And blue curaçao barely exists anymore outside of bad memories and Applebee's.

By the late 1990s, bars had begun to come back to life; bartenders began to take pride once again in the things we now take for granted: mixing a great Manhattan, using fresh lime juice in a daiquiri. Many of us can say we are intimately familiar with the rest of the story, as almost every city with more than 20,000 people now comes stocked with a bar that specializes in craft cocktails. This revival was reactionary in many ways, a call to arms against premade mixers and canned Tequila Sunrises—a back-to-the-land movement applied to cocktails. And American bartenders sought to recreate a part of America's drinking past that seemed banished to the history books for good. Old ingredients that hadn't been used in decades were being revived.

Sherry, however, was a rarity in cocktails until the mid-2000s, when the grassroots efforts of a few—notably Steve Olson and Andy Seymour—helped educate bartenders about sherry. In 2005, Seymour and Olson launched the Vinos de Jerez Cocktail competition, which has since sent dozens of bartenders to Jerez. This, along with several other campaigns, helped ignite a fire within a small community of elite bartenders, which spread quickly across the country. Today, almost every major craft cocktail bar in America has at least one sherry drink on its menu.

Many of the drinks that have inspired the revival of sherry in cocktails are classic nineteenth-century drinks, but sherry's modern ascent as a beloved tool in the barman's arsenal is truly part revival and part revelation. The Sherry Cobbler has returned to its proper place among the most revered—and American— of classic cocktails. The Bamboo and the Adonis have both been riffed on and supplanted on lists like Leo Robitschek's at the NoMad and Joaquín Simó's at Pouring Ribbons. Other drinks, like Jack McGarry of the Dead Rabbit's house Sherry Cocktail, are improved variations on forgotten aperitif drinks, like the New Yorker and the Schnozzle. But some of sherry's greatest contributions to modern cocktailing have come courtesy of drinks that are rooted in the classics, but are totally original, like Robert Hess's Trident (a riff on the Negroni), Phil Ward's Stone Raft (a very distant cousin of the Old-Fashioned), and Joaquín Simó's Flor de Jerez (a relative of the Daisy).

The use of sherry with agave spirits has also been a driving force behind the revival of sherry in cocktails. In 2005, San Francisco bartender Jacques Bezuidenhout won the first Vinos de Jerez cocktail competition with his La Perla, a combination of sherry, tequila, and pear liqueur. The simplicity and balance of the drink landed it on discussion boards and blogs and won hearts across the country. It was one of several drinks that sparked one of the great revelations in twenty-first-century cocktailing: the incredible compatibility of agave spirits and sherry.

In a general sense—whether on crushed ice or mixed with mezcal—it's hard to understate the role the cocktail has played, both in the nineteenth century and today, in exposing the American market to sherry. Like so many changes we're seeing in the beverage world now, the details of sherry's revival look a lot like history repeating itself.

In the late eighteenth and early nineteenth centuries, sherry was mostly a luxury reserved for the rich. It wasn't exactly cheap, but its niche status was less about price and more about the social barrier that kept sherry trapped in the cupboards of the upper class, while the rest of the country was busy drinking rum and homegrown whiskey.

The cocktail—more specifically, the Sherry Cobbler—flung the doors open and democratized sherry. Today, cocktails are playing a similar role by acting as the gateway for consumers who might've otherwise dismissed sherry. In fact, there's no denying that many people who've fallen in love with it as a wine first encountered it in a cocktail. And it's this unique role that bartenders have played in giving sherry a chance to succeed anew in this market that makes its ascendance so unique. It's one of the rare liquids that has inspired equal evangelism in the wine and cocktail worlds. Barring a second Prohibition, it's here to stay.

Working with Sherry

Understanding sherry as a cocktail ingredient begins with seeing how it transforms the drinks you're already intimately familiar with. In educating myself (read: mixing and consuming many drinks for yours truly), I began with simple drinks like the Negroni, the Old-Fashioned, and the Martini and applied New York bartender Joaquín Simó's Mr. Potato Head approach, which is perhaps the modern bar world's most-quoted creed when it comes to mixing cocktails. Each main component of a drink—sweet, sour (or acid), bitter, spirit, water—can be represented by a variety of different ingredients, but if you want it to drink like a balanced cocktail (that is, look like Mr. or Mrs. Potato Head and not an accident victim), you have to make sure there isn't an ear in place of a mouth, or a nose where an eye should be.

To start, it's easiest to use sherry as a "modifier"—which, *very* broadly speaking, is usually typified by an aromatic wine (think vermouth) or a liqueur that is meant to soften the blow of the base spirit. Identify the flavor profile of the ingredient. In the case of French vermouth, or any other ingredient meant to add dryness or acidity, sub in manzanilla or fino. Or in place of Italian vermouth, sub in a blended sherry, like cream or East India—or oloroso or palo cortado for a drier variation—to add depth and richness.

Consider this approach applied to the Negroni, which traditionally calls for equal parts gin, Campari, and sweet vermouth. Replace sweet vermouth with Lustau's East India Solera sherry and gin with rum, keep the Campari, and you've got Jim Meehan's East India Negroni (page 229), a drink that retains the spirit of the original, but leans on deeper, more brooding flavors.

An even simpler example of how swapping in sherry can transform a drink is the original Tuxedo cocktail (page 182), a riff on the classic Martini combination of gin, dry vermouth, and orange bitters. The use of sherry in this drink, and in other variations on the Martini that call for sherry instead of vermouth, changes the aromas and flavors of the drink—the sherry lending a yeasty, briny note in place of the herbaceousness of dry vermouth.

The sweet sherries—pedro ximénez and moscatel—can take the place of liqueurs or can act as a more complex stand-in for simple or demerara syrup. Pedro ximénez adds notes of coffee, chocolate, and raisins, while moscatel offers both sweetness and florality.

Once you become familiar with the spectrum of sherry styles and how they act in basic drinks, sherry's versatility becomes more exciting than overwhelming. "Sherry is like Mr. Potato Head's Darth Vader mask," says Leo Robitschek, head bartender at Eleven Madison Park and The NoMad. "It can work as an eye, an ear, a nose, a mouth."

In other words, the dry sherry styles—fino, manzanilla, amontillado, oloroso, and palo cortado—can, in addition to their role as a modifiers, be used as the base of a drink. In the case of his Remember the Alimony (page 204), Dan Greenbaum, like Meehan, riffs on the Negroni, but uses fino as the base in place of gin, to which he adds an equal dose of the Italian amaro Cynar and repurposes gin from its traditional role, adding just a small dash for aromatics.

Alternatively, these dry sherries can even act as "seasoners"—which is a category that is most commonly used to refer to bitters and their ability to add complexity in very small doses. Even in small amounts, sherry can add a lot of complexity to a drink, or can act as a balancing ingredient, creating a bridge between flavors of sweet, bitter, or citric.

In another one of Meehan's drinks, the Rye Witch (page 210)—an Old-Fashioned variation that calls for rye, the saffron-infused Italian liqueur Strega, and sugar—the addition of a very small amount of palo cortado keeps the Strega's sweetness in check.

These different constructions play out in the following pages, where you'll find a combination of classic sherry drinks from the eighteenth, nineteenth, and early twentieth centuries—each of them tested and adjusted for the modern home bartender—as well as a grip of my favorite modern sherry cocktails peppered with a few drinks I've managed to cobble together on my own.

STOCKING YOUR SHERRY BAR

WHEN USING SHERRY IN COCKTAILS, YOU should adhere to the same standards of freshness as when you consume sherry on its own: use fino and manzanilla within about three days after opening; amontillado, a few weeks; oloroso and palo cortado, up to a couple months. But, admittedly, there is a bit more leeway when it comes to mixing sherry. In fact, some bartenders will tell you that they prefer working with manzanilla and fino that's been open a bit longer, as it begins to show a touch more roundness and a tinge of oxidation—especially in the biological wines that undergo a heavier filtration.

Since most finos and manzanillas come in 375-milliliter bottles, between mixing cocktails and drinking sherry by the glass, in my house a bottle typically doesn't linger open for more than a day or two. But that's just me.

Choosing which fino, manzanilla, amontillado, or oloroso to mix with is just like choosing which whiskey or vermouth to use in your Manhattan. Each style has a small spectrum of expressions within it, based on each producer's style, the age of the wine at bottling, and so on. Mixing with, for example, a more full-bodied, oxidative amontillado like Lustau's Los Arcos will yield a very different drink than mixing with the much leaner, flor-driven Viña AB from Gonzalez Byass. They are the bourbon and rye of amontillados.

Finally, while it's true that the quality of the sherry you choose will certainly affect the finished drink, there is no reason to be mixing with a twelve-year-old fino from Bodegas Tradición or one of the Equipo Navazos La Bota bottlings. You're looking for sherries that are affordable, high-quality representations of their style. Save the top-shelf stuff for the wine glass.

There are certain bottlings within each style that I tend to use most frequently when mixing at home, all of them widely available.

Fino

I am a sucker for **Lustau's Fino La Ina** ($, 750ml). It's full-bodied, and because it has a higher level of acetaldehyde—a by-product of flor aging that imparts a doughy, yeasty quality to the wine—it tends to stand up to bold spirits. If I am trying to cut through or add perceived acidity to a drink, a lighter fino like **Fernando de Castilla's Fino Classic** ($$, 750ml) or González Byass's **Tío Pepe Fino** ($) are what I typically reach for. For fino in Martini-style drinks like the Tuxedo (page 182) or the Coronation (page 183) where the sherry really shines, I go with **Valdespino's Inocente** ($), which is one of my favorite finos, period.

Amontillado

Lustau's Amontillado Los Arcos ($$, 750ml) is full-bodied with strong oxidative notes and bit more viscosity than your typical amontillado. As such, it's great in stirred, boozy drinks that call for brown spirits. A bit lighter and leaner but still showing plenty of oxidation is **Hidalgo–La Gitana's Amontillado Napoleon** ($, 500ml), which is perhaps my favorite all-purpose amontillado. For drinks that you want to add just touch of oxidation to, **González Byass Amontillado Viña AB** ($, 750ml) has a strong flor character and stylistically falls somewhere in between fino and amontillado (though it is labeled as the latter).

Palo Cortado and Oloroso

Palo cortados can often be on the pricier side, but **Lustau's Palo Cortado Península** ($$, 750ml) is a fine—and affordable—palo cortado for mixing. As is **Delgado Zuleta's Palo Cortado Monteagudo** ($$, 750ml), which is a bit lighter with a stronger bergamot and citric component than the ripe and caramelly Península. On the oloroso front, there are few better than **Gutiérrez Colosía's Oloroso Sangre y Trabajadero** ($$); it's supremely balanced, adding both richness and perceived acidity. With dark and golden rums and whiskey, **Lustau's Oloroso Don Nuño** ($$, 750ml)—which has a higher level of glycerol and more bass tones—tends to play nice.

Creams and East India

Emilio Hidalgo's Cream Morenita ($, 750ml) and **Hidalgo–La Gitana's Cream Alameda** ($, 500ml) are my two go-tos in the cream category. While they're both undeniably sweet, neither of them is cloying and both easily add complexity and richness to a drink without weighing it down. On the richer side, **Lustau's East India** ($$, 750ml) is essentially the black strap rum of sherries—it's thick and more concentrated with an oily texture that places it in a category of its own. It's a bit of a bully in drinks, but when you find the right balance, it's one of the most interesting sherries to work with. Lastly, pale cream: while it's not an ingredient I use with great frequency, the best one on the market comes from Bodegas Alvear. The **Alvear Pale Cream** ($, 750ml) is well made and balanced and can work as a nice replacement for something like Dolin Blanc.

Pedro Ximénez and Moscatel

When it comes to pedro ximénez you want to look for a wine that has that classic clingy viscosity, but still shows a range of flavors beyond raisins and prunes. **Valdespino's Pedro Ximénez El Candado** ($, 375ml) is a beautiful example—rich, smoky, and chocolaty. **Hidalgo-La Gitana's Pedro Ximénez Triana** ($$, 500ml) is a fine value; it's a bit fruitier than the El Candado with a briskness that makes it more compatible with drinks shaken with citrus. On the moscatel front, **Lustau's Moscatel Emilin** ($$, 750ml) is rich and full-bodied with lots of dried-fruit character, while **Cesar Florido's Moscatel Pasas** ($) is plenty sweet and rich, but more complex—showing intense floral aromatics and sweet spice.

SHERRY COBBLER

The Sherry Cobbler is an American-born cocktail by most accounts. Simply sherry, sugar, and citrus shaken, poured over crushed ice, and slurped through a straw, the cobbler is thought to have originated sometime in the 1820s or early 1830s. And, like most nineteenth-century drinks, its exact origins have been endlessly debated. One thing is for sure: the Sherry Cobbler was the first drink to introduce the drinking straw to popular consciousness.

Like the straw, ice was not a common element of cocktail anatomy prior to the cobbler. (Neither, by the way, was shaking a drink.) The commercial ice trade did not begin in earnest until the 1830s, and even in the mid-1800s, as Mark Twain recalls in his memoir *Life on the Mississippi*, "Ice was jewelry; none but the rich could wear it." So, even if the protocobbler did originate in eighteenth-century England, as an 1883 article in the *London Telegraph* seemed to suggest, it likely bore little resemblance to the ice-packed cobbler of mid-nineteenth-century America—the version that became the most popular drink of its time.

Cocktail historian David Wondrich is credited with digging up the first known mention of the Sherry Cobbler in the 1838 diary of Katherine Jane Ellice, a Canadian who took note of the drink while traveling in the United States. But its great launching pad to international renown came courtesy of Charles Dickens and his *Life and Adventures of Martin Chuzzlewit* (1843–1844). In a scene now famous among cocktail dorks, Chuzzlewit, reacting to his first Sherry Cobbler, sums up the nineteenth-century sentiment around the drink: "Martin took the glass with an astonished look; applied his lips to the reed; and cast up his eyes once in ecstasy. He paused no more until the goblet was drained to the last drop. 'This wonderful invention, sir,' said Mark, tenderly patting the empty glass, 'is called a cobbler. Sherry Cobbler when you name it long; cobbler, when you name it short.'"

Some 150 years after the Sherry Cobbler's decades-long heyday, it's being rediscovered, both as a classic and as a drink prime for riffing. Get weird with your garnishes or omit them altogether, but whatever you do, just don't forget the straw.

---

1 lemon wheel

1 orange wheel

¾ ounce simple syrup (1:1 sugar:water)

3 ounces amontillado

Garnish: berries in season, citrus, mint, a Lego minifig—anything, really

IN A MIXING GLASS add the lemon, orange, and simple syrup, and muddle. Add the sherry, fill with ice, and shake. Finely strain into a Collins glass over crushed ice. Top up with additional crushed ice and garnish like there's no tomorrow.

ADONIS

• ⌁ —— ··· ○

> "Went to see 'Adonis' with the fellers first thing Wednesday night. Went out between acts, every one of 'em, an' had a ball. Began drinking vermouth cocktails, an' had about six of 'em before the show was over."
>
> —"Celebrating New Year's: How a Dude Calls at the Large Hotels," *New York Times*, January 2, 1885

Of the stirred aperitif drinks of the nineteenth century that involve sherry, there are really two archetypes that are riffed on ad nauseam: the Bamboo (page 181) and the Adonis. Both offer clues to their body type. The Bamboo is lean and tough; the Adonis, a sort of classical beefcake—the brawnier of the two. The drinks, even when variations are applied, still split in these different directions.

What we know about the Adonis is that the drink was named after the Broadway burlesque show by William Gill called *Adonis*, which is often credited as the first-ever Broadway musical. It opened at the Bijou Theater in 1884 and became the *Cats* of the late nineteenth century. While the eponymous drink's exact origin is not confirmed, we do know that by the 1890s it was a regular drink at the Waldorf-Astoria Bar—right around the same time that Louis Eppinger was whipping up Bamboos at Yokohama's Grand Hotel, half a world away. The Adonis didn't quite reach the level of fame that the Bamboo did, but it remained both a regular drink at the Waldorf and a fixture in most nineteenth- and early twentieth–century cocktail books.

While quantities tend to vary depending on which vintage cocktail book you're looking at, the original calls for two parts dry sherry to one part sweet vermouth, a ratio that is the most consistent when swapping different vermouth brands in and out. My go-to here is Carpano Antica and a bold fino like Lustau's La Ina; switching in Dolin Rouge or even Martini & Rossi for Carpano makes for a fruitier drink but a fine one nonetheless.

○···══ ···○

1 ounce sweet vermouth, preferably Carpano Antica

2 ounces fino, preferably Lustau La Ina

2 dashes orange bitters

Garnish: orange peel

ADD THE VERMOUTH, sherry, and bitters to a mixing glass. Fill with ice and stir quickly. Strain into a coupe glass and garnish with the orange peel.

○···══ ···○

ARTIST'S SPECIAL

This drink first appears in Harry McElhone's 1927 *Barflies and Cocktails*, and again three years later in *The Savoy Cocktail Book* (1930) with the caption: "This is the genuine 'Ink of Inspiration,' imbibed at the Bal Bullier, Paris. The recipe is from the Artists' Club, Rue Pigalle, Paris."

In the 1920s the Rue Pigalle—or Quartier Pigalle—was a sordid slice of neighborhood between the 18th and 9th arrondissements, not far from the Moulin Rouge. Between the two world wars this became ground zero for the jazz movement—a kind of Harlem of Paris—and the home base for the likes of Utrillo and Picasso. The Artists' Bar, also called Fred Payne's Bar—or "Freddie's," as Henry Miller called it in the opening of his short story "Burlesque"—played host to everyone from jazz musicians to poets. This remained true of the bar through the Beat era.

The Artist's Special, which is essentially a riff on the Whiskey Sour, had apparently become popular enough that it made its way across the Seine to become a staple at the Bal Bullier, after that room was reimagined in the 1920s, in both décor and activities, in the spirit of Dada.

The redcurrant syrup is adapted from Jerry Thomas's 1862 *Bartender's Guide*. If redcurrants are unavailable, raspberries or sour cherries will make a fine substitute, as will grenadine.

---

1 ounce oloroso

1 ounce blended scotch, preferably Black Grouse

½ ounce lemon juice

½ ounce redcurrant syrup (see below)

Garnish: lemon peel

ADD ALL THE INGREDIENTS but the garnish to a mixing glass. Fill with ice and shake. Strain into a coupe glass and garnish with the lemon peel.

REDCURRANT SYRUP

1 cup stemmed redcurrants

¼ cup raspberries

1¼ cups sugar

7 ounces boiling water

IN A BOWL, combine the currants and raspberries and muddle. Cover with a cloth or kitchen towel and let stand at room temperature overnight. Add the sugar and boiling water and stir to combine. Let cool, and finely strain into a jar or glass bottle. Refrigerate for up to 1 month.

DUNHILL

While the Dunhill makes its most famous appearances in *Boothby's World Drinks and How to Mix Them* (1908) and the *Savoy Cocktail Book* (1930) as the Dunhill's Special, according to Dave Wondrich, the drink was invented at Hatchett's Bar in London's Piccadilly at some point before 1925, when it's first mentioned in Nina Toye and A. H. Adair's *Drinks—Long and Short*.

The drink echoes several classics—the 1:1:1 ratio skews Negroni, while splitting dry vermouth with an oxidized sherry and an olive garnish (or in this case, a blended sherry) seems to wink at the perfect Martini. What it ends up drinking like is something akin to a mellower take on the former, and while early recipes suggest the drink be served up, when using a sherry like Lustau's East India, which is almost oily in texture, it's best to serve it over a big cube, replacing the original olive garnish with a twist of lemon for a little extra cut.

1 barspoon absinthe

1 ounce Beefeater gin

1 ounce Lustau East India Solera

1 ounce dry vermouth

¼ ounce Pierre Ferrand orange curaçao

Garnish: lemon peel

FILL A ROCKS GLASS with ice, add the absinthe, and set aside. In a mixing glass add the gin, sherry, vermouth, and curaçao, fill with ice, and stir. Empty the rocks glass, coating the sides with the absinthe. Add a large ice cube to the rocks glass and strain the stirred ingredients into the glass. Garnish with the lemon peel.

SHERRY FLIP

According to the *Oxford English Dictionary*, the term "flip" is said to have been used as far back as 1695 to describe a mixture of beer, rum, and sugar cooked at high heat—resulting in what is essentially the seventeenth-century version of the worst hangover instigator imaginable. By the nineteenth century, the flip had evolved into a fully upright drink, defined as a combination of a spirit or fortified wine, sugar, and egg, shaken with ice, and served up with nutmeg grated over the top.

Like the Sherry Cobbler, the flip graces many of Dickens's novels. In chapter 21 of *Little Dorrit* (1857), a bishop, sidestepping a physician's recommendation, suggests that Mr. Merdle, who is suffering from depression and "an overtaxed intellect," try his personal cure: "... the yolk of a new-laid egg, beaten up by the good woman in whose house he at that time lodged, with a glass of sound sherry, nutmeg, and powdered sugar."

Dickens himself seemed to have believed the flip could cure his own ailments. On his second and last trip to the United States he kept a grueling schedule, resulting in what he called the "true American catarrh." According to Dickens biographer Fred Kaplan, by the end of the tour, Dickens, who was homesick and depressed, survived almost entirely on Champagne and sherry, often by way of flips and cobblers.

While there are a number of spirits that make for a fine flip, the full-bodied, walnutty character of dry oloroso—and its higher level of glycerol—combined with the creaminess of the egg will get you what Jerry Thomas, in his 1887 version of *How to Mix Drinks*, aptly describes as a "very delicious drink" that "gives strength to delicate people." Sure does. It's a great cold-weather drink and, during the holidays, a less polarizing—and less boozy—stand-in for eggnog.

2 ounces oloroso	**ADD THE OLOROSO,** simple syrup, and egg to a mixing glass. Dry-shake, then add ice and shake vigorously. Strain into a *copita* or small wineglass. Top with grated nutmeg.
½ ounce simple syrup (1:1 sugar:water)	
1 whole egg	
Garnish: nutmeg	

UP-TO-DATE COCKTAIL

German-born Hugo Ensslin was the head bartender at the Hotel Wallick in Times Square, a neighborhood that was, at the dawn of the twentieth century, the cultural heartbeat of New York City. His book *Recipes for Mixed Drinks*, published in 1916, is the last snapshot of New York bartending before Prohibition, documenting well— via a wealth of new ingredients like Dubonnet, crème de menthe, and Bacardi—just how fancy the cocktail had become. While the book is perhaps best known for containing the first-known printed recipe for the Aviation (in all of its crème de violette glory), it's also home to a number of interesting drinks—many of them originals— like this fairly simple concoction.

Manhattanesque in both composition and deliciousness, it welcomes swapping in bourbon if you prefer your whiskey a little sweeter, or swapping in oloroso for amontillado if you fancy a bit more viscosity. I prefer sticking with the original stipulation of rye whiskey and using a fuller-bodied amontillado like Lustau's Los Arcos or the slightly leaner Hidalgo—La Gitana Amontillado Napoleon.

1¼ ounces amontillado

1¼ ounces rye

½ ounce Grand Marnier

2 dashes Angostura bitters

Garnish: lemon peel

ADD ALL THE INGREDIENTS but the garnish to a mixing glass. Add ice and stir. Strain into a coupe glass and garnish with the lemon peel.

BADMINTON CUP

If there were ever a drink name that conjured images of British gents in white lawn-tennis attire, it's the Badminton Cup. "It's really the name that drew me to this drink originally," says Kenny Freeman of Houston's Anvil, who created this riff on George Kappeler's version of the Badminton Cup, featured in his 1895 *Modern American Drinks*. "It reminded me of my grandmother and all of those weird games I'd go and play at her house when I was a kid."

The drink's origins can be traced back to Badminton House in Badminton, Gloucestershire, England, the site of the first badminton game ever played. It started off, in the mid-1800s, as a punch containing sugar, cucumber, claret, soda water, and grated nutmeg. The drink eventually evolved to included everything from Grand Marnier to Cognac. Kappeler's version, which calls for sherry, maraschino, sugar, soda water, claret, cucumber, and a little borage, has been adjusted for the modern palate by Freeman. It is undoubtedly still best consumed in linen attire, as its upper crust birth implies.

4 cucumber slices	**IN A MIXING GLASS,** add the cucumber and muddle. Add the wine, sherry, demerara syrup, and maraschino, shake, and finely strain into a Collins glass with cubed ice. Top with soda.
1½ ounces dry red wine	
1 ounce amontillado	
¾ ounce demerara syrup (1:1 sugar:water)	
½ ounce maraschino liqueur	
Soda	

BAMBOO

The Bamboo is the first original cocktail ever created in Japan. The simple mixture of sherry, dry vermouth, and bitters was the handiwork of a German bartender named Louis Eppinger, the manager at Yokohama's Grand Hotel in the late 1800s and one of the godfathers of bartending in Japan. Having worked in San Francisco around the same time that Jerry Thomas became the world's first "startender," Eppinger became a star in his own right and remained a fixture at the hotel for a decade and a half until his death, in 1907.

There are several theories about the inspiration for the drink. Some say that it's a riff on the martini, with fino sherry replacing gin. Others believe it's a spin on the Adonis, a popular drink of the time that called for sweet vermouth instead of dry French vermouth.

The San Francisco–based writer and bartender William Boothby's 1908 book *World Drinks and How to Mix Them* gives weight to the former theory. His recipe, which has become the American standard (sans olive), calls for equal parts sherry and dry vermouth, with two dashes of orange bitters, two dashes of Angostura bitters, a twist of lemon, and an olive. His dry martini recipe is exactly the same, but subs gin for sherry and drops the Angostura. Whatever the inspiration, according to David Wondrich, by the beginning of the twentieth century the drink had become a staple on American bar menus and found enough fame that it was eventually sold in premixed bottles across the country.

The combination of modern fino and dry vermouth creates a drink that will be appreciated by lovers of the dry martini, but it's a bit one-dimensional in this form. Given what we know about the dry sherries of the late nineteenth century (finos were much older and fuller-bodied, for one), this drink certainly employed something more akin to a young amontillado than a fino as we know it today. Further, it could've even called for a blended sherry. For the modern palate, Joaquín Simó of Pouring Ribbons nails it by sticking with fino and adding a teaspoon of cane syrup to give the drink a bit more texture and balance.

1½ ounces fino

1½ ounces dry vermouth

1 teaspoon cane syrup (2:1 sugar:water)

2 dashes Angostura bitters

2 dashes orange bitters

Garnish: lemon peel

ADD ALL THE INGREDIENTS but the garnish to a mixing glass. Fill with ice and stir quickly. Strain into a coupe glass and garnish with the lemon peel.

TUXEDO

There are a dozen or so sherry-and-gin drinks that start to pop up during the twilight years of the nineteenth century and repeat themselves with very slight variations throughout the first quarter of the twentieth. Of them all, the Tuxedo is the best known. The drink's name refers to Tuxedo Park, a sort of early experiment in country club living established in 1886 about thirty-five miles from Jersey City. There were cottages, lawn tennis courts, a golf course, a clubhouse, and plenty of well-heeled New Yorkers willing to call this sporting paradise home. Tuxedo Park was the birthplace of not only the first complete sewage system in America but also the tailless suit, called—yes, you got it—the tuxedo. The members of this bourgie utopia were called Tuxedoites, and before shuffling home after work they no doubt stopped off at the city's top bars, most notable among them the Waldorf-Astoria Bar, where this drink was said to have been born.

(Note: For all the dorks out there who know their Tuxedos and are wondering where the maraschino and absinthe are: there are several drinks that bear the Tuxedo name, but this version, according to David Wondrich, appears to be the original.)

2 ounces gin, preferably Plymouth or Beefeater 24	ADD ALL THE INGREDIENTS but the garnish to a mixing glass. Add ice and stir. Strain into a chilled coupe glass and garnish with the orange peel.
1 ounce fino, preferably Lustau La Ina	
2 dashes orange bitters	
Garnish: orange peel	

CORONATION COCKTAIL

Like the Tuxedo, the Coronation Cocktail became a category unto itself, with a wealth of variations that seemed to be added to the pot with the crowning of each new English king or queen. While the sherry- and dry vermouth–based version appears most famously in the *Savoy Cocktail Book* (1930) as Coronation No. 1, the recipe dates back to almost thirty years earlier. Though the actual recipe is not printed, it is first mentioned as the creation of one Joseph Rose, a bartender at Murray's Buffett Café in the heart of Newark, New Jersey, in *Mixer and Server, Volume 12*, 1903: "He has numerous friends who keep him busy serving them with popular drinks, several of which he has introduced himself, such as the 'Coronation Cocktail,' the 'Flashlight,' and others."

Three years later the recipe specs popped up in the *Hoffman House Bartender's Guide* (1906), with a caption that also credits the drink to Rose: "This drink, arranged by Joseph Rose, of Murray Bros.' Café, 184 Market Street, Newark, N.J., won second prize in the *Police Gazette* Bartenders' Contest for 1903." The drink, a simple mixture of sherry, French vermouth, orange bitters, and maraschino is one of the more enduring and delicate sherry aperitif drinks. This version is a variation on the drink's original construction, which called for a roughly 5:1 ratio in favor of sherry.

2½ ounces fino
½ ounce dry vermouth
¼ ounce maraschino liqueur
3 dashes orange bitters
Garnish: lemon peel

ADD ALL THE INGREDIENTS but the garnish to a mixing glass. Add ice and stir. Strain into a coupe glass and garnish with the lemon peel.

LINCOLN CLUB CUP

Founded in 1890, the Lincoln Club was housed in a brownstone on Putnam Avenue between Irving Place and Classon Avenue in the Clinton Hill neighborhood of Brooklyn. The building was, as the *New York Times* describes it, "one of the great club buildings of New York, a wild, chunky Queen Anne fantasy of turrets, buttresses, monograms and custom-shaped brick," with a monogrammed "LC" at the top, the "size of a Mini Cooper." It also had, according to the *Eagle and Brooklyn: Volume 2* (1893), "four bowling alleys in the basement" and was "upon a plane with any of the great social institutions of Brooklyn."

The club was, like most of its day, known for its social receptions. And while it's unknown whether this drink, which first appears in George Kappeler's *Modern American Drinks* (1895), was actually served at the Lincoln Club, its combination of sherry, brandy, and Rhine wine (or Sauternes) was certainly of noble birth. My variation on the original subs in Lillet for Sauternes and adjusts the quantities for both a single serving and, in keeping with the drink's original cup form, a batched drink for small groups.

1 lemon wheel

1 orange wheel

2 cucumber wheels

½ ounce simple syrup (1:1 sugar:water)

1½ ounces amontillado

¾ ounce Lillet Blanc

¾ ounce brandy

Dry sparkling wine

Garnish: lemon, orange, and cucumber wheels

ADD THE LEMON WHEEL, the orange wheel, the cucumber wheels, and the simple syrup to a mixing glass, and muddle. Add the sherry, Lillet, and brandy to the glass. Add ice and shake. Finely strain over ice into a Collins glass and top with dry sparkling wine. Garnish with lemon, orange, and cucumber wheels.

DANIEL WEBSTER'S PUNCH

Yes, that Daniel Webster. Though a quick Google search for Daniel Webster's Punch will bring up several variant recipes, they all refer to the same man—the famed Massachusetts senator of yore. In his book *Punch*, David Wondrich attributes the wealth of different recipes floating around to the fact that, at least in part, asking for a glass of Webster's Punch seemed to be akin to a nineteenth-century version of "stump the bartender." No one really knew which version Daniel Webster actually preferred and, thus, riffs abound.

The original version of this recipe, adapted by Wondrich, comes from the *Steward & Barkeeper's Manual* (1869) with the assertion that this was the very punch recipe that Webster gave to his friend, "Major Brooks, of Boston", before his death. True or not, it's a tasty punch and one whose quantities and ice mold can easily be adjusted for season and party size. ··· SERVES 8

3 lemons	**PEEL THE LEMONS,** taking care to avoid as much of the bitter white pith as possible. In a large bowl, combine the sugar with the lemon peels, then lightly muddle and let sit for 20 minutes to allow the citrus oils to infuse with the sugar. Boil 2 cups of water and steep the tea bag in it for 5 minutes. Set aside to cool slightly. To the bowl, add the tea, lemon juice, cognac, sherry, rum, and red wine. Stir to combine. Strain out the lemon peels and refrigerate for at least 30 minutes. Fifteen minutes before serving, add the ice ring. Ladle into cups and lightly top each glass with Champagne.
½ cup sugar	
1 black tea bag	
½ cup lemon juice	
¾ cup cognac	
¾ cup dry oloroso	
¾ cup Jamaican rum	
1½ cups Bordeaux (or any full-bodied red wine)	
Ice ring (see below)	
Champagne to top	

ICE RING

5 strawberries, cut in half lengthwise	**TO A BUNDT CAKE MOLD,** add enough water to fill halfway to the top. Evenly place the strawberries, pineapple, and mint. Freeze overnight.
5 slices of pineapple	
10 mint leaves	

REPOSSESSION

Leo Robitschek, the bar manager at both Eleven Madison Park and The NoMad, took the former from a solid cocktail program that leaned heavily on the classics to one of the most innovative cocktail bars in New York. The Repossession quickly became a staple at the restaurant's bar, but it feels most at home at its newer digs at The NoMad. The room is a mahogany-and-leather ode to a time when its stretch of high-twenties Broadway was studded with brothels and gambling halls and the hotel bar was the capital of the cocktail world. There's a bit of grit to this drink thanks to the interplay between the smokiness of the mezcal, the vegetal notes of the tequila, and the deep, briny nuttiness of the amontillado. The apricot liqueur, which adds the drink's only fruit note, is a classic companion with bass-note bases like sherry or bourbon.

1 ounce reposado tequila

¾ ounce amontillado

½ ounce lemon juice

½ ounce apricot liqueur, preferably Rothman & Winter

¼ ounce cane syrup (2:1 sugar:water)

¼ ounce mezcal

ADD ALL THE INGREDIENTS except the mezcal to a mixing glass. Add ice and shake, then strain into a coupe glass. Pour the mezcal slowly over the back of a barspoon to float.

PALE RIDER

The Pale Rider was born out of Phil Ward's deep hatred of sangria. "This drink is almost a sangria, but sangrias are garbage," says Ward, of Mayahuel in New York City. As most of us know, via early forays into college drink-making, sangria is hard to batch with any consistency and it doesn't keep all that long. It also invariably leads to extreme intoxication. In order to tighten things up, Ward infuses fruit into booze so he can recreate his riffs on sangria with greater consistency. The Pale Rider swaps out fruit for jalapeño and simply adds manzanilla, a small dose of cane syrup, and lime. This is not only a Ward drink to its core—spicy and adamantly savory—but also one that showcases how well sherry performs in even the simplest of drinks.

2½ ounces manzanilla

1 ounce jalapeño tequila (see below)

¼ ounce fresh lime juice

½ ounce cane syrup (2:1 sugar:water)

1 ounce soda

Garnish: 2 slices cucumber

ADD THE SHERRY, tequila, lime juice, and cane syrup to a mixing glass. Add ice, shake, and strain into a wine tumbler over ice. Top with the soda, garnish with the cucumber slices, and serve with a straw.

JALAPEÑO TEQUILA

2 fresh jalapeños

1½ cups silver tequila

CUT THE JALAPEÑOS lengthwise and extract the seeds and membranes; add them to a glass bowl. Discard the rest of the pepper. Add the tequila to the seeds and membranes and infuse for 10 to 20 minutes, depending on the heat of the peppers. Finely strain and bottle. Keep at room temperature for up to 1 month.

BETTY CARTER

When Natasha David and Jeremy Oertel of You and Me Cocktails signed on to create the list for Berlyn—a wacky, bric-a-bracked Fort Greene, Brooklyn, restaurant that bills itself as "new Brooklyn / regional Germanic"—the owner asked that they use the town's historic residents as inspiration.

This drink is the husband-and-wife team's ode to Betty Carter, the American jazz singer who rose to fame in the late 1950s for her improvisational style and talent for scat singing. They began by searching for "flavors that made us think of Carter's kind of music," says Oertel, and ended up with this riff on the Whiskey Sour. Here pedro ximénez sherry takes the place of sugar, and the unlikely addition of floral, bittersweet Amaro Nonino acts as the ad-libbed bridge between the bass tones of the sherry and bourbon and the high-toned delicacy of the lemon.

1½ ounces bourbon, preferably Buffalo Trace

¾ ounce pedro ximénez, preferably Hidalgo–La Gitana Triana

½ ounce Amaro Nonino

¾ ounce lemon juice

ADD ALL THE INGREDIENTS to a mixing glass or shaker. And ice and shake until chilled. Strain into a coupe glass.

FLOR DE JEREZ

Joaquín Simó's Flor de Jerez is a distant relative of the Daisy—a broad category of cocktails generally typified by a base spirit, lemon, a liqueur or sugar sweetener (or both), and, often, seltzer water. Simó, of Pouring Ribbons, wanted to "turn the usual spirit-heavy drink on its head to let the perceived acidity of the sherry shine."

So instead of using funky Appleton Reserve Jamaican rum as the base spirit, he used it as a modifier for a base of amontillado. To that he added lemon for brightness, cane syrup for richness and mouthfeel, apricot liqueur for that sherry-friendly fruit note, and Angostura as a "flavor hub," because, as Simó describes it, "every ingredient can relate to something in the Angostura and it pulls them all together." The drink first appeared on the New York City bar Death & Co's 2010 spring/summer menu and has since found its way around the country.

1½ ounces **amontillado**

½ ounce **Jamaican rum**

¼ ounce apricot liqueur, **preferably Rothman & Winter**

¾ ounce fresh **lemon** juice

½ ounce **cane syrup (2:1 sugar:water)**

Dash of Angostura bitters

FILL A COCKTAIL SHAKER with ice. Add all of the ingredients and shake well. Strain into a chilled coupe glass.

SHERRY COCKTAIL

Irish bartender Jack McGarry made a name for himself at Belfast's Merchant Hotel and later at London's Milk & Honey before crossing the Atlantic in 2011 to open the Dead Rabbit, a three-story bar with a sixty-page menu of over seventy drinks, located in Lower Manhattan.

With the bar's focus on seventeenth-, eighteenth-, and nineteenth-century drinks, sherry became a "natural focal point," and McGarry knew that "these nerdy cocktail guys were going to come in after reading fucking Jerry Thomas's 18-whatever book, and would try and test us." In preparation, he and his staff essentially memorized all of the recipes in all three versions of Thomas's book, among other classic cocktail manuals. In the process, this drink—an amalgamation of the Bamboo (dry sherry, dry vermouth, bitters; page 181), the Vermouth Cocktail (essentially vermouth and bitters), and the Turf Club (gin, dry vermouth, maraschino, absinthe, orange bitters)—was born. It's an ode to the "old-fashioned" drinks of Thomas's first version, via the prominent use of bitters, and the new and improved drinks of the second via the use of absinthe and maraschino as seasoners. There are many drinks that appear to be ghosts of this drink's past life—like the Schnozzle and the New Yorker—many of which are lost, but none is as successful as the Dead Rabbit's house sherry cocktail.

3 ounces oloroso	ADD ALL THE INGREDIENTS except the lemon peel to a mixing glass. Stir and strain into a Nick & Nora glass. Twist the lemon peel over the glass and discard.
¾ ounce Pierre Ferrand Dry orange curaçao	
¼ ounce maraschino liqueur	
2 dashes Angostura bitters	
2 dashes Regan's Orange Bitters No. 6	
1 dash absinthe	
Lemon peel, to express over the drink	

OLD ALHAMBRA

The Old Alhambra was a nineteenth-century New York City saloon, which, in those days, almost always doubled as a whorehouse. It was tucked into what is now called the Flatiron District, a definably uneventful stretch of commercial and high-end residential housing that separates Union Square from Midtown. In its heyday it was the heart of the city—the area that played host to the cocktail movement, grand hotels, and Broadway shows. But it was also considered the tenderloin of New York, referred to by reformers as Satan's Circus, a place where all manner of grit and vice lurked under the guise of entertainment. It was a place where the luxe and the degenerate were entwined.

When coming up with the drinks for New York's The NoMad Hotel, Leo Robitschek first drew inspiration from the history of the area and then created drinks with a nod to the names and places that once defined it. Given the demographic that likely frequented the Old Alhambra, he knew this drink had to be closely based on a "manly, burly" classic. The original Alhambra is an old Moorish fortress in Granada, Spain, and Robitschek says, "I started picturing this old Spanish man drinking something whiskey-related." He ended up with a scotch-and-sherry drink, made burly by the addition of crème de cacao and brightened with the unlikely addition of an expressed grapefruit peel.

1½ ounces Laphroaig 10 Year scotch, or substitute any smoky Islay scotch

¾ ounce Dolin Blanc vermouth

½ ounce Lustau East India sherry

¼ ounce crème de cacao, preferably Marie Brizard

Garnish: grapefruit peel

ADD ALL THE INGREDIENTS but the garnish to a mixing glass. Stir with ice and strain into a coupe glass, then garnish with the grapefruit peel.

BREAD & WINE

Even with the rise of the craft cocktail and its integration into restaurant beverage programs, it's still assumed that spirit-forward drinks don't pair well with food. More often than not, this is true. But the Vinos de Jerez Cocktail Competition requires that bartenders not only submit their drinks, but also articulate what they would pair them with. Charles Joly, now the head bartender at Chicago's The Aviary, submitted his Bread & Wine as a companion to pork belly in 2007 and won the whole thing.

While the drink sticks close to the traditional Whiskey Sour blueprint, the interplay among sherry, scotch, maple, and lemon give the impression in both flavor and texture of consuming a liquid version of a waffle house breakfast. In a good way. But really, how could such a thing be bad?

5 dashes of absinthe

1 ounce Lustau Don Nuño oloroso

1½ ounces Balvenie Doublewood 12 Year scotch

½ ounce lemon juice

¼ to ⅓ ounce maple syrup (depending on tartness of lemon)

Garnish: orange peel

FILL AN OLD-FASHIONED GLASS with ice, add the absinthe, and set aside to season. Combine the sherry, scotch, lemon juice, and maple syrup in a mixing glass. Add ice and shake well. Empty the old-fashioned glass, coating the sides with absinthe. Add ice (preferably a large cube) and strain the drink into the glass. Garnish with the orange peel. No straws, please.

PALO NEGRO

Ivy Mix was born in the wrong country. "I was supposed to be born in either Mexico or Spain—not sure what happened," she says. When Mix, whose name is indeed almost too good to be true, was behind the bar at Brooklyn's Clover Club, she sought to create a drink that combined her two favorite places in the world. "It could have been as easy as mixing tequila and sherry, since they go so well together, but when I think about making cocktails I think of them as a story—you should taste a beginning, a middle, an end." Mix found her climax of sorts in the almost menacing mugginess of Cruzan Black Strap rum, and her falling action in Grand Marnier, which is remarkable in its ability to elevate some of the bergamot flavors that I personally have always associated with palo cortado, Mix's sherry of choice here. Demerara syrup adds a bit more body and Mix's insistence on using lowlands tequila—which typically has more pepper and bite than that of the highlands—cuts right through the center.

To me this drink embodies fall: it's strong, it's stirred, and it just happens to be a staple of the autumn menu at Clover Club—which is just about the best place in Brooklyn to be when the gloves and scarves come out.

2 ounces reposado tequila, preferably Partida

1 ounce palo cortado, preferably Lustau Península

½ ounce Cruzan Black Strap rum

1 teaspoon Grand Marnier

1 teaspoon demerara syrup (1:1 sugar:water)

Garnish: orange peel, cut in the shape of a coin

ADD ALL THE INGREDIENTS but the garnish to a mixing glass. Add ice and stir. Strain into a coupe glass and garnish with the orange peel.

STONE RAFT

"The Stone Raft is a weird one," says Phil Ward of the New York agave den Mayahuel. "I figured that people weren't going to like it or order it, but I thought it was so god-damn good I put it on the menu anyway." A combination of amontillado, mezcal, jalapeño tequila, celery bitters, and a barspoon of agave nectar, the Stone Raft is a distant cousin of the Oaxaca Old-Fashioned, one of the first drinks Ward ever made with mezcal—his "spirit" spirit. The Stone Raft was born out of a long line of riffs on the drink. The adamantly savory combination of herbal-smoky-nutty is unusual, but despite Ward's prediction that the drink would be met with sneers, it went on to become the obsession of many fans of Mayahuel—myself included—and has been a mainstay on the menu since the bar opened.

1½ ounces amontillado
½ ounce jalapeño tequila (page 188)
½ ounce Del Maguey Vida mezcal
1 barspoon agave nectar
2 dashes Bitter Truth celery bitters

ADD ALL THE INGREDIENTS to a mixing glass. Stir and strain into a coupe glass.

LA PERLA

Jacques Bezuidenhout cut his teeth behind the bar at a number of San Francisco restaurants before opening Tres Agaves in 2005. Since then, he's become the jolly South African mascot of the SF bar scene. This drink, which was on the opening menu at Tres, became one of the early anthems to tequila and sherry, catching the attention of a growing community of cocktail weenies online and eventually crisscrossing the country before earning a permanent place in the annals of modern sherry drinks. Bezuidenhout explains this drink as essentially a deconstruction of the flavor profile of reposado—the pear liqueur representing the obvious and the manzanilla lending not only a freshness and bite, but also the flavors of bright green apples he associates with great reposado tequila. The result is an elegant and surprisingly food-friendly aperitif drink.

1½ ounces reposado tequila
1½ ounces manzanilla
¾ ounce pear liqueur
Garnish: lemon peel

ADD ALL THE INGREDIENTS but the garnish to a mixing glass. Stir and strain into a coupe glass and garnish with the lemon peel.

VELO DE FLOR

Flor doesn't really photograph well. It's one of the great lessons that this book's photographer learned while we traveled from bodega to bodega, trying to see if we could get this veil of yeast to work it for the camera. We did not succeed. So, in lieu of an actual photo of flor, I came up with this cocktail after realizing that the gloriousness of shaken egg white is just about as close as you can get to recreating spring or autumn flor. If you're looking for a stiffer drink, you could certainly split the fino with gin, but a forward fino like Lustau's La Ina has a flavor profile strong enough to stand tall when tossed in with simple syrup, citrus, and egg. What you end up with is a drink that is really about the flavor of the fino, beefed up.

2 ounces **La Ina fino**	**ADD ALL THE INGREDIENTS** to a mixing glass and dry-shake. Add ice and shake vigorously; strain into a wine or large coupe glass.
1 ounce simple syrup (1:1 sugar:water)	
1 ounce **lemon** juice	
1 small **egg white**	
Pinch of salt	

TRIDENT

Seattle bartender Robert Hess created the Trident in what was still the prehistoric period of the modern craft cocktail revival. It was 2000 and barely anyone had heard of amaro, let alone an amaro made from artichokes. And sherry? Even some of the savviest sommeliers and bartenders wouldn't have batted an eyelash if a fino were left, half-opened marinating on the back bar. Hess came up with this drink while working for Fee Brothers, and what began as a Negroni variation became what he considers to be one of the most successful drinks in his long career. The drink remains on the list of Seattle's Zig Zag Café and is firmly established as one of the few sherry drinks that have achieved modern classic status.

1 ounce fino

1 ounce Cynar

1 ounce aquavit, preferably Linie

2 dashes peach bitters

Garnish: lemon peel

ADD ALL THE INGREDIENTS but the garnish to a mixing glass. Add ice and stir, then strain into a coupe glass. Garnish with the lemon peel.

REMEMBER THE ALIMONY

Bartender Dan Greenbaum suspects that he was going through a breakup when he created this drink for his now-defunct New York City bar, the Beagle: "Inadvertently, we had a whole breakup-themed menu." The Second Marriage (page 214) was part of the same sad playlist. Greenbaum created this drink as a brighter, lower-alcohol riff on the most famous of bitter drinks, the Negroni. A simple three-ingredient structure is built on a base of fino, to which the bitter Italian artichoke amaro Cynar is added for bite and gin supplies the backbone. The name? A mash-up of the battle cry "Remember the Alamo" and the sort of bitter fallout that only divorce can bring. Season with a tear.

1¼ ounces La Ina fino

¾ ounce Beefeater gin

1¼ ounces Cynar

Garnish: orange peel

IN A ROCKS GLASS with one large ice cube, combine the sherry, gin, and Cynar and stir. Garnish with the orange peel.

PARISH HALL PUNCH

For New York City bartender Damon Boelte, punch will always be associated with church, where on holidays like Easter there was always a bright bowl of punch in the Parish Hall after service. Punch at his Oklahoma church meant a combo of sherbet and ginger ale—the sort of mixture that undoubtedly turned small children into demons. But Boelte remembers savoring it as a kid and admits that the memory of it is so strong that, as a grown man, if he saw a bowl of ginger ale and sherbet he'd "fucking attack it." This is his more sensible, adult version of that parish hall classic— a summery mix of grapefruit-infused sugar, Basque cider, ginger beer, amontillado, seltzer, and Old Tom gin. ··· SERVES 8

Peels of 2 ruby red grapefruits

¼ cup sugar

½ cup Greenhook Ginsmiths' Old Tom Gin (or Hayman's Old Tom if unavailable)

½ cup amontillado

½ cup Basque cider (preferably Isastegi or Sarasola)

½ cup ginger beer (preferably Fever Tree)

¼ cup seltzer water

Garnish: 1 (3-inch) knob fresh ginger, peeled and cut into coins; grapefruit peels

PEEL THE GRAPEFRUITS, taking care to avoid as much of the bitter white pith as possible. In a large bowl, combine the sugar with the grapefruit peels, then lightly muddle and let sit for 20 minutes to allow the citrus oils to infuse with the sugar. After 20 minutes, add the gin, sherry, cider, ginger beer, and seltzer. Stir to combine. Add the ginger and the grapefruit peels to the bowl to garnish. To serve, ladle into punch cups over ice.

PIMM'S COPA

The first Pimm's Cup I ever had was at Employees Only in New York City back in the summer of 2006. It's one of those drinks, with its gang of garnishes, that sparks daydreams of late afternoon sun, porches, and Indian summer. But in true New York fashion I met this drink for the first time on an excruciating date; all unfortunate circumstances aside, though, I still managed to fall in love with it that day and it's become one of the drinks I return to most often. It's primed for riffing and over-the-top garnishing (go ahead). In this iteration, the addition of amontillado gives the drink the sort of depth that makes it feel most at home when the temperature dips.

½ ounce demerara syrup
(1:1 demerara sugar:water)

3 (½-inch-thick) slices fresh ginger, peeled

1 slice cucumber

4 mint leaves

2 ounces Pimm's No. 1 Cup

1 ounce amontillado

¾ ounce fresh lemon juice

Soda

Garnish: mint, cucumber slice,
berries in season

ADD THE DEMERARA SYRUP, fresh ginger, and slice of cucumber to a mixing glass. Muddle well. Add the mint leaves and lightly muddle to release the oils. Add the Pimm's, sherry, and lemon juice, shake, and finely strain over ice in a highball glass. Top with soda and garnish with a small bunch of mint, a cucumber slice, and the berries.

COFFEY PARK SWIZZLE

Alex Day was in his early twenties when he got a job behind the bar at New York City's Death & Co, of which he is now a partner. He came up with this drink just a few months after joining the staff: "I started with the idea of the Queens Park Swizzle, which is basically a fancy mojito with bitters on top." He remembers going downstairs to the walk-in to grab mint and seeing a bottle of Lustau's Los Arcos amontillado. He'd never really used it as the base of a drink before, and "seeing how it worked in this drink was an a-ha moment for [him]." The drink, which is named for Red Hook's Coffey Park, is a simple Caribbean blend of Velvet Falernum, rum, sherry, lime, and a generous float of Angostura—which, depending on your fancy, you can either stir in at once or allow to integrate slowly with each sip.

1 ounce Barbancourt 4-year rum

1 ounce Lustau Los Arcos amontillado

¼ ounce Velvet Falernum

¾ ounce ginger syrup (see below), or substitute 2 nickle-size pieces fresh ginger and ½ ounce simple syrup

¾ ounce lime juice

Angostura bitters

Garnish: mint

ADD THE RUM, SHERRY, falernum, ginger syrup, and lime juice to a pilsner glass. Add crushed or pebbled ice and swizzle. (If using fresh ginger and simple syrup, lightly muddle, shake, and finely strain over crushed or pebbled ice.) Add 3 to 5 dashes of Angostura bitters on top of the crushed ice. Garnish with a mint sprig and serve with a straw.

GINGER SYRUP

½ cup fresh-pressed ginger juice

¾ cup sugar

COMBINE THE GINGER juice and sugar in a small saucepan and heat over low. Stir continuously until the mixture heats through and the sugar dissolves, about 7 to 10 minutes. Remove from the heat and set aside to cool. Transfer to a glass container and store covered in the refrigerator for up to 1 month.

RYE WITCH

The Rye Witch was one of the first sherry cocktails New York City bartender and owner of PDT Jim Meehan came up with while bartending at Gramercy Tavern back in 2006 and 2007. Meehan was constantly trying to find ways to incorporate the wine program into the bar program and, he says, "sherry came to me."

The Rye Witch is a riff on an Improved Old-Fashioned, using the Italian liqueur Strega as an aromatic component and a sweetener (along with a cube of demerara sugar) and palo cortado as the balancing component. To Meehan, styles like palo cortado and amontillado allow you to add richness and complexity, but are also dry enough to serve a "corrective function" to sweet liqueurs like Chartreuse and Strega ("witch" in Italian, hence the name), which can be difficult to work with.

Dash of Fee Brothers orange bitters

Dash of Regan's Orange Bitters No. 6

1 cube (or 1 teaspoon) demerara sugar

2 ounces Rittenhouse rye whiskey

¼ ounce Strega

¼ ounce palo cortado, preferably Lustau Península

Garnish: orange peel

ADD BOTH BITTERS and the sugar cube to a mixing glass and muddle to a paste. Add the whiskey, Strega, sherry, and ice and strain into a chilled rocks glass. Garnish with the orange peel.

FORTIFY YOURSELF

Katie Stipe's introduction to sherry cocktails came courtesy of Jacques Bezuidenhout's La Perla (page 199) almost ten years ago, when she was tending bar at New York City's Flatiron Lounge—part of a crew of bartenders who would go on to become some of the biggest names in cocktails.

Stipe describes this pioneering generation of bartenders as largely eager to build a diverse base of knowledge on what was, at the time, a blank slate. But now that bartenders have a base to work from, she says, they are "looking for a field of study—so you have well-rounded bartenders, but they'll be rum-centric or agave-centric." While she didn't actively choose sherry to become her concentration, it has become exactly that. This drink, which Stipe calls a happy accident, was conceived on the heels of a week spent working sherry into tiki drinks. Stirred, boozy, and aromatic, this is one of those drinks that manages to be as complex as it is crowd-pleasing, delicately balancing the herbaceousness of Chartreuse with the florality of moscatel against a bold and spicy base of rye whiskey and palo cortado.

¾ ounce **palo cortado**

¾ ounce **moscatel**

1 ounce **rye whiskey**

½ ounce yellow **Chartreuse**

2 dashes **orange bitters**

Garnish: **lemon peel**

ADD ALL THE INGREDIENTS but the garnish to a mixing glass. Add ice and stir. Strain into a coupe glass. Garnish with the lemon peel.

MARIAH SHERRY

When coming up with a name for this drink, which is as pink and refreshing as it is bitter and sour, I couldn't help but think of Mariah Carey—all butterflies, cut-off shorts, teary ballads, and temper tantrums. Shrubs are, after all, the angry divas of the cocktail world, vinegar-laced sweet-and-sour concoctions that must be handled with caution. As a lover of all things pickled, fermented, and dressed in vinegar, I went through a heavy shrub phase—this warm-weather, low-alcohol cooler being one of the high points of a very sour summer. This drink combines grapefruit shrub with a bold fino, Aperol (grapefruit's soul mate), a little lime, muddled mint, and soda water—my own angsty rendition of "Dreamlover."

5 to 7 mint leaves

2 ounces fino, preferably Lustau La Ina

¾ ounce Aperol

½ ounce grapefruit shrub (see below)

¾ ounce fresh lime juice

¼ ounce simple syrup (1:1 sugar:water)

Soda

Garnish: grapefruit peel, lime wedge, mint sprig

IN A MIXING GLASS, gently muddle the mint leaves. Add the sherry, Aperol, shrub, lime juice, and simple syrup. Add ice and shake, then strain over ice in a Collins glass. Top with soda. Garnish with the grapefruit peel, a skewered lime wedge, and a sprig of the mint.

GRAPEFRUIT SHRUB

2 ruby red grapefruits

1¾ cups cane sugar

1¾ cups ruby red grapefruit juice

¾ cup apple cider vinegar

½ ounce red peppercorns, crushed

PEEL THE GRAPEFRUITS, avoiding as much of the bitter white pith as possible, and transfer them to a glass mixing bowl. Add the sugar and muddle, then cover and let sit overnight at room temperature. Add the grapefruit juice, taste, and adjust the seasoning, adding more sugar if necessary. Add the vinegar, about ¼ cup at a time, until the taste is to your liking. Finely strain the mixture and pour into a glass container, then add the peppercorns and refrigerate overnight. The following day, strain the liquid through a cheesecloth and discard the peppercorns. Stored covered in the refrigerator, this will keep for up to 4 months.

THE SECOND MARRIAGE

In the world of brown spirits, bourbon and rye make the perfect pair. One is sweet and round, the other spicy and lean—one the yin to the other's yang. When New York bartender Dan Greenbaum set out to create an Old-Fashioned–inspired drink using pedro ximénez as the sweet component, he tried to imagine which spirit might take the place of rye if the perfect pair were to divorce. The apple-based spirit calvados won bourbon's affection as the perfect autumnal substitute for rye.

½ ounce pedro ximénez, preferably Valdespino El Candado

1 ounce calvados or Laird's Old Apple Brandy 7½ Year

1 ounce bourbon, preferably Elijah Craig 12 Year

Garnish: orange peel

ADD THE SHERRY, calvados, and bourbon to a rocks glass over a large ice cube and stir. Garnish with the orange peel.

I AM . . . I SAID

•⋝————⋯○

This drink, plucked from the mind of Morgan Schick, the bar manager at San Francisco's Trick Dog, began as a mash-up of the Mint Julep and the Sherry Cobbler (page 168)—two drinks cut from the same crushed-ice cloth. Schick likes to add a bit of booze to his cobbler to give the drink a bit more backbone, and he decided to go with genever, a Dutch-style gin whose distinct maltiness, Schick knew, would comingle nicely with the nuttiness of amontillado. The addition of curaçao might seem unorthodox in the world of sherry cobblers, but there's historical precedent: toward the latter part of the nineteenth century the cobbler started to embrace a number of embellishments, like pineapple gum syrup, orange curaçao, and port. Where things get weird here is with Schick's menthol tincture, a relatively simple mix of menthol crystals dissolved in vodka—which he came up while reading soap-maker forums. While the drink certainly benefits from the cooling menthol sensation, if you can't get your hands on menthol crystals at your local soap store, the drink is plenty delicious without it.

2 ounces amontillado

½ ounce Pierre Ferrand Dry orange curaçao

½ ounce Bols genever

¼ ounce lemon juice

¼ ounce simple syrup (1:1 syrup:water)

1 drop menthol tincture (see below)

Garnish: mint, half orange wheel

ADD ALL THE INGREDIENTS but the garnishes to a mixing glass, add ice, and shake. Strain over crushed ice into a double rocks glass. Garnish with a sprig of mint and the half orange wheel.

⋯—○•○—⋯

MENTHOL TINCTURE

1 ounce menthol crystals

5 ounces vodka

COMBINE THE MENTHOL crystals and vodka in a small jar. Cap the jar and shake. The crystals will dissolve and infuse after about a day. It keeps, according to Schick, "probably forever."

NEW SPAIN

New York City bartender Sam Ross's Penicillin—a mix of scotch, lemon, honey, and ginger—became one of the few drinks to quickly establish itself within the tiny category of "modern classics." It's a drink I return to often and one I am always pleased to meet on a cocktail list. The Penicillin's foolproof combination of smoky, spicy, sweet, and sour has sparked a whole category of riffs, including this one. I used the same flavor blueprint and subbed in mezcal, amontillado, lime, and agave to give it a muggier, bass-toned Latino updo. What the drink illustrates well is the strong relationship between sherry and spirits like mezcal or scotch, which tend to have an iodine and salt component that is echoed in both fino and amontillado.

1 (½-inch-thick) slice fresh ginger, peeled
½ ounce agave nectar
¾ ounce lime juice
2 ounces amontillado
1 ounce Del Maguey Vida mezcal
Garnish: nutmeg, lime wheel

ADD THE GINGER to a mixing glass with the agave and lime juice and muddle. Add the sherry and mezcal, and fill with ice. Shake, and finely strain over a large cube of ice into a rocks glass. Grate nutmeg over the top and garnish with the lime wheel.

SUPPRESSOR #1

"A few years ago everyone was hot on the how-much-high-proof-alcohol-can-you-fit-in-one-drink thing," says Greg Best. "But Atlanta is a driving town." In reaction to this trend, Best, who rose to fame within the bartending world for his innovative drinks at Holeman & Finch in Atlanta, asked bartenders from around the city to come up with at least one low-alcohol "distance" cocktail. As of this writing, there are around twenty drinks in the Suppressor collection, but this is the original. Best began with pedro ximénez, an ingredient that most would associate with a spirit-forward drink, and sought to turn that perception on its head by integrating it into an elegant julep-inspired drink, fresh enough to combat the brutal Southern sun.

1 ounce Dolin dry vermouth

1 ounce Cocchi Americano

1 ounce Alvear 2008 pedro ximénez

8 drops Bittermens Hopped Grapefruit Bitters

2 heavy barspoons lime juice

Garnish: orange peel, mint sprig

ADD ALL THE INGREDIENTS but the garnish over crushed ice in a julep cup. Garnish with the orange peel and mint.

EL CAPATAZ COBBLER

Sean Kenyon of Williams & Graham in Denver had a friend who complained that the budding trend of using vinegar in drinks was "disgusting and horrible." Kenyon loves peaches and vinegar (or, really, any fruit and vinegar), and this late-summer riff on the classic Sherry Cobbler (page 168) arose from his determination to change his friend's mind. The drink marries his beloved Colorado Palisades peaches to thick and potent Lustau pedro ximénez sherry vinegar. The sweet-and-sour interplay of honey syrup, fruit, and vinegar combined with East India and fino sherries turns the classic fruity cobbler flavor profile upside down, embracing the drink's savory side.

¼ peach

½ orange wheel

½ ounce honey syrup (2:1 honey:water)

1 barspoon Lustau pedro ximénez sherry vinegar

2 ounces Lustao La Ina fino

2 ounces Lustau East India sherry

Garnish: peach slice, dash of sherry vinegar

IN A MIXING GLASS, muddle the peach and orange with the honey syrup and vinegar. Add the sherries and shake without ice. Pour into a goblet and add crushed ice. Stir to frost the glass. Drizzle the peach slice with a bit of vinegar and garnish.

REBUJITO

The first time I visited Andalusia was in 1998 in what was a brutally hot August. I was fourteen and had tagged along on a European trip with a group of friends who'd just graduated high school. There were chaperones, but they didn't do much of a job: I came back with bright red hair and a new appreciation for Camel cigarettes. I can't remember if I drank Rebujitos—more or less the official summer drink of Andalusia—in Sevilla, but it was August and the drink combines Sprite and alcohol, so I can't imagine turning it down. I've certainly had my fair share since. Even in its original form—Sprite and all—it's hard not to fall in love with it, especially when the levante blows. But Evan Zimmerman's fresh, Spriteless version—a staple on his cocktail list at Portland's Woodsman Tavern—is no doubt a far superior, and far more craft cocktail–acceptable version.

2 mint leaves	ADD THE MINT and simple syrup to a mixing glass and lightly muddle. Add the sherry and lemon and lime juices. Shake and strain into a tall Collins glass. Top with soda water and garnish with the lime and lemon wheels and sprig of mint.
½ ounce simple syrup (1:1 sugar:water)	
2 ounces fino	
½ ounce lemon juice	
½ ounce lime juice	
Soda	
Garnish: lemon and lime wheels, mint sprig	

MAISON SHERRY COBBLER

If there is any cocktail category that garnishes with near-irrational abandon, it's tiki. But the cobbler, too, invites one to get carried away. And that's part of its charm. Maxwell Britten, the head bartender at Brooklyn's Maison Premiere, created the bar's signature winter version of the classic cobbler, which calls for not only an impressive four styles of sherry—as well as a warming dash of clove, nutmeg, and cinnamon-infused St. Elizabeth Allspice Dram—but also a garnish regime that could put most tropical drinks to shame. In addition to the requisite berries arranged on top of the drink, it arrives with its own wintry tableau of rosemary, cinnamon sticks, cranberries, and blueberries served on the tea saucer on which the drink is set. For those at home we've left out the tableau, but in conception this is a drink that asks you to go wild, so garnish lavishly.

¾ ounce amontillado

¾ ounce manzanilla

¾ ounce oloroso

¾ ounce pedro ximénez

½ ounce lemon juice

½ ounce pineapple juice

¼ ounce demerara syrup (1:1 sugar:water)

1 teaspoon St. Elizabeth Allspice Dram

1 barspoon blueberry jam

Garnish: 2 halved blackberries, thin half-moon of orange, mint sprig, skewered cranberries

ADD ALL THE INGREDIENTS but the garnishes to a mixing glass. Add ice and shake. Strain over crushed ice into a stemmed pilsner glass. Top with more crushed ice and garnish with the berries, orange, mint sprig, and cranberries. Serve with a straw.

ALE CUP

The original recipe for this drink appears in *Jack's Manual* (1910), where it calls for a simple combination of sugar, lemon, sherry, water, Bass ale, mint, and fresh nutmeg. It was served, like a proper cup should be, from a glass pitcher, and topped off with the ale right before being served. While the original recipe is no slouch, I couldn't help but look at this drink—a tangle of dark ale tumbling down from the top of the glass—and think Dark and Stormy. Rum on the brain, I added an ounce of a bold and funky Jamaican gold from Appleton and a dose of sherry vinegar for bite, for what ends up drinking like a West Indian riff on the original.

2 mint leaves

¾ ounce simple syrup (1:1 sugar:water)

1½ ounces palo cortado

1 ounce gold Jamaican rum, preferably Appleton Estate

¾ ounce lemon juice

1 barspoon pedro ximénez sherry vinegar

Brown ale

Garnish: nutmeg, mint sprig

ADD THE MINT LEAVES and simple syrup to a mixing glass and lightly muddle. Add the sherry, rum, lemon juice, and vinegar. Add ice and shake until chilled. Strain over ice into a Collins glass. Top with ale. Grate nutmeg over the top of the glass and garnish with a sprig of mint.

SHERRY BLOODY MARY

As one of the few entirely savory drinks in the classic canon, the Bloody Mary has always been seen as a morning-after medicine—as the cocktail writer David A. Embury wrote in his *The Fine Art of Mixing Drinks* (1948), it's "a classic example of combining in one potion both the poison and the antidote."

But like many other classics, its origins are sketchy. Theories suggest the drink was created either by Fernand Petiot while he was bartending at Harry's New York Bar in Paris during Prohibition, or the comedian George Jessel in Palm Beach in 1927.

A slew of information unearthed by bartender Jack McGarry seems to suggest that, due to the lack of evidence to corroborate a Paris birthplace, the drink is American in origin, and that Jessel may have been the first to toss vodka and tomato juice together. But it was Petiot, who, while at the St. Regis's Nat King Cole Bar in New York City—not Paris—turned it into the generously seasoned drink we know today.

The Bloody Mary has, of course, gone through many reincarnations with a whole mess of different ingredients. A Smirnoff campaign from the 1970s features a simple drink called the Bloodhound, which called for 1½ ounces of Smirnoff, 3 ounces of tomato juice, and ½ ounce of dry sherry. Today, contemporary British riffs call for a splash of fino or, in the case of the Bloody Bishop, splitting the booze 1:1 sherry to vodka.

1½ ounces vodka

½ ounce fino sherry

4 ounces Bloody Mary Mix (see below)

¾ ounce lemon juice

Garnish: 1 lemon wedge, 1 cubed piece of manchego cheese, 1 cubed piece of dried chorizo, 1 white anchovy, 1 pickled piparra pepper, or whatever fits on a cocktail skewer

ADD ALL THE INGREDIENTS but the garnishes to a mixing glass. Add ice and lightly shake. Strain over cubed ice into a Collins glass. Garnish with the lemon, manchego, chorizo, anchovy, and piparra pepper. Serve with a straw.

BLOODY MARY MIX

2 cups tomato juice

1 teaspoon hot paprika

2 teaspoons sherry vinegar

2 teaspoons Worcestershire sauce

¼ teaspoon cracked pepper

¼ teaspoon salt

2 pinches of cayenne, or to taste

¼ teaspoon celery salt

COMBINE ALL THE INGREDIENTS and store, covered in the refrigerator, for up to 3 days. You'll have enough mix for 4 drinks.

KOJO COCKTAIL

Derek Brown, Washington, D.C.'s poster boy for sherry, first created this drink for the beloved D.C. radio journalist Kojo Nnamdi on the fifteen-year anniversary of WAMU's *The Kojo Nnamdi Show*. Brown drew influences for the drink from his conversations with Nnamdi and from the journalist's roots, adding Velvet Falernum—a spice- and lime-infused staple in Caribbean drinks—as a nod to his home country of Guyana. The drink was first served at a dinner in honor of Nnamdi and can still be ordered off-menu at Brown's bars, Mockingbird Hill and The Passenger.

1 ounce dry gin

1 ounce dry oloroso

½ ounce Velvet Falernum

½ ounce lemon juice

¼ ounce simple syrup (1:1 sugar:water)

1 dash aromatic bitters, preferably Angostura

Garnish: grapefruit peel

ADD ALL THE INGREDIENTS but the garnish to a mixing glass. Add ice, shake, and strain into a cocktail glass. Garnish with the grapefruit peel.

FERDINAND AND ISABELLA'S PUNCH

The many variations on the art and architecture of the flowing bowl make punch the category of drink that transcends season. Yet when I think of punch in all of its (generally) high-proof glory, I think of winter. And what do I dream of in winter? Beaches. And rum.

In most Spanish-speaking Caribbean countries and in Latin America, the solera system is often employed in the production of rum, making it sherry's hard-drinking next of kin. Zacapa 23, a Guatemalan rum aged at high altitude via the solera system, is one of the finest rums on the market—bold and spicy, but lean thanks to its cooler aging locale. Both it and the oloroso in this drink have notes of citrus peel, which is echoed in bergamot-tinged Earl Grey tea and then Caribbean-ized with a strong dose of Angostura bitters and Velvet Falernum. ··· SERVES 16

2 lemons

⅔ cup sugar

3 Earl Grey tea bags

1 (750ml) bottle Ron Zacapa 23 Sistema Solera rum

1 (750ml) bottle Lustau Don Nuño oloroso

1 cup lemon juice

1 cup lime juice

2 teaspoons Angostura bitters

1 cup Velvet Falernum

Garnish: lemon and lime wheels, nutmeg, mint sprigs

PEEL THE LEMONS, taking care to avoid as much of the bitter white pith as possible. In a large bowl, combine the sugar with the lemon peels, then lightly muddle and let sit for 20 minutes to allow the citrus oils to infuse with the sugar. Boil 3 cups of water and steep the tea bags in it for 3 minutes. Set aside to cool slightly.

To the bowl, add the rum, sherry, lemon and lime juices, bitters, and Velvet Falernum. Stir to combine. Add the tea and let cool to room temperature. If serving immediately, add several large cubes to chill. Add lime and lemon wheels and grate some nutmeg over the punch. Ladle into punch cups over ice, garnish with mint sprigs, and serve. If making ahead, bottle and refrigerate. When serving, pour over ice and add grated nutmeg, a lemon or lime wheel, and mint sprigs to garnish.

EAST INDIA NEGRONI

This drink, from Jim Meehan of PDT, really began with the rum. More specifically, it began with Joseph Banks—an eighteenth-century explorer and Captain Cook's sidekick on his first voyage. The 5-Island rum used in this drink is a tribute to Banks and Cook's maiden voyage, as is the East India, an old-school style of sherry that was originally matured in the same way as early madeira (via tumultuous sea voyage on masted ships). "The rum takes its namesake from a dude who would've been on the same ship that the East India sherry would've traveled in," says Meehan.

The interplay of the subtle funk of the rum with the raisiny woodiness of Lustau's East India sherry makes for a cocktail that drinks like a Negroni best consumed near the equator.

2 ounces Banks 5-Island rum

¾ ounce Campari

¾ ounce Lustau East India sherry

Garnish: orange peel

ADD ALL THE INGREDIENTS but the garnish to a mixing glass, then add ice. Stir and strain into a rocks glass with one large ice cube. Garnish with the orange peel.

7

SHERRY AT THE TABLE

Tapas are said to have originated in Andalusia. And like most of the region's accredited firsts—and there are several—tales abound on exactly when, where, and why they came to be. But two stories tend to be repeated with the greatest frequency.

One includes a king, and either heartburn or a sandstorm; the other, a gesture of hospitality and a fruit fly problem. Both are generally adjusted for a dubious inclusion of the storyteller's relative or something that links a certain producer's wines to the first tapa. Growing up with a Spanish grandfather on one side and an Italian one on the other, I am no stranger to such embellishments.

But more importantly, both claim a common impetus: sherry.

The first tale concerns King Alfonso X and dates back to the 1200s. After directed by a doctor to take small bites of food between sips of wine—presumably to curb heartburn or maybe just inebriety—the king enacted a public decree stating that all bars must serve small bites of food to help mitigate public drunkenness.

The second King Alfonso story involves a windy day along the Andalusian coast and a sandy glass of sherry. On a journey through Cádiz the king apparently encountered a savvy tavern owner who offered him a slice of *jamón* to cover the top of his glass amidst what sounds like an afternoon run-in with the levante. When he ordered a second glass, he requested a slice of *jamón*, which he referred to as a *tapa,* a word derived from the verb *tapar,* which means "to cover."

The more common story, though, is that tapas originated six hundred years later, in the nineteenth century, when bars and taverns used to keep saucers over glasses of sherry to both keep the flies out and preserve the wine's aroma. (In other words: same idea, no king.) On top of the saucer, barkeepers would generally offer a small slice of *jamón,* either alone or on top or a piece of bread, as a welcoming gesture. This, as it's told, eventually evolved into a collection of small dishes meant to be consumed in bars, with wine.

Whatever the story, tapas are now part of the international dining vocabulary. And while in the minds of most diners, Spain is still connected to the concept of tapas, the word now refers more to the size of a plate and less to a culture of eating. But it's truly the latter.

As in most parts of Spain, dining out in Andalusia is essentially defined by sustained grazing. Going for tapas means jumping from one bar to the next, enjoying what you believe to be the specialty of each bar before moving on to something new. When in Sanlúcar de Barrameda, it's crispy *tortillitas de camarones* at Casa Balbino, *papas aliñas* at Barbiana, and fried *salmonetes* (red mullet) and blistered green peppers at Bar Navarro—all with a *copita* (or more) of manzanilla at each, and probably a beer in between to reset. The Spanish call this *tapeo*, a noun that essentially translates to "tapas crawl." It is, quite literally, a movable feast.

After eating my way through the Sherry Triangle, I'd throw my chips in on the kingless origin tale. It hints not only at the generosity of the people when it comes to hospitality—Andalusia remains one of the last regions in Spain to still offer a tapa as a free accompaniment to your glass of sherry, after all—but also to the function of sherry in their cuisine. The two are inextricable. And not by decree, but by design.

The cooking of Andalusia is varied—reflecting its role as a cultural revolving door for more than three millennia. The eight-century rule of the Moors had a profound influence on the architecture, art, and music of the region—and on the food. To this day, many of the ingredients brought to this part of Spain by the Moors—almonds, spices, saffron, oranges, artichokes—still dominate Andalusian cooking.

First, though, there is a simple, three-pillar foundation—which is shared by many other Mediterranean cuisines—upon which most of Andalusia's cooking is based: bread, garlic, and olive oil. This foundation is evident in the region's most famous dish: gazpacho, which in its various forms—notably *ajo blanco* and *salmorejo*—epitomizes both the bounty and the simplicity of Andalusian cooking.

The region is also famous for its seafood—its *costa de la luz* (or "Coast of Light," as the coastline is called) is teeming with bluefin tuna, squid, sardines, anchovies, and *langostinos* so sweet they could double as dessert. And while the sea rules, braised rabbit, oxtail, offal (specifically tripe and kidneys), lamb, and wild gamebirds also find their way onto the table in memorable ways.

But no meat is more important in Andalusia than cured *jamón*. The town of Jabugo, in the Andalusian province of Huelva, is home to some of the most prized producers of *jamón ibérico*, while Trevelez, located on the southern slope of the Sierra Nevada mountain range, is one of the most well-known towns for the production of *jamón serrano* (see page 244). In short, they've got their bases covered.

The recipes in this chapter are a collection of snapshots—dishes I associate with sherry or with Andalusia that have colored in my impressions of the region and the wines. Some of them are adaptations of dishes I've eaten at specific bars or restaurants, others are from chefs here in the United States who've drawn inspiration from Andalusia and who have shaped my experience with Spanish food Stateside. They are all tapas, and almost all of them call for either sherry or sherry vinegar—or they are simply dishes I can't imagine eating without a glass of sherry.

TORTILLITAS DE CAMARONES EL FARO

There are few tapas more synonymous with coastal Andalusia—a place with a deep love for frying seafood—than these paper-thin fritters studded with *camarones de Cádiz*. In Sanlúcar, they are a staple, and getting to know the spectrum of *tortillitas* here—from rich and chewy to cracker thin—is a delicious pleasure.

Many believe these *tortillitas* originated in the nineteenth century in the city of San Fernando, just south of Cádiz, where the tiny shrimp proliferate in the marshes and salt ponds along the shore. But the writer and gastronomist Manolo Ruiz Torres suggests a much earlier birth—perhaps dating back as far as the sixteenth or seventeenth century—and a shared parentage with Italy. This recipe is adapted from Fernándo Córdoba, the chef at the Michelin-starred restaurant El Faro, which has locations in both El Puerto and Cádiz. It remains home to the finest *tortillitas* I've tasted.

Predictably, *camarones de Cádiz* are difficult to get your hands on Stateside, but if you have an Asian market near you, dried shrimp are a fine substitute (grab some dried seaweed while you're there). And, of course, there's nothing wrong with regular shrimp chopped into small cubes. They are delicious every which way. · · · SERVES 6

1½ cups all-purpose flour

2 cups water

1½ teaspoons salt (or less if using seaweed)

3 tablespoons chopped parsley

¾ cup sliced green onions, white and pale green parts only

½ cup (about 1¾ ounces) chopped kombu seaweed (optional)

1½ cups chopped raw shrimp (about 12 ounces) or 1 cup whole dried baby shrimp

Olive oil

Garnish: lemon wedges

IN A BOWL, combine the flour with the water and stir. Add the salt, parsley, green onions, seaweed, and shrimp. When all the ingredients are incorporated, the batter should be similar to the consistency of crepe batter—just thin enough to pour.

In a frying pan over medium-high heat, add about ½ inch of oil. When the oil is very hot (test by dropping in a small spoonful of batter in the oil; it should sizzle), add the batter to the oil in 1-tablespoon portions, taking care not to crowd the pan and frying in batches if necessary. Cook, flipping once halfway through, until golden brown and crispy at the edges, about 3 minutes.

With a spatula, remove the *tortillitas* from the pan onto a plate lined with paper towels.

Transfer to a small platter and serve hot with lemon wedges on the side.

CAZÓN EN ADOBO

Adobo and escabeche are the two most common types of acidic marinades used in Spanish cooking, and their use in preserving seafood dates back to antiquity. In Andalusia, adobo shows up most famously in this dish: *cazón*, or dogfish, is cubed and marinated in a mixture of olive oil, sherry vinegar, garlic, and spices. It's then dredged in flour, quickly fried, and served hot with a squeeze of lemon and a (mandatory, in my book) glass of fino or manzanilla to balance out the tangy, decadent fish. · · · SERVES 6

1½ pounds swordfish or monkfish fillet, skin removed

Olive oil

⅓ cup sherry vinegar

1 tablespoon water

3 cloves garlic, chopped

¼ teaspoon smoked Spanish paprika

¼ teaspoon cumin

1 teaspoon oregano

2 bay leaves

¼ teaspoon ground black pepper

⅓ teaspoon salt

Flour

Garnish: smoked paprika, chopped parsley, lemon wedges

CUT THE SWORDFISH into 1-inch cubes and place in a nonreactive bowl. In a separate bowl, mix together 3 tablespoons of the oil and the vinegar, water, garlic, paprika, cumin, oregano, bay, pepper, and salt. Pour this mixture over the fish, turning to coat each piece. Cover with plastic wrap and refrigerate overnight.

When ready to cook, drain the fish well and blot the pieces to remove excess marinade. Put the flour in a shallow bowl and set aside.

In a 12-inch pan over medium-high heat, heat ¼ inch of oil until shimmering but not quite smoking. Dredge the fish pieces in the flour, shaking off any excess, and fry in batches, turning to brown each side, until crisp and golden, about 1½ minutes per side. As the pieces finish cooking, remove them to a plate lined with paper towels to drain.

Transfer to a bowl or small platter, dust with a little paprika and sprinkle with parsley, and serve hot with lemon wedges on the side.

SALMOREJO

When most people think of Andalusia they think of gazpacho, a cold soup of tomatoes, cucumber, peppers, and garlic. It's like liquid summer. *Salmorejo* riffs on traditional gazpacho: it's a thicker, smoother version from Córdoba, which is just over a hundred miles from Jerez as the crow flies. It's great as a soup, but leftovers are a reason to rejoice, as *salmorejo* is easily repurposed as a sauce or vinaigrette. ··· SERVES 6 TO 8

2 cups cubed and smashed day-old bread

4 cups chopped ripe tomatoes (about 8 medium)

2½ tablespoons sherry vinegar

1 clove garlic, minced

¼ teaspoon smoked Spanish paprika

2 teaspoons salt

1 cup plus 1 teaspoon olive oil

1½ to 2 ounces Serrano ham, chopped

3 hard-boiled eggs, chopped

2 slices toasted bread, chopped

IN A LARGE BOWL combine the cubed bread, tomatoes, sherry vinegar, garlic, paprika, and salt and stir to combine. Set the mixture aside and allow the bread to soften in the liquid, about 15 minutes. If the mixture seems dry, add a couple tablespoons of warm water.

Pour the mixture into a blender or food processor and puree on low speed, gradually adding the 1 cup of olive oil. (The mixture will turn bright orange as the oil is introduced.) Transfer to a large bowl, cover, and refrigerate for about 2 hours.

In a 12-inch skillet over medium-high heat, add the remaining 1 teaspoon of oil and heat until shimmering but not quite smoking. Add the ham and fry, turning once halfway through, until crispy, about 3 minutes. As the pieces finish cooking, transfer them to a paper towel–lined plate to drain.

When ready to serve, ladle the *salmorejo* into small bowls or cups and top with the chopped egg, crispy ham, and bread.

CUMIN- AND PAPRIKA-SPICED MARCONA ALMONDS

Almonds were brought to Spain by the Moors, and they've featured in Andalusian cuisine ever since. Typically they are used as a thickener for sauces and, most famously, as the base of *ajo blanco*. Whole Marcona almonds are roasted with sweet or hot smoked paprika—I prefer to use sweet paprika, introduce a little heat via cayenne, and round it out with cumin and salt. In the event of a crippling Marcona almond shortage, regular blanched almonds will do the trick. ··· MAKES 3 CUPS

1 egg white

1½ teaspoons salt

1 teaspoon plus ⅛ teaspoon cumin, for dusting

1 teaspoon plus ⅛ teaspoon sweet or smoked Spanish paprika, for dusting

¼ teaspoon cayenne

3 cups blanched Marcona almonds

PREHEAT THE OVEN to 350°F. Line a large baking sheet with parchment paper. In a bowl, whisk together the egg white, salt, 1 teaspoon of cumin, 1 teaspoon of paprika, and the cayenne. Add the almonds and toss to coat. Spread the almonds out evenly on the prepared baking sheet and roast until golden brown, 20 to 25 minutes, shaking the pan halfway through. Transfer to a plate to cool for about 30 minutes.

In a small bowl, combine the remaining ⅛ teaspoon of cumin and the remaining ⅛ teaspoon of paprika. Sprinkle this mixture over the cooled nuts. Store in a sealed container for up to 2 weeks.

PAPAS ALIÑAS

Papas aliñas translates to "dressed potatoes" or, simply, potato salad. But this is just about the dreamiest potato salad there ever was: warm potatoes tossed in sherry vinegar, olive oil, salt, and onion and then draped ceremoniously with strips of tuna belly packed in oil.

This dish abounds in Sanlúcar, where the finest potatoes in the region are grown in the sandy *arenas* soils near the sea; in my opinion it reaches its height at Bar Barbiana, a tiny jewelbox tavern with ample patio space on the town's main square. While their exact recipe remains a mystery, I was offered two key bits of advice: make sure the potatoes are warm when you dress them, and always, always serve them at room temperature. · · · SERVES 4

4 yellow potatoes

5 to 6 tablespoons sherry vinegar

6 tablespoons extra-virgin olive oil

1 yellow onion, coarsely chopped

¼ cup chopped parsley

1 to 2 tablespoons salt

1 (6-ounce) jar olive oil–packed tuna belly, preferably Tonnino

PLACE THE POTATOES in a large pot and add enough water to cover by 1 inch. Bring the water to a boil over high heat and cook the potatoes, uncovered, for about 20 to 25 minutes or until fork tender.

Drain the potatoes and set aside until cool enough to handle, but still warm, about 10 minutes.

In a small bowl whisk the sherry vinegar and olive oil until combined, then set aside.

Peel the potatoes and cut into 1-inch cubes, then add to a large mixing bowl. Add the onion, parsley, and salt to taste, then drizzle the sherry vinegar and oil mixture over the top. Stir to combine, ensuring that potatoes are evenly coated.

Transfer the potatoes to small bowls and top with a few pieces of tuna belly. Serve at room temperature.

THE MANY CURED HAMS OF SPAIN

IN THE SHERRY TRIANGLE, WHEN YOU'RE feeling under the weather, you drink flor. "Flor is like penicillin," Miguel Gutiérrez of Hidalgo—La Gitana said to me as he scooped some of the veil, in all of its pond-scum glory, into my glass. There's also a special Andalusian cure for sadness, boredom, hunger, anxiety, or any number of common ailments: it's called *jamón*. Ham is a religion in Spain—a source of joy and salvation within the Spanish diet. And there are few things more harmonious than a glass of fino and a slice of ham. If there were a special Spanish password to heaven, it would be "salty-nutty-fatty-sweet"—and *jamón ibérico* would be your ticket in.

In Andalusia, as in most parts of Spain, you will encounter a variety of different types of *jamón*. Their differences are based on three things: the breed of the pig, the pig's diet, and the cut of meat that is used.

Jamón Ibérico

The production of *jamón ibérico* is strictly governed within four DOs, and regulations cover everything from the pigs' diet to how they are kept and killed. By law a pig used for *jamón ibérico* must be at least 50 percent Iberian pig, referred to colloquially as *pata negra* ("black hoof"). As of 2013, the pigs used to make *jamón* are further subdivided according to their diet and breed into three main grades: *jamón*

ibérico bellota de campo, jamón ibérico cebo de campo, and *jamón ibérico cebo intensivo.*

JAMÓN IBÉRICO BELLOTA DE CAMPO: This is the most prized of all of the Spanish hams, noted for its funky, nutty sweetness and high fat content. In order to be classified as such, the pigs must spend at least the last three months of their lives feeding on acorns (*bellotas*) in the *dehesa* (a forested pastureland containing cork trees and holm oaks). In Andalusia, these areas are located in Huelva (DO Jamón de Huelva) and, to a lesser extent, near Córdoba (DO Los Pedroches). The period during which the pigs graze on acorns is called "montanera," which is when they gain about half their weight, consuming upward of twenty pounds of acorns and adding more than one pound of body weight per day. This rapid weight gain, coupled with the flavor that the acorns impart to the pig's body fat, is what makes *bellota* so prized. And because the quality of the ham largely depends on the size of the acorn harvest, *bellota* hams can be as vintage-dependant as wine, which further drives up the perceived value and price. As of 2014, the percentage of Iberian (*pata negra*) breed must be specified and coded by color for *bellota* hams. A black label indicates a 100 percent pure-bred Iberian pig, while red is not pure bred, but must specify the percentage Iberian pig on the label.

JAMÓN IBÉRICO CEBO DE CAMPO: This is ham from free-range, grain-fed pigs that must be at least 50 percent Iberian. These hams can be recognized by their green label.

JAMÓN IBÉRICO CEBO INTENSIVO: This is the lowest quality ham, sourced from commercially raised, grain-fed pigs. They must be 50 percent Iberian, and the ham's label is white.

Jamón Serrano

Regular *jamón serrano* ("mountain ham") comes from white pigs (Duroc or Land-race breed) instead of the black Iberian pig. While it does not have DO status, it is regulated by the Consorcio del Jamón Serrano Español and, if compliant, is protected by the EU's Tradition Specialty Guaranteed (T.S.G.) certification. Histori-cally, *serrano* came from mountainous regions, where the moderate climate allowed the cured hams to age slowly. Today, hams labeled *jamón serrano* can be made anywhere in Spain (which is not true for *jamon ibérico*). However, the best *jamón serrano* still comes from the high-altitude, mountainous towns of Trevélez in Andalusia and Teruel in Aragón.

JAMÓN DE TERUEL AND JAMÓN DE TREVÉLEZ: Both of these high-quality *serrano* hams are protected by different regulating organizations, and both are prized for their high-altitude locales.

Cuts of Jamón and Sausages

JAMÓN: The gold standard, cured from the hind leg of the pig. *Jamón de bellota de campo* represents the highest quality level for this cut.

PALETA: Cured from the front leg and shoulder of the pig, *paleta* is not as moist and tender as *jamón*, but still a fine value. *Paleta de bellota de campo* represents the highest quality level for this cut.

LOMO: The loin of the pig, which, when dry-cured, is called *lomo embuchado*. This lean but flavorful cut is typically seasoned with paprika. The cut's highest calling is *lomo embuchado ibérico de bellota*, a more marbled, nutty loin from acorn-fed black Iberian pigs.

SALCHICHÓN: A relative of French *saucisson* or Italian *salami*, this summer sausage is flavored with garlic, salt, pepper, and various spices, such as clove or oregano. It's typically made with pork and the higher-end versions with *ibérico de bellota*.

CHORIZO: A category of spiced Spanish sausage that comes in a whole kaleidoscope of flavors and preparations, from hot to smoked, thick to thin, hard to soft. The three pillars are pork, garlic, and paprika (which gives *chorizo* its familiar color). The highest classification is *chorizo ibérico de bellota*.

MORCILLA: This famous blood sau-sage contains pig's blood and rice, and is flavored with paprika, garlic, and onion. Try *morcilla* pan-fried and in stews.

ALBÓNDIGAS AL JEREZ

In the three sherry towns, seafood certainly dominates most tables, but there are a few meat dishes that are ubiquitous in the bars here. Tripe served with chickpeas and *morcilla* in a rich tomato sauce is one of my go-tos when the temperature drops; so is oxtail braised in oloroso into a rich, nutty mess of meat. But *albóndigas*, or meatballs, are the most consistent staple. The sauce varies from bar to bar: some taverns serve them in a gravy of sherry, chicken stock, and olive oil; others whip up a sauce of amontillado and tomato with a dash of cream to thicken.

I love both these sauces, and for both recipes, a dry oloroso works if you don't have amontillado. ··· SERVES 6

12 ounces ground beef

12 ounces ground pork

1 clove garlic, minced

¼ cup chopped parsley

½ cup fine bread crumbs

1 egg

2 teaspoons salt

1 teaspoon sweet Spanish paprika

½ teaspoon hot Spanish paprika

Black pepper

2 tablespoons olive oil

Salsa de Jerez *or* Salsa de Jerez con Tomate (see opposite)

IN A LARGE BOWL, combine the beef, pork, garlic, parsley, bread crumbs, egg, salt, both paprikas, and a few grinds of black pepper. Mix thoroughly with your hands and shape into 18 to 20 golf ball–size meatballs, placing on a baking sheet covered with wax paper as you shape them.

In a large frying pan, heat the olive oil over medium-high heat. Add the meatballs to the pan in batches and brown on both sides to create a crust, about 2 to 3 minutes on each side.

Remove the meatballs from the pan and place them on a plate lined with paper towels to soak up excess oil.

Finish the meatballs in the sauce of your choice.

SALSA DE JEREZ

4 tablespoons olive oil

1 cup minced yellow onion

1 clove garlic, minced

1 teaspoon sweet Spanish paprika

1 tablespoon flour

½ cup dry amontillado

1 cup chicken broth

½ teaspoon salt

Garnish: lemon wedges, chopped parsley

IN A MEDIUM-SIZE POT over medium heat, heat 2 tablespoons of the olive oil. Add the onion and garlic and sweat until translucent, about 5 minutes.

Add the paprika, flour, and remaining 2 tablespoons of olive oil and stir well to combine. Let simmer for 2 minutes; the sauce should have the consistency of a roux. Stir in the sherry and chicken broth and bring to a simmer, then turn the heat to low and simmer for 10 minutes. Season with salt to taste.

Add the meatballs and stir to coat them in the sauce. Cook for another 10 minutes over low heat, adjusting the heat to maintain a rolling simmer, to cook the meatballs through. If the sauce gets too dry, stir in a bit of chicken broth.

Spoon the meatballs and sauce into a large serving bowl. Garnish with lemon wedges and a dusting of chopped parsley; serve with toothpicks for spearing the meatballs.

··· — ◦•◦ — ···

SALSA DE JEREZ CON TOMATE

2 tablespoons olive oil

½ cup minced yellow onion

1 clove garlic, minced

1 (28-ounce) can tomato puree

½ cup dry amontillado

¼ cup cream

½ teaspoon salt

Black pepper

Garnish: chopped parsley

IN A MEDIUM-SIZE POT over medium heat, heat the olive oil. Add the onion and garlic and sweat until translucent, about 5 minutes. Stir in the tomato puree and sherry and turn the heat to medium-low. Simmer for 10 minutes.

Add the meatballs and stir to coat them in the sauce. Cook for 15 minutes. Stir in the cream, salt, and a few grinds of black pepper and cook for another 5 to 10 minutes to thicken the sauce and finish cooking the meatballs.

Spoon the meatballs and sauce into a large serving bowl. Garnish with chopped parsley and serve with toothpicks for spearing the meatballs.

GARBANZOS CON ESPINACAS

For chef Alexandra Raij—who, along with her husband, Eder Montero, owns three of New York's most beloved Spanish restaurants, Txikito, El Quinto Pino, and La Vara—this dish *is* Andalusia. "It's a simple dish, but there's something so noble about the care it takes to make it well," she says. She first encountered it at El Rincóncillo, Sevilla's oldest bar, which was founded in 1670. The bar, one of the rare species beloved by tourists and locals alike, looks as though it hasn't changed all that much since the seventeenth century. It's dark and cavernous—clearly constructed as a pre–air conditioning refuge from Sevilla's evil summer sun. This simple chickpea, spinach, and bread stew has long been one of the bar's specialties, and no matter whether it is hot outside, whether it the long bartop is always littered with steaming plates of *garbanzos con espinacas.*

It took Raij longer than she expected to master the creamy texture and richness that makes the dish so addicting, but once she did, it became a staple at her restaurants; and a dish that, she says, "will follow me wherever I go." ··· SERVES 6

8 ounces dried chickpeas

1 onion, halved

1 carrot, peeled

1 head garlic, plus 2 smashed cloves

4 tablespoons kosher salt, plus more to taste

½ cup extra-virgin olive oil

2 bunches spinach, triple washed

½ cup panko bread crumbs

1 tablespoon smoked Spanish paprika

1 teaspoon cumin

⅛ teaspoon cayenne pepper

Garnish: smoked paprika, good Spanish olive oil

IN A MEDIUM-SIZED POT, combine the chickpeas, onion, carrot, head of garlic, and salt, then add enough cold water to cover the chickpeas and vegetables by at least 4 inches. Bring to a boil over high heat, then reduce to a simmer and cook until the chickpeas are creamy inside, about 2 to 2½ hours. Drain the chickpeas, reserving the cooking liquid. Discard the vegetables.

In a separate pot, heat 3 tablespoons of the olive oil over medium heat and, in 2 batches, wilt the spinach. Remove the spinach from the pot and drain it well. Chop and set aside.

Drain the liquid from the pot and wipe it clean. Over medium-low heat, add the remaining 5 tablespoons of olive oil and the 2 smashed garlic cloves. Stir until the garlic becomes golden, about 5 minutes, and remove the garlic cloves. Add the panko to the garlic-infused oil and stir until evenly browned, about 5 minutes.

Add the paprika, cumin, and cayenne, and stir. Add 2 cups of the reserved chickpea cooking broth, turn the heat up to high, and whisk vigorously to break the panko down. Cook until the bread crumbs are dry and starting to stick to the pan, about 10 minutes, before adding another 2 cups of broth. Whisk well, making sure to scrape up any crumbs sticking to the bottom of the pot so that the sauce has no lumps. Cook for another 10 minutes, stirring often.

The sauce should reach a point where it is smooth and creamy, like a roux. Continue tasting the sauce as it breaks down; if it reaches a good balance of salty and spicy flavors but still needs more liquid, add water instead of more chickpea broth. When the sauce is smooth and seasoned to your taste, add the chickpeas and spinach back in and heat through, about 3 minutes.

Season with more salt if needed and serve hot, dusted with paprika and drizzled with good Spanish olive oil.

BRAISED CHICKEN AND CLAMS SOFRITO

Ever since Casa Mono opened ten years ago, I've been warming a seat at the kitchen counter, watching the chefs maneuver around an open kitchen barely bigger than a Halal cart, pumping out some of the best Spanish food in New York. Chef Anthony Sasso has, for years, managed this team and been responsible for some of the restaurant's most innovative dishes.

This is his spin on a simple dish of clams cooked in sherry that he had while in Sanlúcar de Barrameda in 2007. While it'd be delicious sans chicken, it gets the "Sasso treatment" via the addition of chicken thighs braised with the clams and sherry—a common Spanish and Portuguese version of surf and turf. · · · SERVES 4

Olive oil

2 boneless, skin-on chicken thighs, each cut into 4 pieces

Salt

Flour

1 white onion, finely chopped

1 carrot, peeled and finely chopped

1 stalk celery, finely chopped

2 cloves garlic, thinly sliced

2 fresh bay leaves

1 (8-ounce) jar plum tomato sauce

1 cup chicken stock

1 cup amontillado

2 dozen cockles (or manila clams if unavailable), scrubbed

Garnish: plenty of chopped parsley, sherry vinegar

SET A HEAVY-BOTTOMED pot over medium heat and add enough olive oil to coat the pan. Season the chicken pieces all over with salt and dredge in flour; shake off the excess. Evenly brown each piece in the oil; remove and set aside.

Add the onion, carrot, celery, garlic, and bay leaves to the pot. Season with salt and lower the heat to medium. Sweat until the vegetables are soft and slightly caramelized.

Add the tomato sauce, chicken stock, and amontillado. Simmer for about 30 minutes uncovered over medium heat.

Transfer the sauce to a blender in batches and puree until smooth. Return the pureed sauce to the heat along with the browned pieces of chicken.

Cover and cook for another 30 minutes, until the chicken is tender and the sauce thickens to a gravylike consistency. (You may need to add a little water to the sauce if it gets too dry.) During the last 5 minutes of cooking, add the clams, and cover the pot until they have all opened; discard any that do not open.

Garnish with chopped parsley, stir in a splash of vinegar, and serve.

SHERRY VINEGAR

FOR AS LONG AS WINE HAS BEEN MADE in the Sherry Triangle, so too has vinegar. Just not on purpose. In the beginning, the part of the bodega reserved for vinegar aging was a room full of accidents—barrels that, after fermentation, contained high levels of acetic acid bacteria. Because this bacteria (good bacteria, unless you ask wine) can contaminate other casks in its vicinity, the barrels must be removed from their respective soleras and set aside.

While sherry wine vinegar has been used in Andalusian cooking for centuries, it wasn't until well into the nineteenth century that it became a commercial product known outside of the region. This is thanks primarily to the French food industry's undying thirst for it: today, France remains the largest consumer (Spain included) of sherry vinegar.

As of 1995, sherry vinegar has been protected by its own *Denominación de Origen: Vinagre de Jerez*; and as of 2000, its production has been regulated by sherry's Consejo Regulador.

While some barrels still do deviate by accident, modern sherry vinegar production is much more deliberate than it once was. Most of the time the dry wines are purposefully chosen for vinegar production and then inoculated with the acetic acid bacteria. The Consejo Regulador dictates that these dry wines must be of the quality suitable for the production of sherry wine and must be sourced from within the Jerez-Xérès-Sherry DO.

The vinegars are, like sherry wine, matured via the solera system and need good air circulation. As such, vinegar barrels are only filled to 500 of the 600-liter capacity and very loosely sealed. This also oxidizes the vinegar, giving it the intense, nutty tones that have come to define sherry vinegar.

Stylistically, sherry vinegar falls somewhere in between a regular wine vinegar and balsamic vinegar. But as with balsamic vinegar, the fact that the aging barrels are only partially filled leads to evaporation and concentration—and in the case of older vinegars, high levels of acetic acid. All this is to say that the stuff is intense. Unlike balsamic vinegar, which has high levels of sugar to buffer the acid, sherry vinegar is lean and mean—like the dry Riesling of vinegars.

In order for vinegars produced in the region to bear the *Vinagre de Jerez* stamp of approval, they must adhere to one of several requirements:

VINAGRE DE JEREZ: a minimum six months of aging

VINAGRE DE JEREZ RESERVA: a minimum two years of aging

VINAGRE DE JEREZ GRAN RESERVA: a minimum ten years of aging

There are also two types of semi-sweet vinegars, which vary depending on the type of wine used:

VINAGRE DE JEREZ AL PEDRO XIMÉNEZ: vinegar to which PX wine is added

VINAGRE DE JEREZ AL MOSCATEL: vinegar to which moscatel wine is added

HUEVOS A LA FLAMENCA

Huevos a la flamenca (flamenco eggs) is one of the most ubiquitous dishes in Andalusia. A sort of meat lover's *shakshuka*, the dish has many variations, depending on the type of vegetable used and whether it has potatoes or beans. I use asparagus tips or peas when they're in season and chickpeas when they're not, but feel free to get creative here. Just be sure to keep an eye on the eggs: if your oven temperature is unreliable, you'll need to watch carefully to make sure you don't overcook them, since the best part of this dish is the dénouement of runny yolk meeting *morcilla*. ··· SERVES 4

2 tablespoons olive oil

2 (5-ounce) chorizo sausages (about 4 inches each), chopped

2 (5-ounce) morcilla sausages (about 4 inches each), chopped

1 small yellow onion, chopped (about 1 cup)

2 cloves garlic, minced

1 teaspoon sweet Spanish paprika

1 (28-ounce) can chopped tomatoes

Salt

2 marinated piquillo peppers, sliced

¼ cup fresh peas

8 eggs

Toasted bread, for serving

PREHEAT THE OVEN TO 350°F.

In a large saucepan over medium heat, add the olive oil. Add the chorizo and *morcilla* and sear until lightly browned, about 4 minutes. Set aside. Reduce the heat to low, add the onion to the pan, and sweat until translucent, about 5 to 7 minutes. Add the garlic and paprika and cook for another 4 minutes, stirring occasionally. Add the tomatoes, salt, and peppers and simmer over low heat for 10 minutes. Add the *morcilla* and chorizo back to the pan and continue cooking until the sauce thickens, about 7 minutes.

Prepare an ice-water bath. In a medium saucepan, bring 4 cups of salted water to a boil, then add the fresh peas and boil for 3 minutes until bright green but still crisp. Drain the peas and transfer them to the ice-water bath.

Lightly oil 4 *cazuelas* or 6-inch oven-safe earthenware dishes. Add the peas to the tomato sauce and stir to combine. Fill each cazuela about half full with the mixture, then crack two eggs overtop. Bake in the oven for 10 to 15 minutes, until the whites of the eggs are just set but the yolks are still runny. Take care not to overcook the eggs.

Drizzle olive oil over top and serve with toasted bread.

WHERE TO FIND SHERRY

WHERE TO EAT IN THE SHERRY TRIANGLE

El Faro del Puerto ($$$; tasting menu: 49 euros)
Ctra. de Fuentebravía, km 0.5
11500 El Puerto de Santa María
+34 956 87 09 52
Don't miss: *Tortillitas de camarones, marinada con lubina, calamares, arroz negro.*

Aponiente ($$$$; full tasting menu, 70 to 110 euros)
Calle Puerto Escondido, 6
11500 El Puerto de Santa María
+34 956 85 18 70

El Pescaito ($)
Calle de la Atalaya, 9
11500 El Puerto de Santa María
+34 956 85 04 56
Don't miss: *Salmonetes fritos, zamburiñas* (scallops), *langostinos, huevos de choco* (cuttlefish eggs).

Casa Bigote ($$$) and **Tavern** ($$)
Calle Pórtico Bajo de Guía, 10
11540 Sanlúcar de Barrameda
+34 956 36 26 96
Don't miss: *Langostinos, corvina con salsa tártara, almejas a la marinera, atún mechado, acedias fritas.*

Bar Navarro ($)
Calle Menacho, 26
11540 Sanlúcar de Barrameda
Don't miss: *Boquerones fritos, salmonetes, acedias, pimientos fritos, ensalada de atun.*

Bar Barbiana ($)
Calle Ancha, 2
11540 Sanlúcar de Barrameda
+34 956 36 28 94
Don't miss: *papas aliñas.*

Casa Balbino ($)
Plaza del Cabildo, 14
11540 Sanlúcar de Barrameda
+34 956 36 05 13
Don't miss: *Tortillitas de camarones, ortiguillas, berenjenas fritas con langostinos*

Bar La Gitana ($)
Plaza del Cabildo, 15
11540 Sanlúcar de Barrameda
Don't miss: *Ortiguillas fritos, sopa de galera, raya a la naranja agria.*

Bar La Moderna ($)
Calle Larga, 67
11403 Jerez de la Frontera
+34 956 32 13 79
Don't miss: *Papas aliñas,* stew with tripe and garbanzos.

Albalá ($$)
Conjunto Residencial Valdespino, 6
11403 Jerez de la Frontera
+34 956 34 64 88
Don't miss: Stew with *morcilla,* tripe, and garbanzos; *croquetas de rabo de toro.*

Bar Arturo ($)
Calle Guita, 9
11408 Jerez de la Frontera
+34 956 33 00 12
Don't miss: *Adobo, gambas alijo, tomate aliñado.*

La Carboná ($$)
Calle San Francisco de Paula, 2
11401 Jerez de la Frontera
+34 956 34 74 75
Don't miss: *Rape y amontillado, barriga de atún.*

Bar Juanito ($)
Calle de Pescadería Vieja, 8
11403 Jerez de la Frontera
+34 956 34 12 18
Don't miss: *Alcachofas, pochas con langostinos, riñones al Jerez.*

Casa Manteca ($)
Calle Corralon de los Carros, 66
11002 Cádiz
+34 956 21 36 03

El Faro ($$$)
Calle San Félix, 15
11002 Cádiz
+34 956 22 58 58

Taberna el Albero ($)
Calle San Felix, 2
11002 Cádiz
+34 956 22 08 38

La Candela ($)
Calle Feduchy, 3
11001 Cádiz
+34 956 22 18 22

La Isleta de la Viña ($)
Calle san Felix, 11
11002 Cádiz

WHERE TO DRINK SHERRY

Narcissa
New York, NY
narcissarestaurant.com

The Breslin
New York, NY
thebreslin.com

The John Dory
New York, NY
thejohndory.com

Casa Mono & Bar Jamón
New York, NY
casamononyc.com

Hearth
New York, NY
restauranthearth.com

El Quinto Pino
New York, NY
elquintopinonyc.com

Terroir
Multiple locations, NYC
restauranthearth.com/terrior

Tertulia
New York, NY
tertulianyc.com

Apartment 13
New York, NY
apt-13.com

TBD
San Francisco, CA
tbdrestaurant.com

Duende
Oakland, CA
duendeoakland.com

Nopa
San Francisco, CA
nopasf.com

Gitane
San Francisco, CA
gitanerestaurant.com

Aragona
Seattle, WA
aragonaseattle.com

The Harvest Vine
Seattle, WA
harvestvine.com

Belly Wine Bar
Cambridge, MA
bellywinebar.com

Taberna de Haro
Brookline, MA
tabernaboston.com

Toro
Boston, MA and New York, NY
toro-restaurant.com

Merrill & Co.
Boston, MA
merrillandcoboston.com

Bar Vivant
Portland, OR
pixpatisserie.myshopify.com

Woodsman Tavern
Portland, OR
woodsmantavern.com

Olympic Provisions
Portland, OR
olympicprovisions.com

Vera
Chicago, IL
verachicago.com

Telegraph Wine Bar
Chicago, IL
telegraphchicago.com

Mockingbird Hill
Washington, DC
drinkmoresherry.com

Jaleo
Washington, DC
jaleo.com/dc

Mateo Bar de Tapas
Durham, NC
mateotapas.com

Jamonera
Philadelphia, PA
jamonerarestaurant.com

Fino
Austin, TX
finoaustin.com

Stella
New Orleans, LA
restaurantstella.com

SHERRY-FRIENDLY COCKTAIL BARS

Pouring Ribbons
New York, NY
pouringribbons.com

Nitecap
New York, NY
nitecapnyc.com

Mayahuel
New York, NY
mayahuelny.com

The NoMad
New York, NY
thenomadhotel.com

Wallflower
New York, NY
wallflowernyc.com

Maison Premiere
New York, NY
maisonpremiere.com

The Dead Rabbit
New York, NY
deadrabbitnyc.com

15 Romolo
San Francisco, CA
15romolo.com

Trick Dog
San Francisco, CA
trickdogbar.com

Coqueta
San Francisco, CA
coquetasf.com

Zig Zag Café
Seattle, WA
zigzagseattle.com

Mistral Kitchen
Seattle, WA
mistral-kitchen.com

The Varnish
Los Angeles, CA
213nightlife.com

Honeycut
Los Angeles, CA
honeycutla.com

Eveleigh
Los Angeles, CA
theeveleigh.com

Anvil
Houston, TX
anvilhouston.com

Williams & Graham
Denver, CO
williamsandgraham.com

Franklin Mortgage and
    Investment Co.
Philadelphia, PA
thefranklinbar.com

The Passenger
Washington, DC
passengerdc.com

The Hawthorne
Boston, MA
thehawthornebar.com

Barrelhouse Flat
Chicago, IL
barrelhouseflat.com

The Violet Hour
Chicago, IL
theviolethour.com

Bellocq
New Orleans, LA
thehotelmodern.com/
    bellocq

WHERE TO BUY SHERRY

Despana Vinos y Mas
New York, NY
despanabrandfoods.com

Crush Wines & Spirits
New York, NY
crushwineco.com

Astor Wines & Spirits
New York, NY
astorwines.com

Vine Wine
Brooklyn, NY
vine-wine.com

Flatiron Wines
New York, NY
flatiron-wines.com

The Spanish Table
Seattle, WA; Mill Valley, CA;
    Berkeley, CA; Santa Fe, NM
spanishtable.com

K&L Wine Merchant
Redwood City, CA
klwines.com

The Wine House
Los Angeles, CA
winehouse.com

Vinopolis
Portland, OR
vinopoliswineshop.com

Great Wine Buys
Portland, OR
greatwinebuys.com

Liner & Elsen
Portland, OR
linerandelsen.com

E&R
Portland, OR
erwineshop.com

Perman Wine Selections
Chicago, IL
permanwine.com

Lush Wines & Spirits
Chicago, IL
lushwineandspirits.com

Central Bottle
Cambridge, MA
centralbottle.com

Wine Bottega
Boston, MA
thewinebottega.com

ACKNOWLEDGMENTS

FIRST AND FOREMOST, to my editor Emily Timberlake, without whose smarts, dedication, and patience this book would not have been possible. I owe you all of the sherry and champagne, forever. Thank you for making me a better writer and a better editor.

To Ten Speed's publisher Aaron Wehner for wanting to tell this story, for believing I could do it, and for tapping me to launch a magazine with him simultaneously. Thank you/I will never forgive you.

Thanks to Clancy Drake for her expert copyediting and Betsy Stromberg for her incredible design work and even more incredible patience.

To my friend, colleague, publicist, and unofficial guidance counselor Kelly Snowden: Thank you for your unwavering support and advice.

To everyone else at Ten Speed I've had the great pleasure of meeting. Thank you for inviting me into your family.

Thank you to this book's photographer, Ed Anderson, one of the kindest and most humble people I've had the pleasure of meeting. Thank you for bringing your Midwest-meets-California charm to Spain and for bringing this book to life.

Thanks to my agent, Kim Witherspoon, for signing an obscure wine writer with an obscure book proposal and for guiding me through the process. You are both wonderful and completely intimidating, and I wouldn't have it any other way.

To Doña Pilar Plá Pechovierto, Maria del Carmen Borrego Plá, Ana Cabestrero, Jan Pettersen, Antonio Flores, Charlotte Hey, Fernando Hidalgo, Marcelino Piquero, Lorenzo García-Iglesias, Juan González Salguero, Federico Sanchez-Pece Salmeron, José Luis González Obregón, Carmen Pou Riutort, Juan Carlos Gutiérrez, Edmundo Grant, Ignacio Hidalgo, Javier Hidalgo, Montse Molino, Steve Cook, Eduardo Ojeda, Jesus Barquin, Jaime Gil, Maria

Alvear, Rafael Delgado, Adela Córdoba, and the rest of the sherry producers, bodega owners, and employees in the sherry region that invited me into their homes and bodegas and told me their stories. This book is yours and so am I.

To my friend Alberto Orte for his passion for sherry, his incredible knowledge, and his generosity. Thank you for being my unofficial guide and advisor on so many occasions.

To Álvaro Girón Sierra, who knows more about sherry than anyone on this planet. This book would not have been possible without your generosity and your willingness to sit with me on the phone for hours at a time. Your passion for sherry is boundless and infectious.

To César Saldaña for his willingness to field all of my questions and to pore through piles of documents to find the answers. Thank you for never tiring.

To André Tamers for never getting annoyed with my incessant emailing (or at least pretending like he wasn't). Thanks for your insight and for hedging on sherry when everyone thought you were a nut for doing so. This book surely wouldn't have come to be without the work you did to pave the way.

To Kerin Auth, preeminent sherry cheerleader. Thank you for your translating skills, knowledge, and support the whole way through.

Special thanks to Peter Liem and Jesús Barquín, two of brightest minds in the wine world, for writing what is—and remains—the most comprehensive book on sherry written in at least a century. Your work has allowed a book like mine to exist.

I am indebted to each and every one of the bartenders and bar owners who were willing to answer my calls, emails, and endure my interrogation. So thank you Jim Meehan, Alex Day, Phil Ward, Joaquín Simó, Natasha David, Jeremy Oertel, Bobby Heugel, Kenny Freeman, Jack McGarry, Leo Robitschek, Charles Joly, Ivy Mix, Jacques Bezuidenhout, Katie Stipe, Morgan Schick and the Bon Vivants crew, Greg Best, Evan Zimmerman, Maxwell Britten and the whole team at Maison Premiere, Derek Brown, Chantal Tseng, Sean Kenyon,and Damon Boelte.

A special shout out to Dan Greenbaum, who is a well of cocktail information and one of sherry's most tireless champions within the drinks world. Thank you for letting me borrow your bar, your shaking skills, and your brain.

Thank you to the lovely crew at Donna, for lending their gorgeous space, and to Natasha David for filling the pages of this book with beautiful drinks and beautiful hair. Another extra thank you to my friends at Maison Premiere for also lending their space, and to Jesse Carr for spending his morning making drinks with us.

To David Wondrich, renaissance man, for always returning my calls and emails with more historical information then he ever needed to provide. You are a national treasure.

Thank you to all of the staff at Casa Mono & Bar Jamón for being such a formative part of my experience with sherry. I will be bellying up to your bar for as long as you let me.

To Anthony Sasso, my friend and Casa Mono's chef for his support and guidance, and for helping cook and style the food for the book.

To Ashley Santoro, for putting up with my shit. Thank you for being there every step of the way and for being a major force in my sherry education from the beginning. And thank you for speaking enough Spanish to ensure that I didn't make a fool out of myself in every train station, restaurant, bar, or taxi cab.

To Alex Raij. I will be forever touched by your willingness to help me without even knowing me. One of the best outcomes of this book has been getting to know you.

To Leslie Pariseau, my friend and *PUNCH* partner in crime for holding down the fort when I was on the brink(s) of a breakdown. Without you, I could not have done this. Thank you for your kindness, your creativity, and all of the emotional support.

For their support, advice, and inspiration throughout my career, a special thank you to August Cardona, Jon Bonné, Levi Dalton, Alice Feiring, Eric Asimov, Michael Madrigale, Jordan Mackay, Talitha Whidbee, Colu Henry, Jordan Salcito, Pascaline Lepeltier, Ray Isle, Joe Campanale, Josh Greene, Becky Teitel, Jennifer Cacicio, Nicole Moke, Whitney Schubert, and Micheline Gaulin.

To my cousin/sister Jacquelyn Morris for her support and love.

To all of the friends and family who have been affected by my disappearing off the face of the earth for nearly twelve months: Thank you for being right there when I resurfaced.

Last and hardly least, to my parents for teaching me what it means to work hard and love even harder, and for never asking me to get a more practical job. I love you.

INDEX

Copyright © 2014 by Talia Baiocchi
Photographs copyright © 2014 by Ed Anderson

All rights reserved.
Published in the United States by Ten Speed Press, an imprint of the Crown Publishing Group, a division of Random House LLC, a Penguin Random House Company, New York.
www.crownpublishing.com
www.tenspeed.com

Ten Speed Press and the Ten Speed Press colophon are registered trademarks of Random House LLC.

The map on page 11 appears courtesy of the Consejo Regulador de las DD.O. Jerez-Xeres-Sherry.

Library of Congress Cataloging-in-Publication Data

Baiocchi, Talia.
  Sherry : a modern guide to the wine world's best-kept secret, with cocktails and recipes / Talia Baiocchi.
    pages cm
  Includes index.
  1. Sherry. I. Title.
  TP559.S8.B29 2014
  663'.226094688—dc23
                          2014011853

Hardcover ISBN: 978-1-60774-581-5
eBook ISBN: 978-1-60774-582-2

Printed in China

Design by Betsy Stromberg
Cover design by Headcase Design

10 9 8 7 6 5 4 3 2 1

First Edition

SPECTRUM OF SHERRIES

LIGHTEST IN COLOR & BODY	**· MANZANILLA/FINO ·** *Pale gold, lean, and salty.*
	· AMONTILLADO · *Fino plus oxidation. Nutty, salty.*
	· PALO CORTADO · *If amontillado and oloroso had a love child.*
	· OLOROSO · *The yin to fino's yang. Brawny, nutty, caramelly.*
HEAVIEST IN COLOR & BODY	**· CREAM ·** *A blend of sweet and dry styles, generally PX and oloroso.*
	· MOSCATEL · *Amber-colored, floral, spicy.*
	· PEDRO XIMÉNEZ (PX) · *Black as night and sweet as hell.*

DRY

SWEET